THE WORKS OF AGENCY

The Works of Agency

On Human Action, Will, and Freedom

HUGH J. MCCANN

CORNELL UNIVERSITY PRESS

ITHACA AND LONDON

First published 1998 by Cornell University Press.

Printed in the United States of America

Library of Congress Cataloging-in-Publication Data

McCann, Hugh.
    The works of agency : on human action, will, and freedom /
by Hugh J. McCann.
        p.   cm.
    Includes bibliographical references and index.
    ISBN 0-8014-3528-5 (hardcover : alk. paper). —
ISBN 0-8014-8583-5 (pbk. : alk. paper)
    1. Act (Philosophy) 2. Agent (Philosophy)   I. Title.
B105.A35M39   1998
128′.4—dc21   98-28463

Cornell University Press strives to use environmentally responsible suppliers
and materials to the fullest extent possible in the publishing of its books. Such
materials include vegetable-based, low-VOC inks and acid-free papers that are
recycled, totally chlorine-free, or partly composed of nonwood fibers.

Cloth printing   10 9 8 7 6 5 4 3 2 1

For My Parents
Hugh and Mary

Contents

IV
PRACTICAL RATIONALITY

Preface

This book brings together eleven of my essays on human action, six of them previously published, the other five of more recent vintage. My hope is that taken together they will be found to represent a unified and coherent position on some of the foundational issues about action that have been the focus of philosophical attention in recent years. The essays that have appeared before are concerned largely with questions of ontology and etiology, in particular the subject of volition. I have modified them slightly, mostly for the sake of unity and to avoid unnecessary repetition. But I have also done some softening and modification of a few points on which, over the years, I may have managed to learn a little. The more recent essays are more concerned with matters having to do with intention formation and the freedom of the will, but I have also filled in some gaps left by the earlier papers. The essays are arranged chronologically within each part of the book.

I am grateful to the editors of the following journals for permission to reprint the papers that appeared previously: "Individuating Actions: The Fine-Grained Approach," *Canadian Journal of Philosophy* 13 (1983), 493–512; "Is Raising One's Arm a Basic Action?" *Journal of Philosophy* 68 (1972), 235–50; "Volition and Basic Action," *Philosophical Review* 83 (1974), 451–73 (copyright 1974 Cornell University; reprinted by permission of the publisher); "Trying, Paralysis, and Volition," *Review of Metaphysics* 28 (1975), 423–42; "Intrinsic Intentionality," *Theory and Decision* 20 (1986), 247–73 (copyright © 1986 by D. Reidel Publishing Company; with kind permission from Kluwer Academic Publishers); "Settled Objectives and Rational Constraints," *American Philosophical Quarterly* 28 (1991); 24–36.

I have worked on the positions defended in this book for a number of years, and it is not possible to remember and thank everyone from whose influence and encouragement I have benefited. I owe a special debt to the late Alan Donagan for fostering my early development, and to Hector-Neri Castañeda, whose insight and perseverance in discussion did much to improve my thinking. In addition, I have enjoyed fruitful discussions and exchanges with Frederick Adams, Myles Brand, Michael Bratman, Robert Burch, Lawrence Davis, Robert Kane, Jonathan Kvanvig, Keith Lehrer, Lawrence Brian Lombard, Michael Loux, Alfred Mele, Sidney Shoemaker, the late Irving Thalberg, and Michael Zimmerman. Some of the ideas presented here received their first formulation while I was supported by an NEH Fellowship for College Teachers and Independent Scholars in 1987–88. Thanks also go to Herman Saatkamp and Robin Smith for helping me secure time to work, and to Kris Frost of the Santayana Edition at Texas A&M University for help in preparing the manuscript. Alfred Mele's criticisms of the previously unpublished parts of this book have been especially valuable. Above all, I thank Robert Audi, whose encouragement has been the incentive for more than one of the papers in this volume, and whose patient and selfless criticisms have enhanced most of the others.

HUGH J. McCANN

College Station, Texas

THE WORKS OF AGENCY

Introduction

The theory of human action represents a kind of philosophical cross-roads, at which several pathways of perennial interest intersect. The problem of how action is individuated is of interest for general ontology, and for understanding the metaphysics of time and change. Action theory is also important to our understanding the relation between mind and body, action and perception being the two major arenas in which, as thinking beings, we interact with the world. Action is especially important here because it involves the mysterious phenomenon of agency, the operations of which resist representation in terms of familiar causal processes, and may require irreducibly teleological conceptions in order to be understood. This in turn raises problems in the philosophy of science: about how broadly nomic causation applies to the world, and about what, in the end, the true relationship between motive and behavior is. Issues concerning rationality in choice and behavior also come up here: what counts as a good reason, and when is an intention rationally formed? Finally, action theory has bearing on important topics in ethics: the nature of responsibility, weakness of will, and the general relationship between practical rationality and the rightness or wrongness of actions.

It is, of course, impossible even to address more than a few of these issues in one volume. The essays that follow are grouped under four headings, and focus primarily on the ontology and etiology of action, and the phenomenon of intention formation. They begin with an effort to address issues of ontology.

Part I: The Ontology of Action

The focal concern of action ontology is the phenomenon wherein by acting just once, agents are often able to accomplish what appear to be a number of actions. When Booth assassinated Lincoln, for example, he moved his finger, thereby firing a gun, thereby shooting Lincoln, thereby killing him. And that is only the beginning; he also committed treason, broke the law, plunged the nation into mourning, and so on. The question is, how many actions did Booth perform? Those who emphasize the unity of agency in such cases hold there is only one: Booth's basic action, often claimed to be his moving his finger. And they hold that all the other things Booth can be said to have done are merely redescriptions of this basic action in terms of its consequences, legal standing, and so on. At the opposite end of the spectrum are those who emphasize the multiplicity of act properties displayed by Booth when he performed his infamous deed. For these philosophers, Booth performed many distinct actions—perhaps even as many as there are true descriptions of things he did.

A number of philosophers have sought a compromise between these extremes. The two papers that begin this collection constitute one such attempt. It is grounded in a combination of claims having to do with the linguistics of change, and the way events relate to time. The linguistic foundation is a modification of some of Zeno Vendler's work on the functions of English nominals.[1] Vendler divides nominals into two broad classifications, *perfect* and *imperfect*, which he holds refer to events and facts, respectively. In perfect nominals—expressions like *Booth's assassination of Lincoln* or *John's singing of the Marseillaise*—the verbal element has been transformed completely into a noun. The linguistic evidence that these structures designate events is convincing. It would be correct, for example, to say of Booth's assassination of Lincoln that it occurred at a certain time, or of John's singing of the Marseillaise that it began, lasted, and ended. Since these are characteristics typically associated with events, it seems clear that perfect nominals are event designators.

But the other side of Vendler's distinction is not as clear-cut. Imperfect nominals, in which the verbal element still functions as such, are diverse. They include *that*-clauses, and these are clearly fact oriented: it is a fact that Booth shot Lincoln—a fact which, like others, we may believe or doubt, assert or deny, and so on. But this heading also comprises imperfect gerundive constructions—expressions such as *Booth's killing Lincoln* or

---

[1]   See Zeno Vendler, *Linguistics and Philosophy* (Ithaca: Cornell University Press, 1976), esp. chap. 5; and my "Nominals, Facts, and Two Conceptions of Events," *Philosophical Studies* 39 (1979), 129–49.

John's singing the Marseillaise—whose behavior is quite different. Booth's killing Lincoln is not the kind of thing we can believe, nor can we assert John's singing the Marseillaise; we can and do, however, refer to them as events and actions. What is deceptive is that these entities seem not to have characteristics usually associated with events, such as beginning, lasting, and ending. This, I maintain, is because change can be conceived in two entirely different ways with respect to time. Perfect nominals designate events conceived as temporally *persistent* individual accidents or tropes. Such entities count as characteristics of individual things, and they relate to time just as substances do: they come to be, change, and so on. Imperfect gerundives, by contrast, refer to events conceived as temporally *extended* processes. These entities do not even happen, in the strict sense of the word, and they do not persist through time. Rather, time is analogized to space in their conception, and they are spread through stretches of it. Hence they lack the features associated with individual accidents. Moreover, the evidence is that events of this second type are more susceptible of identity claims than are those designated by perfect nominals. The stage for compromise is thereby set: both the fine-grained actions of those who emphasize the multiplicity of Booth's deeds and the coarser entities of those who emphasize that he acted but once appear to be legitimate.

This solution is developed in the two papers included here. Chapter 1, "Individuating Actions: The Fine-Grained Approach," makes the case for the multiple actions called for by philosophers such as Jaegwon Kim and Alvin Goldman[2]—actions that, as "property exemplifications," turn out to be the individual accidents referred to by perfect nominals. The crucial necessary condition for the identity of act tokens of this kind—namely, that they be instances of the same act type—is interpreted to apply only to the core, verbal elements of perfect nominals. So John's singing of the Marseillaise and his loud singing can be identical, but Booth's killing of Lincoln and his firing of the gun cannot. The functional role of such entities is to enable us to differentiate among the many things that "go on" in episodes of action. There must, after all, be something fine-grained in the world answering to the many descriptions we can give of things an agent "does" in a single exercise of agency. If we deny that, we will soon find ourselves speaking of such things as aspects of action, or the like, and those will turn out to be fine-grained after all. Individual accidents *are* aspects of the agents who display them, and so seem best suited to fill this role. In addition, the behavior of perfect nominals with respect to objec-

2 Jaegwon Kim, "Events as Property Exemplifications," in M. Brand and D. Walton, eds., *Action Theory* (Boston: D. Reidel, 1976), 159–77; Alvin I. Goldman, *A Theory of Human Action* (Englewood Cliffs, NJ: Prentice-Hall, 1970), chap. 1.

tive phrases and attributive adjectives gives evidence that the entities they designate do obey the property exemplification theory's fine-grained identity requirements.

Accepting fine-grained actions does not, however, commit us to holding that these are the only actions, and there are reasons for postulating another sort as well. In Chapter 2, "The Individuation of Action and the Unity of Agency," I argue that fine-grained actions do a poor job of accounting for the fact that in accomplishing the many things he did, Booth acted just once. Concepts such as Goldman's "level-generation" seem not to locate a legitimate generative relation among actions, nor is it clear that such a relation would solve the problem. And it is implausible to suppose the many perfect nominals that pick out actions of Booth's simply redescribe his basic act. A satisfying account of the unity of agency does become available, however, if we accept temporally extended actions, since these have more tolerant identity conditions. It is suggested that fundamentally, temporally extended actions consist in dynamic processes of physical interaction reaching from agents into the world. If that is so, then any overt action consists in a segment of such a sequence, and a lot of identity claims philosophers have wanted to make become permissible. But not all. As Irving Thalberg and others have argued, Booth's moving his finger, pulling the trigger, firing the gun, and so on are not identical; rather, they are successively longer segments of a causal chain that begins in Booth.[3]

Part II: The Foundations of Action

Theories of the ontogenesis of human action tend to fall under two, radically different headings. On one view, bodily acts like raising an arm or moving a finger count as direct or *basic actions:* roughly, actions not done *by* doing anything else. What counts as the action is the motion of the bodily part in question, and it does so by virtue of being appropriately caused by a motivational state of the agent: one of intending, perhaps, or some combination of desire and belief. To proponents of this theory its advantages are that it does not ground physical action in any sort of mental doing, thus meshing with certain versions of materialism, and that it promises to reduce human agency to a causal sequence involving only nonactional events. The opposing view does not seek to reduce agency at all. It treats overt action as grounded in interior doings of the agent, and

---

[3]   Irving Thalberg, *Perception, Emotion, and Action: A Component Approach* (Oxford: Basil Blackwell, 1977), chap. 5.

ultimately in mental activity of the sort traditionally known as volition. The four papers in Part II present a comprehensive defense of the volitionist position.

A useful way to begin is to see that quite apart from the issue of mental acts, there is no hope whatever for the claim that overt movements are ontogenetically basic. That is the point of Chapter 3, "Is Raising One's Arm a Basic Action?" I argue that even rather stringent conditions for an action to count as more basic than overt movement are satisfied by exertional actions—that is, acts of tensing and flexing muscles. When overt movements are performed, exertional acts serve as causal means to them, and they are viewed as means by their agents. What makes it possible for this to be overlooked is, first, that most overt movements are performed with no trouble. As a result, it is easy to forget that we have to put forth physical effort in order to move. The need for effort does show up in cases where one is said to *try* to make a movement, however, and not every case of trying to move is one where the agent anticipates difficulty in advance. Where no difficulty is expected, there is every reason to believe that whatever constitutes the agent's attempt is simply the normal means for making movements of the type at issue. And unless the agent is paralyzed, what constitutes the attempt is an act of physical exertion.

A second factor that permits exertional acts to be ignored is that since they involve the tensing of muscles, we tend to expect them to be described in physiological terms. But most of us know little about physiology, thus it might be thought that an agent could never intend an act of muscle tensing, and so could not conceive it as a means to moving. Such actions can be and are intended, however, via their felt characteristics. They remain difficult to describe, because we have little language for describing inner sensations. But an action need not be described in order to be intended; it has only to be conceived. Exertional actions can, therefore, be undertaken as causal means to performing overt movements. Furthermore, our ignorance of physiology notwithstanding, the simple truth is that we all know we perform such actions all the time.

But even exertional actions are not basic. What is foundational to our ability to produce change in the world is the activity of volition. Chapter 4, "Volition and Basic Action," is dedicated to a theoretical defense of this claim, based on the usefulness of volition for answering a famous question of Ludwig Wittgenstein's: "What is left over if I subtract the fact that my arm goes up from the fact that I raise my arm?"[4] Ordinarily, we answer this kind of question by invoking some more basic action of the agent. For example, we might say Lincoln's death belongs to the action

---

[4] Ludwig Wittgenstein, *Philosophical Investigations* (New York: Macmillan, 1953), sec. 621.

which is Booth's killing Lincoln by virtue of the fact that it was caused by Booth's action of shooting Lincoln. But if overt movements are basic, the same kind of move is foreclosed in their case; there simply is no more fundamental action. Yet, like Booth's act of killing Lincoln, overt movements always consist in bringing about some nonactional change, such as the motion of an arm or finger. Moreover, even if we agree that overt movements are grounded in exertional activity, the same problem will reappear: we still must account for the difference between my muscles tensing and my performing an action of tensing them.

But if the entire sequence through which overt actions are performed begins with volitional activity, the problem is solved. That is because volition, being a kind of thinking, does not *consist in* bringing about nonactional changes. It consists, rather, in framing mental *content* in a distinctive modality of thought: it is the activity of willing the exertional changes the agent sees as necessary to bringing about an intended sequence of change in the world. The intended changes may, of course, occur as *consequences* of the volitional activity, but they are not intrinsic to it in the way the upward motion of my arm is intrinsic to raising it. Moreover, though volition does have the characteristics of action, those characteristics are not gotten by a relation to some other mental state or occurrence. On the contrary: volition is by its nature an exercise in voluntariness, and it is intrinsic to our willing an event that we intend to do exactly that. Thus volition neither is nor involves any event about which Wittgenstein's type of problem can be raised.

Chapter 5, "Trying, Paralysis, and Volition," is more empirically oriented. It offers an a posteriori argument for the volitional theory, based on what occurs in clinical tests of the ability of paralytics to perform movements. The treatment here involves a more thorough analysis of trying, which in some accounts substitutes for volition as the activity foundational to all overt action. I argue, however, that even though it is fair to say trying attends all overt doing, trying should not be taken as a *species* of action equivalent to volition. Rather, *trying* is a general term for the business of going about the performance of an action, and an agent's attempt consists in as much as he accomplishes, or could reasonably have been expected to accomplish, toward the action at issue. When John Hinckley tried to assassinate Ronald Reagan, his attempt consisted not merely in mental activity, but in shooting Reagan. As for tests for paralysis, they are of course based on the subject trying to perform various requested movements. And the only thing that can reasonably be taken to constitute such an attempt, especially when paralysis is complete, is volitional activity. The testimony of victims of paralysis indicates that is precisely what occurs.

Notwithstanding the arguments in its favor, the volitional theory has been widely resisted. But the opposite approach, which seeks to understand the foundations of action in terms of causation by motivational states, has to date been a failure. Besides their inability to accommodate attempts to perform overt movements, theories of this kind founder on the problem of causal deviance. Bodily changes like the motion of a limb or digit are not, in any case, what we call "actions." But even if they were, they could not count as such in virtue of being caused by states of intention or desire, simply because such a causal sequence can occur without any action at all being performed. One of many examples is Donald Davidson's case of the mountaineer, whose desire to rid himself of the weight and danger of a companion he is supporting so unnerve him as to cause his grip on the rope to give way, so that the companion is lost.[5] The last paper in Part II, "Agency and the Problem of Causal Deviance" (Chapter 6), is an examination of recent efforts to circumvent such cases. One strategy for excluding them is to demand a close match between the behavior that occurs and the desire or intention out of which it arises. Unfortunately, however, we cannot demand a complete match: intentional action is possible even when the bodily changes it involves are not precisely what was intended. Moreover, in some situations—and Davidson's example may be a case in point—the content of a desire or intention may be simple enough that behavior can easily match it without being actional.

The most common approach for dealing with causal deviance, however, holds that the key to bodily changes counting as action is that they exhibit *sensitivity* to changing circumstances—that is, that they be caused by the agent's motivational states in such a way that as the environment changes, behavior is adjusted in ways suitable to satisfying the agent's intention or desire. And it is true that intentional action often has this feature. But not always: some actions are clumsy and wooden, and others are too quick or simple to exhibit sensitivity. But they are actions all the same. By contrast, it is not impossible for bodily motions to exhibit considerable sensitivity to environmental feedback, yet not count as action. Even without the aid of science fiction, examples of this kind can be constructed. But it is also possible to imagine alien interveners: external agents who with the aid of futuristic electronics are able to read my desires or intentions, and then control my motor functions with all the nuance and subtlety we may wish to imagine—yet without my performing any action at all. There appears to be no effective way to eliminate such examples. If that is correct, then efforts to deal with Wittgenstein's ques-

---

[5]   Donald Davidson, "Freedom to Act," in Ted Honderich, ed., *Essays on Freedom of Action* (London: Routledge & Kegan Paul, 1973), pp. 153–54.

tion in terms of motivational causation fail, and the volitional theory of
the etiology of action is without a convincing competitor.

Part III: Intention, Will, and Freedom

The free will problem has to do with the pathway from reasons to action.
If, following Davidson,[6] we think of a reason as a combination of a motive
to achieve some end and a belief as to how that might be done, then the
question is how reasons need to be related to actions in order for the latter
to be free and responsible. But the path from reason to action is not simple:
between the two there usually intervenes a state of intending, in which the
agent has the settled purpose of performing the action his reasons call for.
In such cases, intentions are formed by acts of decision and executed
through the activity of volition. Both decision and volition are therefore
important to freedom. Decision is important because it is the primary
means by which we enshrine certain of our reasons in intentions for the future, thus selecting from among the actions available to us the one we will
perform. But volition is important also—partly because we feel that our actions as well as our decisions are "up to us," but also because not all action
arises out of a prior deliberation and decision. When that is the case, volition becomes our primary means of intention formation.

There are, of course, divergent views about free will. Libertarians hold
that decision and action are, at least usually, exempt from nomic causation, and that if this were not so we would not be free or responsible. De-
terminists, on the other hand, hold that a satisfying account of intentional
action is not possible outside the context of nomic determination, and
mostly seek an account of freedom that is compatible with determinism.
By and large, determinist theories of action tend not to emphasize the
concept of deciding, and they may seek to reduce intention to a combination of desire and belief. I think it is fair to say that through most of the
twentieth century, determinism has been ascendant. One reason, no
doubt, is that it appears more scientific. Libertarians have long faced the
objection that an uncaused decision or action would violate sound principles of explanation, and so count as a kind of random event for which
no one could be responsible. But there is another problem as well: it has
been argued that apart from a causal account, we cannot even understand what it *is* to act *for* a given reason, or *out of* a certain intention.[7] If

---

[6]   Donald Davidson, "Actions, Reasons, and Causes," *Journal of Philosophy* 60 (1963),
685–86.
[7]   Ibid., pp. 692–93.

this is right, then the problem for the libertarian is not just to explain action: it is to show how there can be a legitimate pathway from reasons to action that is not causal.

The first two papers in Part III are dedicated to this latter problem. Chapter 7, "Intrinsic Intentionality," is concerned with the relationship between intention and volition. I argue first that intention is a legitimate phenomenon in its own right. It cannot be reduced to a combination of the agent's motives and beliefs, nor to the (essentially cognitive) judgment that an act would be best overall. When an intention to *A* is present prior to action, its content provides a plan of action that is put into effect through the agent's volition. In such cases, action commences when the agent begins to will the sequence of exertional changes presented in his intention as appropriate for achieving *A*. But the intention does not cause the willing, nor is a prior intention necessary for willing to be intentional. Rather, willing is intrinsically intentional: it is not possible for me to will the sort of exertion necessary, say, to hitting a golf shot without intending to will it, and without intending thereby to set in motion the sequence of events to which I envision it leading. In the case of playing golf, the plan for making the shot is almost always presented in a prior intention. But even if it were not, simply to engage in volitional activity would be sufficient for my being in the state of intending to do so, and of intending to achieve the objectives to which it is directed.

The intrinsic intentionality of volition is what accounts for our ability to perform intentional actions that are not preceded by deliberation or decision. Impulsive actions and acts performed in sudden emergencies may not be prompted by any prior intention. Still, they are intentional, because the volitional activity in which they are grounded is. All that is required for volition to occur is that a suitable objective be presented to the agent. That can occur with the onset of a sudden desire, or simply with the recognition that one's situation calls for a certain sort of action. Furthermore, even when volition is prompted by a prior intention to *A*, it should not be thought that the volitional activity must give rise to a second intention to *A*. It is not possible to have two intentions with exactly the same content. So when volition is prompted by a prior intention it only ratifies that intention; it does not create a second.

If this is correct, we get a noncausal account of what it is to act out of a prior intention. The issue is not whether volition is caused by the prior intention, but whether it is directed at producing the goals that intention embodies. A similar account applies to the formation of intention. There, the question is whether, when an agent decides to *A* for a certain reason, we can give an account of the *for* without invoking nomic causation. In Chapter 8, "The Formation of Intention," I argue that this relation, too, is essentially teleological rather than causal. In general, one's reasons for deciding to *A* are just one's reasons for *A*-ing: if my desire to get my son an ice cream cone is a reason for taking him to Swensen's, then it is also a reason for deciding to take him there. Thus, if I decide to take my son to Swensen's *for* this reason, it will explain both the decision by which my intention is formed and the eventual act by which the intention is carried out. And the explanation will be teleological, not causal. When my "desire" to get my son an ice cream cone is cited as my reason for taking him to Swensen's, it is not my mental *state* of desiring that is invoked as explanatory, but rather its *content*—a thought, which might be expressed as, "Would that I by my son an ice cream cone." This is not an event or state, but a proposition-like entity, which cannot cause anything. Rather, it explains my action by exhibiting my practical reasoning, by displaying the perceived good at which my action was aimed.

Furthermore, when we are uncertain what the reasons for an action may have been, we do not settle the question through considerations associated with nomic causation, such as the strength of motives or how uniformly they are followed. Rather, we focus on what motives were reflected in the agent's intention. The reason for this is that intentions always duplicate the reasons out of which they were formed: if we know the intention with which I took my son to Swensen's, we know what my reasons were; and if we know my reasons, we know my intention. And that is the clue to what decision is about. The functional role of deciding is to take the incipient action plans our reasons present to us and recast them into intentions. When I decide to take my son to Swensen's out of a desire to get him an ice cream cone, that desire is copied, as it were, into my intention: it becomes a settled objective of mine, an end I am committed to achieving. I resolve not just to take my son to Swensen's, but to do so for the sake of that objective.

But I also *decide* for the sake of that objective. This is in part because, like volition, decision is intrinsically intentional. I cannot decide without intending to decide, and without intending to decide exactly as I do. But that is not all: because to decide is to adopt a commitment to action, to decide to *A* is actually to *progress* toward *A*-ing in a certain definitive way. *A*-ing becomes a part of my agenda, along with whatever good and evil it may involve. To decide is, therefore, to take an intentional step toward the objectives my reasons for *A*-ing represent—which is, simply, to decide for the sake of those reasons. And of course there is nothing about nomic causation in any of this: nothing about there being causal laws afoot, nothing about the strength of my reasons, nothing to suggest I might not have decided differently in precisely the same circumstances. It does not follow that my decisions are not nomically caused. But whether they are caused or not, we do not have to invoke causation to provide an account of what it is to decide for a reason.

If this position is correct, both the formation and execution of intention can be understood in noncausal terms, and the way to a libertarian account of the will is at least partially open. But there remains the traditional objection: that an uncaused act of will could only be a kind of accident, a violation of principles of rational explanation. Actually, there are two aspects to this complaint. One is that an uncaused act would be a *practical* accident—an occurrence which befalls the agent unforeseen and unchosen, in which he is passive, and for which he could not be responsible. But nothing like this follows from an act's not being caused. Moreover, this complaint is refuted by the intrinsically actional character of operations of the will. It is simply a part of the phenomenology of deciding and willing that they are experienced as exercises of intentional agency. If they are anything like what we take them to be, it is not even possible for them to be accidents in this sense.

But—and this is the other aspect of the objection—such acts would still lack a deterministic explanation, and so might be viewed as anomalous, as ontological discontinuities in the world. Chapter 9, "Agency, Control, and Causation," is an effort to address this problem. I defend the view that responsible freedom requires alternative possibilities, and that this idea cannot be done justice by a compatibilist analysis. Only operations of will that display libertarian freedom are free in any sense that matters. As for the complaint that they must count as explanatory anomalies, that has been overestimated. It is true that teleological explanation of actions must eventually give out. Once we have summed up all of an agent's reasons for *A*-ing, we can give no further answer if asked why he chose to *A* for those reasons, rather than do something else for some other set of reasons. But this defect afflicts any type of explanation. Even if the empirical world were deterministic through and through—which the evidence indicates it is not—nomic causation cannot explain why we have this world rather than some other, or no world at all. And unlike nomic explanation, teleological explanation does offer natural stopping points, in the ends an agent takes to be valuable for their own sake. That is much more satisfying than the situation that obtains in physics, where undetermined events have at best only statistical explanations.

We need to be clear, furthermore, on just how it is that nomically determined events are explained. Natural causation is often viewed as a sort of process—which we take to be described by scientific laws—in which the events of the past either produce or necessitate future ones, so that once the past is in place, the existence of the future is guaranteed. And then it seems easy to fault free decisions and actions, because their existence comes with no similar guarantee. But this alleged contrast is entirely groundless. As Hume pointed out, there is no process by which past events confer existence on future ones, nor do we observe any form of "natural" necessitation.[8] Moreover, scientific laws—classical ones, at least—do not even purport to describe such a process. In fact, they are not even diachronic: they describe simultaneous interactions in which dynamic properties such as energy and momentum, which the laws treat as conserved rather than created, are transferred from one entity to another. Assuming the world continues to exist, future events will then emerge naturally and predictably from those that went before. But they will not be produced by them. In that respect, the idea of natural causation is on the same footing as agent causation: neither is a process in its own right, and neither guarantees the existence of anything. It turns out, then, that free exercises of the will differ from the rest of the world *only* in being nomically discontinuous with it. The problem of their provenance is of a piece with that of the provenance of things in general.

Part IV: Practical Rationality

This section consists of two papers on topics having to do with rationality in intention formation. The first topic is whether it is ever rational to form intentions that are inconsistent with each other, or with our beliefs about what we can accomplish. It might be thought that rationality prohibits this, since we seldom if ever avow intentions we believe we cannot satisfy. Yet we do sometimes pursue objectives we believe we cannot achieve. To cite an example of Michael Bratman's, I might try to remove a large log that has fallen into my driveway, even though I believe it is too heavy for me.[9] There is nothing irrational in this, since there is always a chance I will succeed. Moreover, If I do succeed I will have moved the log intentionally. To hold, therefore, that I cannot intend to do what I believe I cannot do commits us to claiming an agent can *A* intentionally without having intended to *A*. Nevertheless, this has been maintained. In Chapter 10, "Settled Objectives and Rational Constraints," I argue that such views are mistaken. Although it is usually unacceptable to have intentions one cannot fulfill, to prohibit them entirely only forces us to postulate other

---

[8]   David Hume, *An Inquiry Concerning Human Understanding*, ed. Charles W. Hendel (New York: Liberal Arts Press, 1955), pp. 74–75.
[9]   Michael E. Bratman, *Intention, Plans, and Practical Reason* (Cambridge: Harvard University Press, 1987), p. 39.

mental states—such as having a purpose or goal—that are alleged to be different from intending, but which have the same action-guiding role. This drives a wedge between intention and practical rationality, by prohibiting agents from intending objectives they are rational to pursue. And it invites efforts to reduce intending to other mental states. Furthermore, the states postulated as alternatives to intending themselves turn out to be subject to the same constraints of rationality that apply to intending, and so are indistinguishable from intention in this respect after all.

The final topic is practical reasoning itself. The primary focus of Chapter 11, "Practical Reasoning and Weakness of Will," is whether practical reasoning is no more than a branch of theoretical reasoning, with strictly propositional content, aimed at reaching judgments about what action one should perform. I argue that even when it is aimed at intention formation, deliberation must involve more than this. There is also *intrinsically* practical reasoning, in which intentions actually *are* formed, and whose content includes not only our beliefs, but also such things as desires, felt obligations, and intentions. If this kind of reasoning is ignored, intention formation may be preceded by reasoning, but in itself it is a strictly nonrational procedure, in which it is left to the agent's motivational states to produce a state of intending, which one can only hope will match his judgment as to what he should do. If there is intrinsically practical reasoning, on the other hand, intention formation can be a ratiocinative procedure, in which the agent decides by drawing a conclusion from the reasons on which his decision is based.

This approach to practical reasoning also sheds useful light on the phenomenon of akrasia, or weakness of will, in which the agent forms an intention opposed to his better judgment or to his beliefs as to what is obligatory. Part of what makes this possible is that the argument through which an intention is formed requires as its major premise an optation—that is, a desire, intention, or felt obligation. This rules out judgments, which are not optations but propositions. As a result, our beliefs about what we should do can enter decision making only as minor premises, and only if they connect logically with an appropriate motive—that is, with some optation to do what we should simply because we should, or as a means to some other end. But motives of the first kind may be weak, and those of the second kind usually represent misplaced values. Ironically, therefore, our beliefs as to what is best or obligatory turn out to be rather poor reasons for acting. An agent who is not motivated to perform an action by its good-making properties themselves—and so has no need of better judgment—is not likely to perform it because it matches his better judgment, either.

I

THE ONTOLOGY OF ACTION

1

Individuating Actions:
The Fine-Grained Approach

When John Wilkes Booth moved his finger, thereby firing a gun, thereby killing Lincoln, did he perform three discrete actions, or were there relations of identity or inclusion among them? Most treatments of this problem have tended to assume there is but one sort of entity properly to be called an action, and hence that one answer to this question must be established to the exclusion of all others. The favored answer has been that Booth's actions are not discrete, or indeed even overlapping, but identical.[1] It is possible, however, to adopt a more conciliatory spirit, in which a place is sought for talk of discrete or fine-grained actions in such cases as well as for entities of the coarser sort most have favored.[2] If, as I believe, this attitude is correct, then it is important to pursue the case for

---

[1] This view is most closely associated with Donald Davidson. See especially "The Logical Form of Action Sentences," in Nicholas Rescher, ed., *The Logic of Decision and Action* (Pittsburgh: University of Pittsburgh Press, 1967), pp. 81–95; and "Agency," in Robert Binkley, Richard Bronaugh, and Ausonio Marras, eds., *Agent, Action, and Reason* (Toronto: University of Toronto Press, 1971), pp. 1–25. See also Jonathan Bennett, "Shooting, Killing and Dying," *Canadian Journal of Philosophy* 2 (1972–73), 315–24; and Jennifer Hornsby, *Actions* (Boston: Routledge & Kegan Paul 1980), chap. 1.

[2] See Jaegwon Kim, "Events as Property Exemplifications," in Myles Brand and Douglas Walton, eds., *Action Theory* (Boston: D. Reidel, 1976), pp. 159–77; and especially the writings of Hector-Neri Castañeda on the subject, including *Thinking and Doing* (Boston: D. Reidel, 1975), chap. 12; and "Intensionality and Identity in Human Action and Philosophical Method," *Nous* 13 (1979), 235–60. I have argued for such an approach in "Nominals, Facts, and Two Conceptions of Events," *Philosophical Studies* 35 (1979), 129–49.

fine-grained actions, if only to show that we should not opt prematurely for a view that is mistakenly one-sided. Moreover, it is important to demonstrate the usefulness of fine-grained actions for dealing with problems that cannot be handled with coarser entities. In what follows, therefore, I shall argue that however justified we may be in finding unity such sequences of action as Booth's, we must also find difference, and that the way to do so is by speaking of discrete actions. I shall claim these actions are in fact entities of a metaphysical sort that is, if not widely accepted, by no means new—namely, what are often called individual accidents, abstract particulars, or tropes—and that everyday language for describing action respects such entities. Finally, I shall try to show that such entities are indeed necessary for dealing with issues important to understanding action. In particular, they make possible an account of what it means to speak of actions "under descriptions," and they provide a better account of the use of attributive adjectives than other theories can offer.

Understanding Fine-Grained Identity

In their most usual formulation, fine-grained theories treat events, and states too, as exemplifications by substances of properties at a time. In the case of actions the properties are act properties, and a criterion for individuation is provided according to which two actions are identical just in case they involve the same agent, the same property, and the same time.[3] Now I would not claim this criterion captures conditions *sufficient* to individuate anything, or even that such criteria are generally available. I do think, though, that it captures, or comes near to capturing, necessary conditions for the identity of what, on one conception, count as actions, and that is enough for present purposes. For implicit in this criterion is the principle that different act properties guarantee different actions. Whether this is so is the main point of dispute between fine-grained theorists and their opponents, and that is a dispute about necessary, not sufficient, conditions for act identity. If it can be shown that there are actions for which such a principle holds, the fine-grained theorist will be substantially vindicated and the nature of those actions at least partially understood. I shall confine myself, therefore, to the question whether the conditions cited are ever necessary for act identity, and leave alone the matter of sufficient conditions.

[3] Kim, "Events as Property Exemplifications," pp. 160–61; also Alvin I. Goldman, *A Theory of Human Action* (Englewood Cliffs, N.J.: Prentice-Hall, 1970), p. 10. It is possible to employ differing individuational bases yet divide actions with as much fineness. See, for example, Myles Brand, "Identity Conditions for Events," *American Philosophical Quarterly* 14 (1977), 329–37.

When we try to specify how these conditions are to be interpreted, problems arise. Talk of agents exemplifying properties at times is, of course, second-order talk, aimed at achieving generality. It is meant to imply not that an action consists primarily in an exemplification relation between an agent and an act property, but rather that when agents do exemplify such properties, there will be found in the world some item in which a specific agent, a specific act property, and a specific time are involved. But the nature of the involvement is problematic. One approach is to treat the action as a complex in which all the elements are parts.[4] Thus the action that occurred when Booth killed Lincoln would be held to include not just the property killing, but also Booth and the time of the killing. But as regards the time, at least, this approach seems to me a mistake. For one thing, neither in reporting nor referring to actions are we generally at pains to mention times. More important, actions are the sort of things we want to say occur at times or are found in temporal locations. But times do not occur at times, nor is the temporal location of an action located in itself. So an action should not include a time. Rather, the demand that identical actions must involve the same time should be understood as requiring a relation of occurrence between the action and a time in which the time is distinct from the action, not a constituent of it.

A similar problem arises with respect to the role of the agent. Adjusting for the fact that the time of an action is extrinsic to it, we might say that in itself a fine-grained action is just an exemplification by an agent of a property. Again, however, we can ask whether the agent belongs to the action or the action to the agent. On the first approach, we would treat what occurs when Booth kills Lincoln as a kind of ontological unit in which Booth is inseparably embedded. To do this is to understand the agent as a constituent in his own actions, so that if, as it were, an action were to disappear in toto from the field of change, the agent would go with it. I think this conception might have value for understanding coarser sorts of entity, but for fine-grained actions it is not as useful as the second alternative, which is quite different. We can treat Booth's act of killing as belonging to him if we understand it to be an instance of the general act property killing, one that counts as a feature of Booth in much the way that, say, the whiteness of a sheet of paper is a feature of it. The relationship here is one not of constituency but of ontological dependence, and it raises no problems about the agent continuing after the action ceases to be. Of the two conceptions it is the more immediately plausible, and I shall argue below that this relation between agent and act is in fact the appropriate one for fine-grained actions.

---

[4]   This was Kim's early view: "Events as Property Exemplifications," p. 160.

This sort of difficulty does not arise with respect to the property involved in an action, since presumably it, or an instance of it, is intrinsic. But if identity of properties is required for identity of actions, some understanding of property identity is needed, and this too is a contested matter. Disagreement can be forestalled to some extent by judicious selection of examples. No one has claimed that the act properties in our case of killing display relations of identity or inclusion. But it is instructive to see how distinctness of properties might be argued for in relatively easy cases such as this, and to see what options are available to the fine-grained theorist when the going gets rough. Sticking, then, to necessary conditions, surely for two properties to be identical it is a requirement that, necessarily, they be coinstantiated in all their occurrences.[5] And this secures at least the nonidentity of the act properties involved in most examples used in discussions of act individuation. A little imagination can easily produce examples to show that neither moving a finger, firing a gun, nor killing Lincoln requires any of the others. Similarly, to take another favorite case, one can raise an arm without signaling a turn, and vice versa. But nonidentity is not distinctness: a table and its legs are not identical, but neither are they distinct, the legs being part of the table. So even though most discussants have been prepared to allow distinctness for the properties so far mentioned, there is still the possibility of a common element. And even if we ignore that possibility, what exactly are the properties in question? Is it, for example, just firing and killing, or must we say firing the gun and killing Lincoln?

The significance of these points emerges in more obviously problematic cases. Suppose John sings, that what he sings is the "Marseillaise," and that he sings loudly. Obviously, one can sing loudly without singing the "Marseillaise," and vice versa, and one need do neither just to sing. Thus we cannot claim identity here. On the other hand, to speak of three distinct act tokens on John's part is to ignore an obvious descriptive overlap, and to proliferate entities to an extent even fine-grained theorists wish to avoid. Moreover, this move leads straight into trouble, for both in singing loudly and in singing the "Marseillaise," John sings. So if all the act tokens here are distinct, we have a total of three acts of singing on John's part, which alone is difficult to accept. Worse, one of those acts of singing appears to have had no volume, although in it a song was sung, while another had volume without a song, and the third had neither. But clearly there can be no singing without volume, nor can there be singing without some sort of song. To insist on distinct tokens in this

---

[5] Peter Achinstein, "The Identity of Properties," *American Philosophical Quarterly* 11 (1974), 262–63.

case, therefore, is to risk winding up with no defensible tokens at all. We must find a way to allow nonidentity for act properties such as singing loudly and singing the "Marseillaise," while not insisting on distinctness for their tokens.

There is more than one way to do this, but I think the best approach is simply to explicate the condition that identical act tokens require identical act properties in terms of what is signified by verb forms alone.[6] The usual device for referring to act properties is a gerund, or a gerundive phrase in which supplementary objects and/or modifiers are provided: thus *singing, singing loudly, singing the "Marseillaise."*[7] And of course the distinctive feature of these properties is that in them the verbal element is the same. When this is the case, the verbal element may be understood as signifying a kind of core property, which is determinable in various ways. The supplementary expressions then specify that property along one or another line of determination.[8] Lines of determination may diverge, as they do here. Singing the "Marseillaise" is determinate as to what is sung, singing loudly as to volume. And since a property determinate in one respect may still be determinable in another, determinations can be combined: we can speak of singing the "Marseillaise" loudly. The key point, however, is that determinations gotten through the use of various objects and modifiers always represent elaborations on a common, core element, signified by a verb. It is really this that gives trouble in the singing example. It is possible to think of the *property* of singing in abstraction from volume and what is sung, and of each of the properties of singing loudly and singing the "Marseillaise" in abstraction from one of these things. But there can be no case in which any of these properties is actually *instantiated* that is not settled in all such respects. Hence it becomes redundant to expect different tokens for each determination of a core act property. Token difference must be made to depend on difference in core properties alone, rather than determinate versions of them.

I propose, therefore, to interpret the third of the fine-grained theory's conditions for act identity as holding it to be necessary for acts to be identical that they involve the same core act property, where such properties are understood to be signified by the verbal elements of property-

---

[6] The approach to be described is adapted from Romane Clark, "Concerning the Logic of Predicate Modifiers," *Nous* 4 (1970), 311–36.

[7] This is not the only device, but it is by far the most common, and keeping to it helps avoid such property designating expressions as *the act Booth performed*, which can refer to a property without signifying or expressing it. See Goldman, *A Theory of Human Action,* pp. 12–13.

[8] For a discussion of determination, see Arthur N. Prior, "Determinables, Determinates and Determinants," I and II, *Mind* 58 (1949), 1–20 and 178–94.

designating expressions.[9] This interpretation allows that singing the "Marseillaise" and singing loudly, though admittedly capable of separate instantiation, may yet be found on occasion to be instantiated in but one token. And it in no way weakens the claim that properties such as firing a gun and killing Lincoln differ in a more fundamental way. Moreover, this approach makes it possible to avoid deciding what is the precise relationship between core act properties and their determinate versions, which is not at all a simple matter. For instance, it might be thought that singing the "Marseillaise" and singing loudly are complex properties that include the property singing. There is some rationale for this interpretation, since determinate properties imply their determinables: from the fact that John sang loudly we can infer that he sang. On the other hand, if the term *singing* is excised from the expression *singing loudly*, what remains is an expression referring to nothing at all. So if singing is a "part" of singing loudly, it is certainly not on an equal footing with any other parts. Furthermore, if we think of act types as sharing part–whole relations, it becomes natural to expect the same of their tokens and so to anticipate that John's act of singing will be part of his act of singing loudly.[10] For this last sort of claim I see no rationale at all. Act tokens have to be things in the world, not *entia rationis*, and so cannot share logical relations. And the spatiotemporal features of John's act of singing loudly cannot be assumed to be any different from those of his act of singing, so that the latter could constitute a segment of the former. Letting core properties alone figure in the fine-grained requirement for token identity helps avoid this trap, since by not addressing the issue of the precise relation between core act properties and their determinates, it does not prejudge the corresponding issue in the case of act tokens.

There is, however, a potential problem in understanding the property identity requirement in terms of verb forms alone. As mentioned, this treatment does not harm the claim that properties such as firing a gun and killing Lincoln are utterly distinct. It may even help focus on why such properties have tended to be so viewed, for something having to do with core properties seems to be at work in that. Besides being capable of separate instantiation, act types such as firing a gun and killing Lincoln are versions of, respectively, firing and killing, which taken alone seem utterly different. Unlike the case with different types of singing, it looks as though each of firing and killing could be done without doing anything that characterizes the other as a specific act type. But the same does not al-

[9]   Core act properties are signified by Clark's "core predicates," "Concerning the Logic of Predicate Modifiers," p. 320.
[10]   Kim, "Events as Property Exemplifications," p. 170; Goldman, *A Theory of Human Action*, p. 39.

ways hold of act types designated by nonsynonymous verbs: Lincoln was also assassinated, and assassinating requires killing. Perhaps, then, Booth's act of assassinating Lincoln is actually identical with his act of killing him, and is simply described so as to allude to the fact that Lincoln was a prominent person. If so, one cannot always rely on nonsynonymous verbs of action as a guide to identity. This problem can be ignored for the moment: it does not loom large in the most commonly discussed examples, and in any case, the insight that act types such as firing a gun and killing Lincoln are distinct seems to me correct. But the idea that nonsynonymous verbs of action signify different core act types is not without problems,[11] and the possibility of their not always doing so will recur.

Individual Accidents

The fine-grained theory has now been taken to hold that for actions to be identical, they must represent cases of display of the same core act property, must involve the same agent, and must occur at the same time. Are there actions that divide according to this criterion? I think there are, but that those are not the only actions. Thus it will not do to adopt the classic approach of the theory and argue simply that all the things we call actions are fine-grained.[12] Neither is it necessary, however, to treat fine-grained actions as a class of entities that cannot be assimilated to any other, for in fact such actions are nothing new. This can be seen by considering whether any types of entity are spoken of in other philosophical contexts that might also count as fine-grained actions. As might be expected, there is more than one candidate.

One possibility, suggested by Hector-Neri Castañeda, is that fine-grained actions are, or at least can be assimilated to, facts. Castañeda holds that "the exemplifying of a property by an agent at a time is the sort of thing philosophers call true propositions, existing states of affairs, or facts."[13] Moreover, he claims that facts or truths are not universal or abstract, and empirical facts are not just in the mind but, in a certain sense, out there in the world. For, says Castañeda, such facts occupy time, in the sense that they occur at the times that, by the fine-grained theory, are con-

[11] Compare Clark, "Concerning the Logic of Predicate Modifiers," p. 323. I discuss this topic more fully in "The Individuation of Action and the Unity of Agency," Chapter 2 of this book.
[12] The classic example is Goldman, *A Theory of Human Action,* pp. 2–6. There have been criticisms of Goldman's arguments, including Castañeda, "Intensionality and Identity," pp. 239–44. See also Norvin Richards, "*E Pluribus Unum:* A Defense of Davidson's Individuation of Action," *Philosophical Studies* 29 (1976), 191–98.
[13] Castañeda, "Intensionality and Identity," p. 236.

stitutive of them. Seemingly, therefore, facts would satisfy the fine-grained theory's demand that events be particular and occupy time. So Castañeda suggests that the fine-grained theory's act tokens are dispensable in favor of facts or, to put it precisely, "dispensable in favor of certain converging materially equivalent classes of truths, namely, those about the same agents and times and with synonymous act types."[14] This approach, he says, has the advantage of not postulating events as entities in addition to facts, thereby avoiding proliferation. Moreover, it might well secure agreement from proponents of other theories of act individuation, who presumably would not deny that many truths, even an infinity of them, are made to obtain when an agent does something.

Some of what is implicit in this account seems to me correct, in particular the idea that, like fine-grained events, facts have stringent identity conditions. But I do not think the parsimony Castañeda rightly aims for is best achieved in this way. Booth's exemplifying the property of killing Lincoln in 1865 is not a fact at all, except in the broad sense in which anything real, including you or me, counts as a fact, and that sense has no reductive force. Rather, the fact is that Booth killed Lincoln in 1865. Now this is clearly something objective, in the sense that we have no choice as to whether it is so, though whether it counts as a particular I doubt. But it is just as certainly not objective in the sense of occupying time, for it is sheer nonsense to say the fact that Booth killed Lincoln, or that he killed him in 1865, occurred or took place at any time.[15] Facts do not do that sort of thing. Events do, and they do other things facts cannot. For example, John's act of singing the "Marseillaise" had to begin, last, and end. The fact that he sang it did not, and indeed if it is a fact at all, it is as real now as ever. Facts can also do things events cannot. They can be true, and putative facts can be false. Neither events nor putative events can be either of these things. Facts, but not events, share logical relations, and they can be the objects of propositional attitudes such as believing, supposing, and judging. But we do not believe, suppose, or, in this sense, judge events. Finally, the facts that John sang, that he sang the "Marseillaise," and that he sang loudly cannot be accounted the same, for they contain different information. Thus they divide more finely than is called for by the version of the third requirement for act identity adopted in the last section, which demands only identity of core act properties. In effect, this condition is based on the hope that there will be fewer fine-grained events involving core act properties than there are facts involving those properties. If we

---

14   Ibid., p. 237.
15   See Zeno Vendler, *Linguistics in Philosophy* (Ithaca: Cornell University Press, 1967), chap. 5, for this and a number of the points that follow. I discuss Vendler's views more fully in "Nominals, Facts, and Two Conceptions of Events."

say fine-grained events simply *are* facts, we shall have to abandon that hope.

In fairness to Castañeda, it should be pointed out that if the requirement of property identity is explicated in terms of properties that include determinations, such as singing loudly, and if we then speak of tokens of this property as having tokens of singing as parts, we get a situation that seems more suited to facts than to events. As we have seen, the entailment relation between the fact that John sang loudly and the fact that he sang invites talk of inclusion relations among properties; and of course, the same applies to the facts themselves. Moreover, it is not entirely clear whether Castañeda holds that facts just *are* fine-grained events or merely wishes to suggest substituting facts for such events, in view of what he perceives to be their similarities. His arguments point in the former direction, but his conclusion is the latter, weaker one. All the same, I think the above objections tell too heavily against the idea. Facts just are not events, nor are events facts. And they are so vastly different that for the fine-grained theorist to give up his events in favor of facts would be to surrender his position almost entirely. That would be premature, since we have seen that facts cannot do the things events can, such as begin, last, and end; and we have yet to discuss whether fine-grained events can do things other sorts cannot. Let us therefore consider whether there is not another class of entities some of whose members count as fine-grained events. I think there is: the class of entities that, in discussions of the problem of universals, are variously called individual accidents, tropes, aspects, or abstract particulars.

Individual accidents are instances of universal properties and, as such, are every bit as particular as you or I.[16] I have already mentioned an example: the whiteness of a sheet of paper. This is of course not a fact, for it is not true or false, or anything we can be said to believe. Nor is it a property, in the sense of a universal, for the whiteness of a particular sheet of paper is not predicable of many. Indeed, properly speaking, it is not predicable of anything: the paper is not its whiteness, or a whiteness. Rather, the whiteness is an instance of the quality white, and an aspect of the paper. As such it cannot exist apart from the paper, and so must be conceived as distinct from the whiteness of any other piece of paper, even one of exactly the same shade. Hence it is particular, although since it depends

---

[16] For treatments of individual accidents, see G. F. Stout, "The Nature of Universals and Propositions," in Charles Landesman, ed., *The Problem of Universals* (New York: Basic Books, 1971), pp. 153–66; the papers by Stout and G. E. Moore from the symposium "Are the Characteristics of Particular Things Universal or Particular?" also in Landesman, pp. 167–83; and Nicholas Wolterstorff, *On Universals* (Chicago: University of Chicago Press, 1970), especially chap. 6.

for its existence on the persistence of the paper, it does not count as an independent entity in the way substances do. Moreover, the whiteness of the paper can be designated in accordance with the category of its corresponding universal. That is to say, just as white is a quality, so the instance of it that is the paper's whiteness may be called a quality of the paper. Thus if one is prepared to accept individual accidents, it is possible quickly to isolate a class of entities that can properly be called actions. For whenever an act type such as killing or singing is exemplified, there will be a particular instance of it, a killing or a singing, that belongs to the agent as an individual accident and counts as an action of his. Finally, though more argument will be required, there is reason to think from the outset that such entities will obey fine-grained principles of individuation. For in terms of content, it is in no way apparent that there should be any more to a sheet of paper's whiteness than is signified by the term *whiteness*. And in the same way, there may be no more to a particular instance of killing or singing than the term for it signifies.[17]

Are there individual accidents? The difficulty with this claim is that it is often associated with efforts at solving the problem of universals, or explaining the notion of substance, and such efforts have been strongly criticized.[18] But these issues need not be gone into here. For even if, as I am inclined to agree, individual accidents cannot alone solve these foundational metaphysical problems, it does not follow that they do not exist or that they cannot solve other problems. And I think it can be shown that no matter what ontological status we accord to properties conceived as universal, we simply cannot do without individual instances of them. Indeed, the need for these shows up especially clearly in the case of act properties. It is not enough simply that there be properties in order that they be displayed; rather, their display requires that something appear in the world. Now if what appears is not a particular token of the property, the only alternative is that it be the property as such—that is, in its status as universal. But that is not possible. Suppose John sings. If he does, there will occur in the world an action on John's part that begins when he begins singing, lasts while he sings, and ends when he finishes singing. We have already seen that facts have none of this character; universals have none of it either, for they are supposed to be eternal. Universals do not occur at all, properly speaking, and they neither begin, last, nor end. Also, as we noted earlier, what occurs when John sings has to have volume. Properties do not: the property singing is neither loud nor soft. Finally, if

17   Many authors take this view of individual accidents as a matter of course. See especially Wolterstorff, *On Universals*, p. 134.
18   See especially David M. Armstrong, *Universals and Scientific Realism*, vol. I (New York: Cambridge University Press, 1978), chap. 8.

what is found in the world when John sings is nothing other than the property singing, then it must be identical with what occurs when anyone else sings. In the same way, what occurs when Booth kills must be identical with what occurs when anyone else kills. But that is not possible either. John's singing may be loud while mine is soft, a difference that, if they are the same, the indiscernibility of identicals would forbid. And though it is certain that Booth committed an act of killing, it is ridiculous to say that all who have ever killed committed the very same killing. If they did, why are they not responsible for Lincoln's death?

One might, of course, try to avoid these problems by saying something to the effect that the property of singing is loud in one of its instancings but not in another, or loud as displayed by John but not as displayed by me. In the end, however, I do not see how this can help. Instancing and displaying a property are, after all, themselves properties, and hence not loud or soft any more than the properties instanced. What, then, can this sort of talk mean, unless we think of instancing as involving the production of a token of the property at issue? But this too commits us to individual accidents, for again properties as such are eternal and so are not produced. In short, these circumlocutions are of no avail for avoiding individual accidents, for we can make sense of them only by accepting such entities anyway. *Something* has to be found persisting through time when John sings and has to have volume. I do not know what it means to say a property as displayed has these features, unless in its display there is produced an instance of it, one distinct from instances of the same property that have different dates.

On metaphysical grounds alone, then, it can be argued that there must be particular instances of act properties. But that is not all. The language for speaking of events indicates that we have referring expressions for just such entities. These are expressions such as *the singing, John's singing of the "Marseillaise," the singing of the "Marseillaise,"* or, in the case of Booth, *the killing of Lincoln, the shooting,* and so on. They represent a subclass of what Zeno Vendler calls "perfect nominals," examples of which are available for other sorts of change as well as action. The distinguishing feature of perfect nominals is that in them the verbal element is completely nominalized. This is indicated by the fact that when such constructions contain an object, it is always in the objective genitive, and by the fact that the possessive subject is eliminable in favor of an article.[19] In both these features, such expressions differ from nominals such as *John's singing the "Marseillaise,"* which, similar though it may appear, obeys entirely different rules. And the behavior of perfect nominals whose verbal elements signify ac-

---

[19]   Vendler, *Linguistics in Philosophy,* pp. 130–31.

tion indicates that they are names for individual accidents in that category.

That perfect nominals are names for actions is clear, for it is always possible to say of John's singing of the "Marseillaise," or the singing, or Booth's killing of Lincoln, both that they are events and that they are actions. And the actions referred to are not universals but instances of them, for the killing of Lincoln occurred in 1865 and is now past, and the singing can be said to have begun, lasted, and ended. These nominals must, then, refer to tokens, for we have seen no such predicates apply to types. Furthermore, these act tokens have the character we would expect individual accidents to have, in that they can be thought of as belonging to agents. That is why possessive subjects in perfect nominals can be exchanged for articles. That we can go from talk of John's singing of the "Marseillaise" to talk of the singing of it, and similarly for the acts Booth performed, indicates that the agent is not really a part of what is referred to by these expressions. Rather, the same instance of singing or killing can be referred to whether or not the agent is mentioned, and indeed it can be predicated of the instance of singing that it was done by John and of the killing that it was done by Booth. Thus when we speak of Booth's killing of Lincoln, we speak of an action of which Booth is the possessor, in the way characteristic of individual accidents.

In this respect, individual accidents of action clearly fall under the second of the two accounts mentioned earlier that the fine-grained theory might give of the relation between agent and action. The actions perfect nominals designate belong to agents, rather than the other way around. Since they do, there is no problem about the action ending while the agent continues to exist. These actions also fit nicely the interpretation adopted earlier of the fine-grained theory's other requirements for identity. They bear the expected occurrence relation to times: it can always be said of a killing or a singing that it occurred at a certain time. Finally, and most important, perfect nominals behave in such a way as to indicate that treating the property identity requirement as applying to core act properties alone is correct. For as long as the core property is the same, there is no problem about claiming identity for instances of variously determined versions of it, where the instances are designated by perfect nominals.

The possibility of making such claims was pointed out by Judith Thomson and further developed by Jaegwon Kim.[20] It is not that perfect nominals cannot signify all that is signified in names for act types. On the contrary, corresponding to *singing loudly* there is the perfect nominal *the*

---

[20] Judith Jarvis Thomson, "Individuating Actions," *Journal of Philosophy* 68 (1971), 778; Kim, "Events as Property Exemplifications," p. 169.

loud singing. Both signify loudness. Similarly, we can think of *the killing of Lincoln* as corresponding to *killing Lincoln, the firing of the gun at time* t as corresponding to *firing the gun at* t, and so on. In all such cases, the conceptual content of the paired expressions is basically the same. But the way in which it is signified is quite different. In *singing loudly,* loudness is signified by an adverb as a determinant for a core act property. The generic property singing is thereby transformed into a specific version of itself, a property determinate with respect to volume. Nothing like this holds for *the loud singing.* Here *singing* is a noun, which refers to an instance of the property singing, and loudness is signified by an adjective. Now the general rule for adjectives is that they express characteristics of the things designated by the nouns they modify. Thus, just as to speak of a red book is to speak of a book that has the characteristic of redness, so also to speak of a loud singing is to speak of a singing that has the characteristic of loudness. In the same way, the killing of Lincoln is a killing that has the property of being of Lincoln, in the sense that he is the victim, and the firing of the gun at time *t* is a firing that is of the gun and that occurred at *t*.

There are, of course, intricacies in this, but the general principle at work should be clear: what act property names treat as determinants of core properties, the corresponding perfect nominals treat as accidents of accidents. So as loudness is what determines singing in the property singing loudly, so loudness is a characteristic of the individual accident that is John's singing. And of course the very same singing may also have the characteristic of being of the "Marseillaise," for it must be a singing of something. So even though the properties of singing loudly and singing the "Marseillaise" cannot be considered identical, the tokens of them designated by perfect nominals in the case of John can and should be. While they signify much more, all that is referred to by the full expressions *the loud singing* and *the singing of the "Marseillaise"* is the singing. This is a much cleaner solution to the problem of the relationship between instances of different determinate versions of the same core act property than is the alternative of calling for inclusion relationships among them. It begins to appear, therefore, that the actions referred to by perfect nominals are just what, on one reasonable interpretation, the fine-grained theory calls for.

Individual Accidents as Fine-Grained

It is not yet clear, however, that these actions are fine-grained. To be sure, taking them as such helps clarify the theory of fine-grained acts, but even in this enterprise the major success comes through claims of identity, not of distinctness. And though it may be natural to take individual acci-dents as relatively thin entities, and thus as differentiated according to core act types, none of the foregoing considerations really requires us to take them that way. What is to prevent the particular instance of killing that is Booth's killing of Lincoln from being identical with the instance of firing that is his firing of the gun, and the instance of moving that is his moving of his finger? Similarly, why cannot a particular raising of an arm be identical with a signaling of a turn? This sort of thing is, after all, common in the case of substances, which are also instances of types. The same man can be a painter and a sculptor, or a grocer and a golfer, even though no one would claim these properties are identical. Why, then, cannot the same action be both a firing and a killing? It would simply be a matter of treating actions as identical under different descriptions, just as we do substances.

I think it can be shown that whatever other "actions" there may be, those named by perfect nominals simply do not admit of such identity claims. Moreover, far from its being the case that fine-grained actions can be avoided by talk of identity "under descriptions," the fact is that such talk makes no sense at all unless there are entities with just the sort of thin-ness fine-grained actions are supposed to have. Indeed, we have a general need for such entities, and the case of substances illustrates it as well as any. Granting that the same person may be equally a painter and a sculptor, part of what it means to describe this as identity under different descriptions is that it is possible to recognize the person as one but not the other. Thus I may know only that Jim is a painter and you only that he is a sculptor. Since these are different descriptions, no amount of deducing will close the gap between your knowledge and mine. What makes this differential recognition possible? Clearly, not just that we are able to *conceive* of Jim under either characterization; the characterizations must also be correct. And that requires that there be something about Jim that an-swers to each of them, for it is not just in virtue of being Jim that he counts as both a painter and a sculptor. That is, Jim has to have different *features* that serve to permit differential recognition. And these features will di-vide up just the way fine-grained actions do—that is, according to type. So just as what is signified by *painter* and *sculptor* differs, we should expect Jim, who is an instance of both, to have different individual features—painterness and sculptorness, if you will—that differ in accordance with type. It is because he has both that he counts as both a painter and a sculptor, and it is because they are different that someone might recognize him under one characterization but not the other.

In short, I suggest that even though in the case of substances the same thing may satisfy more than one description, it does so only because it has characteristics that are individuated according to fine-grained principles. It is this, I think, that allows a reasonable account of knowing a thing qua this but not qua that, and I know no other way to account for it. The same holds in the case of action. What we are able to know about an episode of action divides up logically in terms of descriptions—that is, in terms of the act properties brought to realization on that occasion. Thus one can know that John raised his arm but not that he signaled a turn, and vice versa, and similarly with Booth firing a gun and killing Lincoln. To be in such a knowledge situation is tantamount to recognizing in the case of Booth an instance of firing but not of killing. Here too, it seems to me, the possibility of differential recognition requires different features in the cases themselves, answering to the different conceptions an onlooker might have. The case of John must include features in which the different act types of raising and signaling are found realized, and that of Booth must do the same with respect to firing and killing. Only if these features are different can we account for the fact that a person might recognize one but not the other.

Now none of this would exclude such features, which themselves have to be fine-grained, being related in important ways to entities of a coarser sort. Just as Jim may be both a painter and a sculptor, there may turn out to be entities here that can properly be called "actions" and that answer to more than one description. The point is that even if we call for such coarse-grained actions, we will have to explain their differential recognizability, and that will require a treatment paralleling the one for differential recognition of substances. *Something* in the cases in question has to be finely individuated, for only if that is so can talk of actions being recognizable qua this or qua that receive an adequate account. Since such thin entities are needed, it is natural to let the items that perfect nominals designate serve that need. They are certainly realizations of act types, and their apparent status as individual accidents encourages us to treat them as finely individuated. There is, however, more to encourage this belief. The behavior of perfect nominals themselves with respect to objects and modifiers also indicates that their designata are in fact finely individuated.

As I have pointed out, perfect nominals always cast objects and modifiers in adjectival form, so that they express characteristics predicable of the act token to which the verbal element refers. This is generally recognized to be the case for terms such as *loud*: the perfect nominal *the loud singing* would be used to refer to a token of singing that can be said to be loud or to have the characteristic of loudness. But we have seen that it applies also to expressions signifying objects. Just as we may say of a singing that it was loud, it is also perfectly proper to say of it that it was of the

"Marseillaise," for one of the features that distinguishes this case of singing from others is that in it an instance of the "Marseillaise," rather than some other song, was produced. In the same way, the killing of Lincoln had the characteristic that Lincoln, rather than someone else, was its victim, and similarly for the other acts in our examples. Having the object it does is, then, a characteristic of the action a perfect nominal designates. This, I think, leads to an insoluble problem for the view that, in our examples, the actions that perfect nominals designate are identical. For if Booth's killing of Lincoln is identical with his firing of the gun, then these actions must have the same objects. It follows that the firing was not just of the gun but also of Lincoln, and that the killing was done to the gun as well as to Lincoln. But Lincoln was not fired and the gun was not killed, so these acts cannot be identical. Similarly, in the case of signaling, it was the turn that was signaled and the arm that was raised. If the signaling of the turn and the raising of the arm were the same, then the arm would have had to be signaled and the turn raised, neither of which occurred. So these acts are not identical either.

Like other arguments for the fine-grained theory, this one appeals to the indiscernibility of identicals, and the standard way of evading such arguments is to claim that the contexts at issue are opaque. But I do not think this is a comfortable line of reply in this case. For one thing, there is no independent reason for thinking these contexts—*. . . of the turn, . . . of the gun, . . . done to Lincoln*, and so on—are anything but extensional. Moreover, to treat them otherwise is to lapse into just the sort of qua talk I have claimed individual accidents can be used to help explain, and to render such talk more mysterious than ever. We would have to say, for example, that qua firing the killing was indeed done to the gun and that qua killing the firing was done to Lincoln. But it is not even clear what this would mean. What is killed, one usually supposes, must die. If the gun was killed qua being fired, did it also die qua being fired? Or is it rather that the gun did not have to die, since it was only killed under another description? Both accounts seem to me nonsensical, and the general problem of explaining talk of acts "under descriptions" would only be moved back a step by this procedure. Eventually, we would have to say something to the effect that only in its aspect as firing did the alleged unitary action have the gun as object, and only in its aspect as killing was it done to Lincoln. These "aspects" would have to be fine-grained anyway, so we would not in the end have avoided appealing to such entities. Better, therefore, to let the actions designated by perfect nominals stand as fine-grained from the beginning. There is clear evidence that they are such, and I have argued that they are aspects, at least of individuals. More robust entities, when needed, should be sought elsewhere.

The behavior of perfect nominals with respect to attributive modifiers seems to me also to indicate that they designate fine-grained acts, although here the case is not as clear. Donald Davidson pointed out that in a case where Susan crosses the Channel by swimming it, we might wish to say her swimming of the Channel was fast but her crossing of it slow. This creates a problem for claims that these actions are identical, since it cannot hold without qualification that the same act is both slow and not slow.[21] The account I suggest avoids this problem, for such things as speed and slowness can be predicated of actions only when they are referred to by perfect nominals.[22] Hence, if *Susan's swimming of the Channel* and *her crossing of it* refer to different events, there is no contradiction, since the contrary predicates never apply correctly to the same entity. As with grammatical objects, this solution is better than treating contexts such as . . . *is fast* and . . . *is slow* as opaque. It might, however, be objected that a better solution can be had here if we speak of the same action as belonging to more than one class of comparison. With substances, the phenomenon of opposite predicates applying to the same entity is common. The same individual, for example, can be both a tall man and a short basketball player. There is no contradiction here, because the class of men and the class of basketball players are different, and tallness in relation to one group is not the same as it is in relation to the other. Perhaps in the same way, a single action can be both a fast swimming of the Channel and a slow crossing of it. If so, we can claim identity for these actions, even though the core verbal elements of the perfect nominals used to refer to them are not the same.[23]

I am inclined to think this objection is misconceived. One thing that enables us to say that the same individual is both a tall man and a short basketball player is that the man's height is fixed independently of either of these descriptions. Height is something an individual has simply by virtue of being a physical entity and so can be expected to remain the same across different classes of comparison. But if we take this approach in the case of Susan, we encounter a problem. What we need is a description of her behavior that is neutral as between her swimming of the Channel and her crossing of it but that allows us to assign it a determinate time of occurrence. But nothing of that sort seems to be available. The only likely candidate is Susan's acting per se. But her acting per se will not have had the same duration as the swimming and the crossing unless it

---

[21]   Davidson, "The Logical Form of Action Sentences," p. 82.
[22]   Vendler, *Linguistics in Philosophy*, p. 137.
[23]   Davidson appears to have something like this in mind. The suggestion is developed by Gilbert Harman in "Logical Form," in Davidson and Harman, eds., *The Logic of Grammar* (Encino, Calif.: Dickenson, 1975), pp. 294–95.

ceased when they did, and there is no reason to believe that it did. It is much more likely that Susan moved continuously from swimming to walking out of the water, drying herself off, sipping tea, and talking to reporters.

It might be suggested, however, that if we cannot find anything in Susan's behavior that is neutral as between the swimming and the crossing, we can still proceed by giving one description priority over the other. And there is a case to be made here. One could argue that the relation between swimming the Channel and crossing it is like that between assassinating Lincoln and killing him. Swimming, at least when the verb is transitive, involves traversing some distance; and swimming the Channel entails crossing it, just as assassinating Lincoln entails killing him. So if we are uncomfortable with treating Booth's actions of assassinating and killing Lincoln as distinct, we may feel the same about Susan. It may be that her swimming of the Channel just *is* her crossing of it. Perhaps when we speak of her act of swimming, we are in fact referring to the crossing but describing it in terms of an accidental feature of it—namely, that it was accomplished by swimming. Now it is certainly true that Susan's act of crossing the Channel was both slow by comparison with crossings of the Channel in general, yet fast by comparison with crossings accomplished by swimming. So perhaps to say that her swimming of the Channel was fast is simply to take note of this latter fact.

But if this is to be our ground for the claim that Susan's actions are identical, then that claim remains consistent with the fine-grained theory, for the above argument does not deny that Susan's action is fine-grained. Rather, it holds that to call the act a swimming of the Channel is to give a nonessential description of it, and that we are closer to describing it in terms of a core predicate of action if we call it a crossing of the Channel. Nothing in that prevents Susan's crossing of the Channel from being a fine-grained, individual accident of hers, which itself has the accidental feature of having been accomplished by swimming. Hence this approach to attributive adjectives poses no threat to the claim that the actions we are discussing are fine-grained. Even so, I distrust it. Granted, there is room for flexibility here. Nonsynonymous verbs of action need not always signify completely distinct types, and it may be that in cases like that of Susan, or when Booth is said to have both killed and assassinated Lincoln, claims of identity among tokens are permissible. But we get just as good a treatment of Susan's case if we give her acts of swimming the Channel and crossing it equal standing and let each have its own class of comparison. The mere fact that to swim the Channel is to cross it by swimming does not seem to me reason for denying swimming status as a core predicate of action. To do so is in effect to hold that no action can be essentially a swimming. Yet swimming is a type of bodily movement, which is usually considered a paradigm of action.[24] I prefer, then, to treat attributives along the lines I have suggested.

In any case, the totality of evidence seems to me to weigh strongly in favor of the claim that there are fine-grained actions. Individual accidents in the category of action are, I have argued, required for an adequate ontology, and perfect nominals whose verbal elements signify action seem to me to designate just such entities. The role these expressions play in talk of action provides evidence that their designata do obey the fine-grained theory's crucial condition of individuation: different types guarantee different tokens. Hence, whatever other "actions" there may be, perfect nominals seem to mark a class of actions about which, in its chief contention, the fine-grained theory is correct.[25]

[24] For more on this issue, see "The Individuation of Action and the Unity of Agency," Chapter 2 in this book.

[25] I am especially indebted to Hector-Neri Castañeda, Robert Audi, Irving Thalberg, Myles Brand, Lawrence Davis, and Robert Burch for discussions of these matters, as well as to the editors of *The Canadian Journal of Philosophy* for helpful comments on an earlier version of this essay.

2

The Individuation of Action and
the Unity of Agency

My purpose in this chapter is to make the case for a type of action that obeys coarse-grained conditions of identity; that is, which may receive multiple descriptions using different core verbs of action. Such actions represent a very different class of event from the fine-grained actions I have defended elsewhere,[1] and which many have thought provide for a sufficient ontology of action. Here I argue that fine-grained acts are not sufficient. By themselves, they do not permit an adequate account of the unity of agency—that is, of the fact that in effecting the multitude of things that may be done in a given episode of action, the agent acts just once. Fine-grained actions do not "generate" others in any useful sense, nor is it plausible to think they can all be collapsed into one "basic" act. An adequate account of the unity of agency requires a conception of change quite different from that which underlies fine-grained theories, but which does not force us to reject fine-grained events. I shall offer such a conception, explaining how coarse-grained actions differ from fine-grained ones and how they assist us in understanding unity of agency. Finally, I shall argue that coarse-grained actions do not always collapse into one, either. When one such action serves as a causal means to the performance of another, the former usually counts as a temporal segment of the latter.

---

[1] See "Individuating Actions: The Fine-Grained Approach," Chapter 1 in this book.

The Limitations of Fine-Grained Actions

The point of fine-grained events is to tease apart the rich variety of alterations that may occur in a single episode of change, and to track the various transformations that may be manifested as they take place. Fine-grained events are suited to this role because they are real, ongoing facets of the world and because they have the kind of ontological "thinness" necessary to enable us to study and comprehend particular lines of change in the world without the confusion that would result if everything had to be clumped together. This is especially useful for understanding human action, since action usually involves initiating whole sequences of change in the world, so that a lot can "get done" in a single episode. What gets done in these cases are individual actions. If we think of act types like firing a gun or signaling a turn as universals, then fine-grained actions are simply the individual instances of universals that occur when act types are realized. Such abstract particulars, or "tropes" as they are sometimes called, are naturally taken to be as "thin" as the universals they instantiate: the essential features of a particular firing of a gun are just what is signified in the corresponding act type, and similarly for one's signaling of a turn.

The refinement of fine-grained actions enables us to acquire detailed understanding of particular episodes of behavior without confusion. Not all that is important to firing a gun is important to killing someone, nor are the important features of extending an arm always those of signaling a turn. Speed, efficiency, and expertise in one action need not be measured the same way they are for another, even when both acts are accomplished in the same exercise of agency. We can accommodate such facts if we think of the firing as distinct from the killing, and the extending of the arm as distinct from the signaling of the turn. To be sure, the refinement can be carried to excess. We need not think of the particular action that is John's singing of the "Marseillaise" as distinct from his loud singing. Just as the same core verb of action can take different modifiers, so the same individual accident of action can itself display different features. In the end, however, the fine-grained theory of act individuation is inspired by the principle that different act types require different act tokens. And if that principle is to have significant bite, it needs to be held onto in the case of what is signified by the core verbs used to designate act types. So the instance of firing a gun that occurred when Booth shot Lincoln is not the same as the instance of killing Lincoln that occurred on that occasion. These are distinct individual accidents of Booth. And when Mary extends her arm to signal a turn, her extending of her arm is distinct from her signaling of the turn.

It is just at this point that the fine-grained theory runs into trouble. For while we may count the instances of the different act types realized in the behavior of Booth and Mary as distinct individual accidents of theirs, the fact is that each agent acted only once. That is at least part of the significance of the fact that Booth killed Lincoln *by* firing the gun and that Mary signals *by* extending her arm. Now if Booth's firing of the gun is a distinct action from his killing of Lincoln, then our first instinct ought to be to say that in the episode in question Booth acted twice, and similarly for Mary. But the reason these examples stand as single episodes of action is precisely that this is false. There was just one exercise of agency through which Lincoln was assassinated, and only one through which Mary signaled the turn. That point seems in danger of being lost if we multiply actions in the way the fine-grained approach seems to demand.

Proponents of the fine-grained theory have a response here. They can point out that besides the many specific act universals manifested in the behavior of Booth and Mary, there are also some that are more general, one of which is acting itself. And though many specific deeds can be imputed to Booth and Mary in the examples in question, it is not at all obvious that we need ascribe more than one individual accident of acting to them. If that is right, then to postulate many actions need not be to call for many actings. I think there is value in this point. It shows that the fine-grained theory is able to *respect* the fact that the agents in our examples achieve all that they do in one exercise of agency. But it does no more than that; in particular, it does not *explain* how the achievement is possible. We need to consider what resources the fine-grained theory has for fulfilling this need.

Level-Generation

Perhaps the key to understanding the unity of agency is to explain what it is to do one thing *by* doing another. The most influential treatment of this topic remains Alvin Goldman's theory of "level-generation," according to which the various deeds accomplished in a given episode of action all arise out of the agent's *basic action*, which is in turn performed directly—that is, not by doing anything else.[2] Level-generation is supposed to be a transitive, asymmetric, and irreflexive relation through which more basic actions give rise to less basic ones. The idea is that Booth's act of firing the gun produced or gave rise to his act of killing Lincoln via this relation, that his act of firing was in turn generated by his pulling of the

---

[2]   Alvin I. Goldman, *A Theory of Human Action* (Englewood Cliffs, N.J.: Prentice-Hall, 1970), chap. 2. Carl Ginet, *On Action* (New York: Cambridge University Press, 1990), chap. 3 offers a similar account that is not tied to the notion that actions are fine-grained.

trigger, and so on back to his basic action. As for what level-generation consists in, the core requirement is that for action A to generate action B there must be a set of conditions C^* such that:

(1) The conjunction of A and C^* entails B, but neither A nor C^* alone entails B.

(2) If the agent had not done A, he would not have done B.

(3) If C^* had not obtained, then even though the agent did A, he would not have done B.[3]

The idea here is that A and C^* must be severally necessary and jointly sufficient to entail B, and that both must also figure in B's occurrence, in that in the absence of either B would not have occurred. As for the makeup of C^*, that varies depending on the type of level-generation at issue, for there is more than one. The case of Booth is one of *causal generation*, for which the crucial condition may be expressed as follows:

A causes an event b, and B consists in the agent's causing b.[4]

That is, Booth's action of firing the gun causally generates his act of killing Lincoln, in that it causes Lincoln's death, and Booth's act of killing Lincoln consists in his causing Lincoln's death. As for Mary's act of signaling a turn, it is *conventionally generated* by her act of extending her arm out the car window. The crucial condition for conventional generation is:

A is performed in circumstances C, and there is a rule R saying that A done in C counts as B.[5]

So it is the presence of a rule saying it counts as signaling a turn that enables Mary's act of extending her arm out the window, in the circumstances in which it occurred, to generate her signaling the turn. Finally, consider a case where by jumping six feet three inches, Smith outjumps George. This falls into a kind of catchall category called *simple generation*, for which no independent positive condition is cited. Causality and conventions are not supposed to be involved, but aside from this we are told only that in simple generation, "the existence of certain circumstances, conjoined with the performance of A, ensures the performance of B."[6] In

---

[3] Goldman, *A Theory of Human Action*, p. 43. There are two further conditions, framing restrictions as to what pairs of actions qualify for the level-generation relationship; the issues these involve will not figure in the discussion that follows.

[4] Ibid., p. 23.

[5] Ibid., p. 26. I have simplified the condition somewhat.

[6] Ibid., p. 26.

the case of Smith outjumping George, the crucial circumstance is that George has just jumped six feet. The important thing to realize, however, is that there is no specific difference associated with simple generation; the passage just cited is little more than a restatement of the first clause of condition (1) for level-generation of all types.

The appeal of level-generation is that it points to the right facts. It is indeed because Booth's act of firing the gun caused Lincoln's death that we say he killed Lincoln, and it is because of the conventions for signaling that when Mary extends her arm, she signals. Still, the theory does not offer a satisfying account of the unity of agency. For one thing, it is far from clear that any one relationship underlies our use of the term *by*, or that those which do underlie it always run in the same direction. To cite a familiar example, it is surely by moving my fingers in a certain way that I tie my shoelaces; indeed, this looks like a paradigm case of causal generation. But if someone were to ask me to move my fingers in precisely that way, I could do so only by tying a shoelace, which indicates a relation running the opposite way.[7] Yet the asymmetry of level-generation forbids having a pair of acts generate each other. Now it must be noted in fairness that Goldman does not present level-generation as a complete explication of a supposedly univocal *by*-relation.[8] Still, this example presages trouble for the asymmetry requirement.

One situation in which the trouble emerges is where there is only one way to perform a conventional action. To cite Goldman's own example, suppose that extending her arm out the car window were the only way for Mary to signal a turn. In that case, her act of extending her arm would still conventionally generate her signaling. But the condition that this is the only way to signal, together with the fact that she does signal, entails that Mary extended her arm. So we seem to have a relation of simple generation in the opposite direction. Goldman's third general condition for level-generation is intended to resolve this problem.[9] That condition requires that if C^* had not obtained, then even if the agent had done A he would not have done B. This is intended to leave intact the claim that Mary's act of extending her arm generates her signaling, but to rule out a generational relation in the opposite direction. For that to be accomplished, the first of the following statements must be true, and the second false:

(a) If extending her arm were not a way to signal, then even if Mary had extended her arm she would not have signaled.

[7] Annette Baier, "The Search for Basic Actions," *American Philosophical Quarterly* 8 (1971), 161–70.
[8] *A Theory of Human Action*, p. 21.
[9] Ibid., p. 42.

(b) If signaling did not involve extending her arm, then even if Mary had signaled she would not have extended her arm.

But it is not clear that (a) is true. Presumably, Mary signaled at least in part because she is a conscientious driver. If that is so, then even if extending her arm were not a way to signal she might yet have signaled by other means, whether or not she extended her arm. She would not, of course, have signaled *by* extending her arm. But to invoke that point would be to beg the question, since this is the relation level-generation is supposed to elucidate. And as for whether (b) is false, that seems even more implausible. If we take Mary's case to be a normal example of intentional action, she would surely have extended her arm as a *means* of signaling. If the act no longer counts as a means, then the reasonable supposition is that she would not have extended her arm, even had she signaled. So the counterexample appears to stand. Nor are others hard to find. In the case where Smith outjumps George by jumping six feet three inches, we need only change the latter act to one of Smith jumping more than six feet and the same sort of problem will arise.

As defined, then, the concept of level-generation fails to locate an asymmetric or irreflexive generative relation among actions. Nor is it likely to do so, if it must include anything as broadly framed as simple generation. The circumstances surrounding a given exercise of agency can, after all, be elaborated as richly as one wishes. And that will often make it possible to conclude both that if an agent *A*'s she will *B*, and vice versa. But even if we confine our attention to causal and conventional generation, there is something wrong here. The actions of the fine-grained theory are, after all, particular events in the world. Now the usual relation by which events are thought to give rise to others is that of event causation—although in fact there is long tradition according to which even this idea is spurious. But whatever we may think about event causation, it would certainly be a surprise if there were yet other relations by which one event could produce another. And neither conventional nor causal generation appears an apt candidate.

Conventional generation is suspect even in its description, which says the generating act "counts as" the generated one, given an appropriate rule. That bespeaks a relationship not of production but of identity, and even if it is a misstatement it is implausible to think a generative process is put in place by the formulation of rules. Our *fiat* may have the effect of putting additional actions into the world, given a suitably abstract notion of action, but it is hard to see how it could confer productive capacity on actions that are already there. Causal generation fares no better. In the accepted sense of *cause*, what was caused by Booth's act of firing a gun was Lincoln's death. But the fine-grained theory does not find Booth's act of killing Lincoln to be identical with either of these events, and it would deny that it is caused by them, in the usual sense. But then why say the shooting "causally generates" the killing? To do so is simply to take facts on which everyone is agreed and treat them as constitutive of an ontological relationship on which they would not agree, and the reality of which seems intuitively quite dubious.[10]

Finally, it should be observed that even if level-generation were an ontological reality, it would do little to account for the unity of agency. There are cases in which one action of mine can legitimately be claimed to give rise to another—for example, where by placing the alarm clock by my head at night I cause myself to reach out the next morning to turn it off. But these are *not* cases that display unity of agency; they are clearly situations in which the agent acts more than once, so that the unity problem does not arise. The effect of the theory of level-generation is to treat examples like those of Booth and Mary as analogous to the one where I cause myself to turn off the alarm. Far from accounting for unity of agency, then, this approach obscures it. So even if level-generation could serve as an productive relation among actions, it would do so only at the expense of compounding our problem.[11]

The Identity Thesis and Abstract Particulars

If generative relations among fine-grained actions do not account for the unity of agency, the only alternative is some sort of identity theory. A way must be found to allow the same action to take many descriptions, so that the many things done in one episode can be seen to count as one action, or at least to be nested one within another so that a single exercise of agency will be found at the core. Now it might be thought that this can be done while still treating actions as abstract particulars—that is, as individual accidents of agents that instantiate act universals. We have seen that when act universals are signified by expressions using the same core verb, even

[10]   A defender of level-generation might respond that these criticisms expect too much, that the theory seeks not to posit ontogenetic relations but to provide an orderly understanding of the *facts* that underlie the unity of agency, and hence of various fundamentally conceptual pathways by which we might contrive to do one thing "by" doing another. Fair enough, and the theory is certainly a valuable step in that direction. But if that is the goal, then there is no reason to expect level-generation to be asymmetric and irreflexive. Conceptual pathways don't always run in one direction, nor do recipes for accomplishing actions.

[11]   I discuss the issues of this section at greater length in "The Trouble with Level-Generation," *Mind* 91 (1982), 481–500. See also Hector-Neri Castañeda, "Intensionality and Identity in Human Action and Philosophical Method," *Nous* 13 (1979), 235–60; and Goldman's rejoinder, "Action, Causation, and Unity," *Nous* 13 (1979), 261–70.

the fine-grained theory can permit identity claims. Singing, singing the "Marseillaise," and singing loudly may all be instantiated in the same individual accident, which we can refer to indifferently either as John's singing, his loud singing, or his singing of the "Marseillaise." What permits this is that the features which, in act universals, are treated as determinations of a common, core predicate turn out in the particular instances of those universals to be aspects *of* accidents—in this case, aspects of the single abstract particular that is John's act of singing.[12] Hence the fine-grained theory's key principle—that different act types must be instantiated in different tokens—can be preserved without calling for multiple instantiations of the same core universal in single exercises of agency. One simply confines the principle that different types require different tokens to core predicates only. And it might be thought that a related strategy can be employed throughout the range of cases we have been considering.

This would be so if the true core predicates of action were relatively few, and disclosed themselves only with analysis and study. And it is possible to make at least some progress with this idea. At times, the main verbs in expressions signifying act types appear to pack non-core features into what would otherwise be core predicates of action. The case where Smith outjumps George is a good example. Outjumping entails jumping: to outjump someone is simply to jump farther than they do. And if, when Smith jumped six feet three inches, we were told that he had thereby jumped farther than George, rather than that he had outjumped him, we would treat the case like that of John's singing. We would speak of a single act of jumping on Smith's part, which had two characteristics: it was a jumping of six feet three inches, and a jumping of a distance greater than George had jumped. So here is a case where actions that at first appear distinct may be viewed as identical. And there may be many others. In Booth's case, it is true not only that he killed Lincoln but also that he assassinated him. But it seems prodigal, even on a fine-grained approach, to treat these as separate actions. Perhaps we should say the killing *was* the assassination, assassinations being nothing more than killings of prominent people.

If we find this line of thought plausible so far, we might be willing to carry it much further. Consider again Mary's act of signaling, which the characterization of conventional generation treated as consisting in her extending of her arm. Some might argue that there is good reason for this, in that nothing an agent does can count essentially as an action of following conventional rules. It can, of course, be the case that human gestures of a certain type more or less naturally signify some content, but it can only be

---

[12] For more on this topic; see "Individuating Actions: The Fine-Grained Approach," Chapter 1 in this book.

an accidental feature of them that they are enshrined in our conventions as a means of so doing. In this sense, the argument would run, no action can count essentially as a signaling. Now it seems reasonable to expect that a legitimate core act property would embody only essential features of any action that instantiates it. But then it appears that signaling cannot be such a property, nor can an instantiation of it constitute the essential heart of Mary's particular act of signaling. That must lie in something more natural—say, in her action being one of extending her arm. Thus when we speak of Mary's signaling of a turn, we are in fact referring to her extending of her arm. It is just that we do so under an accidental description, one that applies to her act in virtue of its satisfying the rules for signaling a turn.

If this line of thinking is correct, then any conventional action will turn out to be identical with some nonconventional one. And of course a similar move can be made regarding actions accomplished through causal means. It is an accidental feature of Booth's act of firing a gun that it caused Lincoln's death, and once we know it did so we know that Booth killed Lincoln. Perhaps, then, to say Booth killed Lincoln is simply to describe his act of firing the gun in terms of this causal consequence. And the analysis can be repeated. When he killed Lincoln, Booth stood at the beginning of an entire chain of objectives related as causal means and end: his act of killing Lincoln was accomplished by firing the gun, which was in turn accomplished by his pulling the trigger, and so on. But if each of these is just an accidental description of some more basic doing performed by Booth, then the supposedly numerous actions the fine-grained theory attributes to him were in fact only one action, which is successively described in terms of more and more remote consequences as we move out the causal chain. The implications of this are far-reaching, for it seems clear that in the end the use of causal means represents our only way of effecting changes in the world, and so can be expected to underlie virtually all overt action. Thus, if conventional and so-called simply generated acts are also just more basic acts redescribed in terms of their accidental features, it looks as if the unity of agency can easily be explained. For once all the accidental descriptions have been stripped away, we will be left with just one sort of doing—bodily movement, perhaps—that is foundational to all overt action, and can now be claimed to be all that we ever do when we act.[13]

[13]   Thus Davidson: "We must conclude, perhaps with a shock of surprise, that our primitive actions, the ones we do by not doing something else, mere movements of the body— these are all the actions there are. We never do more than move our bodies: the rest is up to nature." "Agency," in Robert Binkley, Richard Bronaugh, and Ausonio Marras, eds., *Agent, Action, and Reason* (Toronto: University of Toronto Press, 1971), p. 23. Similar views have been held by a number of authors, notably G. E. M. Anscombe, *Intention*, 2d ed., (Ithaca: Cornell University Press, 1963), pp. 37–47; and Jennifer Hornsby, *Actions* (London: Routledge & Kegan Paul, 1980), chap. 1–3.

There are, however, serious problems with this procedure. We shall eventually see that even with actions that are legitimately taken as coarse-grained, the project of reducing all that is accomplished in one exercise of agency to a single basic action is ill-advised. But even if the project were well conceived, it is inappropriate to individual accidents. For one thing, it produces a highly distorted view of the universals of action they instantiate. Ordinarily, we think of killing as a legitimate species of action—that is, as a determinate version of the genus acting or doing,[14] which conveys an essential feature differentiating instances of this sort of action from those of other species, such as pulling a trigger. Killing is, essentially, bringing about a death or causing a death, whereas pulling a trigger is, again essentially, causing the depression of a trigger. But on the present view this is all wrong. In its essence, an action can be neither a killing nor a pulling of a trigger, for properly considered neither of these is a species of action. On the contrary, the term *killing* refers to the genus acting and appends to it an accidental feature of some of its instances—namely, that they cause deaths. If we want to express things perspicuously, we should say not that killing is causing a death, but rather that it is performing an action which causes a death, and similarly for pulling a trigger. That way we make it clear that *killing* signifies no essential features that could differentiate one action from another, and that the same action whose accidental features render it a killing can have others that render it a pulling of a trigger.

I think, however, that this view of act universals is mistaken. Act types like killing and pulling a trigger are in fact paradigms of species of action, because for better or worse the ordinary notion of action is one in which agents are treated as causes—that is, as initiators of change in the world. Exactly what that comes to is, of course, a mysterious matter; and it is certainly true that in order for a person to count as the agent-cause of a non-actional change like a death, there must be a sequence of events in which some action of the agent serves as an event-cause of the change in question. But that such a sequence is required does not entail that it enters into the analysis of the corresponding act universal, or even that it instantiates it. The universal may simply frame the agent-causal relationship, with indifference as to how it is accomplished—the more so since causal means may not be all that is involved. When that is so, the individual accident that instantiates the universal should not be identified with any other. Similar considerations apply to signaling: here the universal involves bringing it about that information is indicated. There is no suggestion as

---

[14]   For the sake of simplicity I ignore the point that not all cases of killing are founded in exercises of agency—for example, if one falls from a scaffold and hits someone, inadvertently killing him.

to how, or whether the means is natural or strictly conventional. But then we need not accept the claim that no fine-grained act of Mary's can be essentially a signaling. Mary's extending of her arm cannot be, of course; but her signaling of a turn is a perfect candidate.

If this is correct, then identity claims among fine-grained actions are in order at most for ones which instantiate act universals like assassinating Lincoln or outjumping George, where the core verb in the expression signifying the universal indicates clearly the nature of the act whose accidental features have entered into its description. There is, moreover, value in limiting identity claims in this way, because it preserves the usefulness of fine-grained actions for keeping track of all that goes on in single episodes of action. Different fine-grained actions have different accidental features. A killing is usually a felony; the pulling of a trigger is not, even when it causes a death. The loudness of John's singing is a feature of that act only; it does not belong to his act of exhaling, even though it is by controlling the amount of air he exhales that John determines the volume of his singing. And Mary's extending of her arm may have been an act her physical therapist told her to avoid, even though her signaling of a turn was not. Treating instances of different act universals as distinct makes it possible to account for such facts without lapsing into the sort of talk that has Booth's action being a felony qua killing but not qua moving a finger, or John's act being loud in its aspect as singing but not in its aspect as exhaling. Fine-grained actions already *are* aspects, which come to characterize agents in episodes of action. The lapse into qua-talk simply shows that if we collapse them all into one we will have to come up with some other tool to fulfill their function.

Finally, there is a linguistic point to be made. In discussing the identity thesis I have been stubbornly referring to fine-grained actions using the expressions I have argued elsewhere are appropriate for this purpose—that is, perfect nominals.[15] One distinguishing feature of such nominals is their exclusive use of the objective genitive rather than a straight object. *Mary's signaling a turn* is not a perfect nominal but an imperfect one—an imperfect gerundive, to be precise—because when it has a straight object *signaling* still functions as a verb, not a noun. Now if it is perfect nominals that signify individual accidents, then in Mary's case we have to speak of her signaling *of* a turn and her extending *of* her arm as the events which instantiate the corresponding universals. Similarly, the abstract particular that Booth manifested when he killed Lincoln was his killing *of* Lincoln, not his killing Lincoln, and so forth. And I think it has to be admitted that this kind of lo-

---

[15]   See "Individuating Actions: The Fine-Grained Approach," Chapter 1 in this book; and "Nominals, Facts, and Two Conceptions of Events," *Philosophical Studies* 35 (1979), 129–49.

cution gives identity claims an odd sound. One feels more comfortable with imperfect gerundives: that is, with the claim that Mary's extending her arm is identical with her signaling a turn. The idea that her extending *of* her arm is identical with her signaling *of* the turn has a peculiar ring. Extendings, one wants to say, cannot be identical with signalings, because extendings *must* be "of" things like arms; signalings, by contrast, must be "of" information, commands, and the like. Similarly, although I shall soon disagree with the claim that Booth's pulling the trigger was identical with his killing Lincoln, the *language* of that claim is to my ear acceptable. The same does not hold for the claim that Booth's pulling *of* the trigger was his killing *of* Lincoln. Rather, with perfect nominals each deed appears to be directed solely to its peculiar object, so that when the objects are different the acts are not interchangeable. This reinforces the thesis that with individual accidents of action, wholesale identity claims are out. But the contrast here with imperfect gerundives points toward another kind of event, and with it a much more useful approach to accounting for the unity of agency.

Coarse-Grained Actions

Our discussion so far indicates that the language of fine-grained action is that of perfect nominals—in which the main element of an act, signified by the core verb of an act universal, is frozen, as it were, into the form of a noun, and all else that belongs to the action is expressed through adjectival modifiers. Thus portrayed, an action is an abstract particular: an instance of the universal, with the descriptive features the modifiers signify. But, as is indicated above, perfect nominals are not our only linguistic tool for referring to events and actions. There are also imperfect gerundive nominals: expressions such as *John's singing loudly, Booth's killing Lincoln,* and *Mary's signaling a turn.* John's singing loudly counts as an event, just as his loud singing does. Booth's killing Lincoln was an action on his part just as his killing *of* Lincoln was, and similarly for Mary's signaling a turn.[16] The difference is that the actions designated by imperfect gerundives are more amenable to identity claims—indicating that they are entities of a kind quite different from individual accidents. We need to examine some of the differences.

Linguistically, the fundamental difference is that the verbal element in imperfect gerundives still functions *as* a verb. One consequence is that

[16] I differ here from Zeno Vendler, who classifies imperfect gerundives with *that* clauses as designating facts. Vendler, *Linguistics in Philosophy* (Ithaca: Cornell University Press, 1967), chap. 5. For arguments against this view see the Introduction to this book and "Nominals, Facts, and Two Conceptions of Events," pp. 134–35.

while the possessive subject in these expressions can be exchanged for a pronoun, it cannot be exchanged for an article. So we can speak both of Booth's killing Lincoln and of *his* killing Lincoln, but there is no *the* killing Lincoln, even though there was the killing *of* him. I have already mentioned a second consequence: in imperfect gerundives objects are kept straight, rather than being given in a prepositional phrase. Finally, whereas in perfect nominals modifications of the core verbal element are treated adjectivally, in imperfect gerundives they are presented adverbially—that is, through predicate modifiers. So in the language of perfect nominals we would speak of John's loud singing of the "Marseillaise" or of Mary's clumsy signaling of a turn, but with imperfect gerundives we speak of John's singing the "Marseillaise" loudly or of Mary's clumsily signaling a turn.

This last difference is especially important, because it helps account for our uneasiness with identity claims that employ perfect nominals. Adjectival modifiers, which perfect nominals require, need not always attach directly to the verbal element; they can also appear as predicate adjectives. So we are not confined to speaking only of John's loud singing of the "Marseillaise"; we can also refer to the singing alone and say that it was loud, that it was of the "Marseillaise," and so on. But then it becomes unnatural to identify the singing with John's exhaling, even though it was (largely) by exhaling that John sang. For if the acts are identical they ought to have the same features, yet it seems clear that the exhaling was not loud, did not have the "Marseillaise" as its content, and so on.[17] Similarly, it is wrong to identify Mary's signaling *of* the turn with her extending *of* her arm, given that the two acts had different objects, and that the former might have been clumsy and inexpert and the latter not.

This problem disappears, however, when we turn to our other type of nominal. With imperfect gerundives, modification *has* to be adverbial, and that cuts off predication. This is not to say imperfect gerundives take no predicates at all. John's singing the "Marseillaise," Booth's firing the gun, and Mary's signaling a turn can still be called events and actions. And they may surprise us, cause various consequences, and so on. But modifications that apply to the core action—that is, its determinations as to time, place, manner, and so on—can only be given adverbially. So even if John sang the "Marseillaise" loudly, it is bad English to say of his singing the "Marseillaise" that it was loudly, or even that it was loud. We can get loudness into the picture only by treating it as a *determination* of John's singing—as a way

---

[17]   Strictly speaking, of course, John has to do more than exhale in order to sing. He must also create the different tensings of his vocal folds the various notes of the song require. But it is even less plausible to speak of the combination of the exhaling and this activity as having the features the singing did.

in which he sang—not as a predicate of it. That is, we must speak of his singing the "Marseillaise" loudly, or of his singing loudly. Similarly, though Mary's signaling *of* a turn might have been clumsy and inexpert, it is wrong to say her signaling a turn was that way; we have to speak of her clumsily and inexpertly signaling a turn.[18] Note, however the effect of this limitation: it turns out that when imperfect gerundives are properly employed, the expressions that signify determinations of core act properties come into play only in alignment with the appropriate verb. The result is that we can make identity claims with much greater freedom. We can identify John's singing not just with his singing loudly and his singing the "Marseillaise," but also with, say, his exercising his voice.[19] And we can identify Mary's extending her arm with her signaling a turn—even, if the signal was inexpert, with her inexpertly signaling a turn. We can do so, moreover, while denying that she extended her arm inexpertly.

Obviously, this is not just a linguistic matter. The greater latitude imperfect gerundives offer for making identity claims indicates that they refer to a different kind of entity, one with different identity conditions, from those to which perfect nominals refer. That is, even though John's singing *of* the "Marseillaise" and his singing the "Marseillaise" may both be called events and actions, they conform to altogether different conceptions of what an event is. The former is an abstract particular—an individual instance of a core act property that counts as an aspect or characteristic of its agent. Like the subjects they characterize, these entities persist through time: John's singing of the "Marseillaise" lasts as long as he is engaged in singing. And they may change with respect to their determinations. The same singing that begins loudly may end softly; it may begin with timidity and end with confidence, or commence in one location and terminate at another. The same does not hold of his singing the "Marseillaise." Predicates that imply the possibility of intrinsic change seem not to apply to what imperfect nominals designate. Indeed, such entities cannot properly be said to begin, last, end—or even, in the full sense of the term, to occur.[20] Nevertheless, it is appropriate to speak of them as events and actions.

The idea of events that lack these traits may sound paradoxical, but I think the conception is legitimate. Besides understanding change in terms of ongoing features of persistent substances, it is possible to comprehend

[18] If the circumstances were such that it was an error on Mary's part that she signaled at all, we might want to say her signaling a turn was clumsy, or clumsy *of her*. But in that sort of case the clumsiness is not a determination of the signaling, but rather a trait of Mary that was manifested in her act.

[19] Out of context, *John's singing* could qualify either as an imperfect nominal or as an imperfect gerundive. To make the identifications given above is to give it the latter interpretation.

[20] Vendler, *Linguistics in Philosophy*, pp. 138–39.

it as a temporally *extended* process in which substances participate. On this model of events, time is analogized to space, and all change is portrayed as laid out within it just as physical objects are spread through space. Such an account would construe John's singing the "Marseillaise" as consisting in the entire temporal sequence of change in which his singing *of* the "Marseillaise" takes place, with characteristics such as loudness built into the process as determinations of a core element, rather than as predicative features of a persisting individual accident. Thus conceived, actions still count as changes, but they do not change; indeed, nothing that is temporally extended ever changes, or even happens, in the full sense of the term. That is not possible, because time enters into the conception of such entities as a dimension they occupy, rather than as a measure of becoming. Temporally persistent entities—substances and their particular characteristics—come to be and pass away. Temporally extended items simply exist, tenselessly, along with whatever determinations they may have. Thus, loudness is present in the process that is John's singing the "Marseillaise" for whatever may be the stretch of time through which John sings loudly, and is otherwise absent. Neither it nor the core activity it determines begins or ceases to exist, in the sense that implies an actual happening. The world of temporal extension is one of fixity, in which the things that come to be and pass away in the world of temporal persistence are enclosed in stable realities, which occupy stretches of time rather than enduring through them.

What I suggest, then, is that imperfect gerundive nominals refer to events and actions conceived as temporally extended processes, rather than to individual instances of event and act universals. The linguistic behavior of imperfect gerundives indicates that they refer to a much more robust sort of reality than fine-grained events. Identity claims can be made more freely with these entities, without the conflicting predications that crop up when we make such claims about individual accidents. And while they do count as events and actions, the items imperfect gerundives designate appear to lack the features of becoming associated with individual accidents. It is reasonable, moreover, to expect human agency to involve entities of greater density than abstract particulars. In the end, after all, we are able to effect changes in the world only through causal means—that is, by way of the dynamic interactions among physical entities whose fundamental nature is described for us by science. However much we accomplish by way of overt action, it has to be accomplished in the transfers of energy and momentum that serve as the basic workings of the world and underlie all of its transformations. To be sure, most of us cannot describe these processes in very sophisticated terms. Still, it is reasonable to think they are there and to treat them as grounding the unity of our experience. That, I suggest, is what happens when the language of imperfect gerundives is employed. When we speak of John's singing the "Marseillaise" or Mary's signaling a turn, we are speaking of a temporally extended process that begins with an exercise of fundamental agency on John's or Mary's part and which, over time, reaches dynamically into the world, resulting in the change or changes definitive of the act in question. Such sequences can, of course, be extended indefinitely, since one exercise of agency can have many consequences. And since in any part of the sequence much can be accomplished, temporally extended doings will often take more than one description. The result is coarse-grained action: the same sequence that counts as John's singing the "Marseillaise" might also count as his exercising his voice, and Mary's extending her arm can also be her signaling a turn.

Individuating Coarse-Grained Actions

If this conception is accepted, we get a much more satisfying account of the unity of agency than we are able to provide in terms of individual accidents. Single episodes of agency count as such not just by virtue of the agent acting only once, but also because the various things he does are bound together in a unified natural process he thereby initiates. But there remains a difficulty: we need to determine how much of the process constitutes any given action. This is especially problematic where actions are accomplished by causal means. Booth killed Lincoln by shooting him; he did the latter by firing a gun, which he did by pulling a trigger, and so on. The question is: How much of the causal series Booth initiated does each of these acts consist in? Do they consist in successively shorter segments of the extended process, or should we opt for the sort of view that appeared untenable in the case of individual accidents, and hold that Booth's temporally extended actions all collapse into one, fundamental exercise of agency on his part?

I think the first of these options is the correct one.[21] The second is prompted in part, no doubt, by the view that it is overt bodily actions—things like Mary's extending her arm or Booth's moving his finger on the trigger—that constitute our fundamental exercises of agency. If bodily

---

[21]   Its defenders include Fredrick Stoutland, "Basic Actions and Causality," *Journal of Philosophy* 16 (1968), 467–75; and Lawrence H. Davis, "Individuation of Actions," *Journal of Philosophy* 67 (1970), 520–30, although Davis moves closer to a single action view in *Theory of Action* (Englewood Cliffs, N.J.: Prentice-Hall, 1979), chap. 2. Other champions of the component theory are Irving Thalberg, *Perception, Emotion, and Action: A Component Approach* (Oxford: Basil Blackwell, 1977), chap. 5; Judith J. Thomson, *Acts and Other Events* (Ithaca: Cornell University Press, 1977); and Carl Ginet, *On Action*, chap. 3.

movements are our "basic actions" and all other actions are just those movements redescribed, human action promises to be a nicely localized and easily observable phenomenon, a readily available target for efforts to understand the nature of agency. In fact, however, this expected advantage is not going to be forthcoming, because bodily movements do not count as fundamental exercises of agency. On the most plausible interpretation of what it is for an action to be basic, overt movements can be shown to be accomplished through more fundamental acts that lie within the agent and that on any given occasion need have no overt manifestation.[22] To insist on collapsing all overt action into whatever action is basic, therefore, would actually be to conceal all action within the agent, leaving only its external effects to be observed. Yet that seems wrong. When we see someone extend an arm or move a finger we feel we are observing their actions, not just consequences of them.

But even if we grant that bodily movements are basic, there is no decisive argument for identifying them with all the actions to which they serve as causal means. Often cited as persuasive is the point that once the bodily movement is complete, the agent need do no more in order to accomplish the succeeding acts in the series. And that is certainly true if what we mean is that the agent need not engage in any further exercise of fundamental agency. But it does not follow that the exercise of agency is identical with every act accomplished through it. Furthermore, when we try to frame a set of identities that would make such a claim plausible, trouble arises. An argument of Donald Davidson purports to accomplish such a result. Recast to cover the case of Booth, it might appear as follows:

(1) Booth's moving his finger = Booth's doing something that causes Lincoln's death.
(2) Booth's doing something that causes Lincoln's death = Booth's causing Lincoln's death.
(3) Booth's causing Lincoln's death = Booth's killing Lincoln.
(4) Therefore, Booth's moving his finger = Booth's killing Lincoln.[23]

A similar set of identities can, of course, be formulated for Booth's other deeds, and indeed for any action accomplished by causal means. So if this set of identities is correct, then assuming causal means are in the end our only tool for bringing about changes in the world, the thesis that the only actions we ever perform are our basic actions would seem pretty secure.

[22] These points are argued for in Part II of this book.
[23] Davidson, "Agency," p. 22. There is considerable affinity between the argument under scrutiny and so-called "big fact" arguments, which Davidson also employs. See, for example, "Causal Relations," *Journal of Philosophy* 64 (1967), 694–95.

In fact, however, the set of identities is fallacious, for consider a similar argument:

(1′) Lincoln's dying = Lincoln's undergoing a death that is caused by an action of Booth's.

(2′) Lincoln's undergoing a death that is caused by an action of Booth's = Lincoln's being caused to die by Booth.

(3′) Lincoln's being caused to die by Booth = Lincoln's being killed by Booth.

(4′) Therefore, Lincoln's dying = Lincoln's being killed by Booth.

The steps of this argument parallel exactly those of the preceding one, so if the first argument is above reproach then this one should be as well. Yet its conclusion seems quite implausible. Much worse, however, is that we now need but one further premise:

(5) Booth's killing Lincoln = Lincoln's being killed by Booth,

and the two arguments combined yield an obviously unacceptable result:

(6) Booth's moving his finger = Lincoln's dying.

Pretty clearly, something has gone wrong.

One might, of course, insist that premise (5) is wrong, that it is a mistake to identify Booth's killing Lincoln with Lincoln's being killed by Booth. But I cannot see that as anything but an ad hoc move. If we are going to make identity claims among events at all, this one has as much plausibility as any, and I can see no reason to deny it apart from a desire to save the identities argument from the present difficulty. What *is* implausible, though, is the claim that Lincoln's dying is identical with his being killed by Booth. The argument for that conclusion is fallacious, because it employs the *that*-clause in *Lincoln's undergoing a death that is caused by an action of Booth's* ambiguously. For premise (1′) to be plausible, we have to take the *that*-clause as strictly informational. It simply expresses a true proposition concerning the event which was Lincoln's dying or undergoing death—namely, that it is caused by action on Booth's part. The item in the world that answers to that proposition—that is, the process consisting in Booth's action causing Lincoln's death—remains *extrinsic* to what the right side of (1′) refers to. As a result, both sides refer only to the event that was Lincoln's dying, and the identity claim is correct. But for (2′) to come out right, precisely the opposite has to occur. Lincoln's undergoing a death that is caused by Booth's action can plausibly be taken as identical with his being caused to die by

Booth only if we take Booth's action's causing the death as *intrinsic* to what is referred to on the left side of this identity. But then the *that*-clause ceases to have a strictly reportorial use; in effect, we are speaking of Lincoln's undergoing a death *and* that event being caused by Booth's action. Provided we do so, (2') comes out true. But then the link with (1') is lost, and the full set of identities fails to go through.

The same difficulty afflicts our first argument. We might expect this argument to be problematic, since we have already seen that doing something that causes a death and causing a death are different universals of action.[24] In the realm of coarse-grained events, however, the expressions signifying these universals may still assist us in locating identical actions, provided they are used unambiguously. The problem is that here they are not. Regarding premise (1), Booth's moving his finger is plausibly taken as identical with his doing something that causes Lincoln's death only if the movement's causing Lincoln's dying is taken as extrinsic to what is referred to by *Booth's doing something that causes Lincoln's death*. But when we turn to premise (2), that part of the process has to be taken as intrinsic to what is referred to. We must now interpret *Booth's doing something that causes Lincoln's death* as referring to Booth's doing something *and* that deed causing Lincoln's death. Again, therefore, we are able to secure the second identity only at the expense of severing the tie to the first, and the full argument comes out invalid.[25]

There is, then, no compelling argument for reducing everything that is done in a single episode of action to whatever we take to be the agent's basic action. Rather, the correct approach seems to be the first of those mentioned above. If it is correct to think of coarse-grained actions as temporally extended sequences of change, then the natural thing is to take any given action as consisting in as much of the causal chain extending from the agent into the world as is required for that action to be accomplished. In Booth's case, this means that his moving his finger is the sequence that begins with the fundamental exercise of will in which that act is founded and ends with the finger's moving. His firing the gun consists in a lengthier sequence that ends with the gun's discharging, and his killing Lincoln is constituted by the still lengthier sequence that terminates in Lincoln's dying.

Understanding cases like that of Booth in this way makes possible a satisfying solution to some well-known difficulties regarding the timing of

---

[24] Contrast the argument of Davidson's on which (1) through (4) is based (*Ibid.*), where the premise that is the analog of (2) is that these universals are identical.

[25] Carl Ginet has criticized arguments like this in very similar terms. *On Action*, pp. 59–60. On Ginet's view, such arguments are valid, but premises like (2) and (2') are simply false. The issue seems to me to be somewhat more complex.

causal actions. Philosophers who oppose collapsing all of Booth's actions into one have pointed out that to do so commits us to holding that his act of killing Lincoln was over once his basic action was complete. That would have to have been on the night of April 14, 1865, when Booth fired the fatal shot. Yet Lincoln did not die until the morning of April 15. We would have to claim, therefore, that Lincoln died sometime after he was killed—that is, that it was true that Booth had killed him before it was true that he was dead. Yet the statement "Booth has killed Lincoln" seems to *entail* "Lincoln is dead," which on the night of April 14 was false. Thus, it seems, Booth's act of killing Lincoln was not complete until well after his basic action.[26] For their part, proponents of the single action view have countered that while it may not have been an act of killing at the time it was performed, Booth's basic action might have *become* an act of killing the next day, when Lincoln died.[27] Furthermore, it may be argued, to hold that Booth's act of killing Lincoln was not over until Lincoln had died commits us to holding that the act was "going on" the whole while. But if that is so then it ought to have been correct to say of Booth, "He is killing Lincoln" long after he had turned his attention to escaping. Indeed, we ought to have been able to say this even after Booth himself was dead, if he had been killed during the interim. Yet surely these claims are false.[28]

If the view I espouse is correct, opponents of the single action view have the better of this dispute. The fact that it would have been wrong to assert that Booth had killed Lincoln until it was true that Lincoln was dead is reflected in the fact that the temporally extended action which is Booth's killing Lincoln extends through time to the morning of April 15, when Lincoln died. That is a longer stretch of time than that occupied by such acts as Booth's moving his finger or his shooting Lincoln, which terminate the night before. Nor is it possible for these earlier segments of the process to *become* his killing Lincoln, for as temporally extended entities they cannot become anything. It is temporally persistent entities that become, but we have already seen reason for denying that the corresponding individual accidents are identical. As for the point that Booth cannot be said to be killing Lincoln during the entire stretch of time the corresponding tem-

---

[26] For this sort of argument see especially Judith J. Thomson, "The Time of a Killing," *Journal of Philosophy* 68 (1971), 115–32.

[27] This view has been defended by a number of authors. See especially Jonathan Bennett, "Shooting, Killing and Dying," *Canadian Journal of Philosophy* 2 (1973), 315–23. Also Robert Grim, "Eventual Change and Action Identity," *American Philosophical Quarterly* 14 (1977), 221–29; and J. F. Vollrath, "When Actions Are Causes," *Philosophical Studies* 27 (1975), 329–39.

[28] Norvin Richards, "*E Pluribus Unum*: A Defense of Davidson's Individuation of Action," *Philosophical Studies* 29 (1976), 195–96; see also Lawrence B. Lombard, *Events: A Metaphysical Study* (London: Routledge & Kegan Paul, 1986), pp. 151–152.

porally extended act occupies, that is quite correct. But it is not damaging, because the present continuous tenses signify that something is "going on" or "happening," which temporally extended events do not do. Again, it is individual accidents that do that—in Booth's case, his killing *of* Lincoln. And it is true that this accident can be attributed to him in the present progressive tense only while he is actively engaged in the deed. What this shows is that the individual accident and the corresponding temporally extended event relate differently to time. The former does not last through the entire temporal interval that the latter occupies. But that is a perfectly acceptable result; it only reflects the fact that we are dealing here with two entirely distinct sorts of entity, representing different ways of conceptualizing change.

It remains to be observed that temporally extended events provide for a natural treatment of our other examples, also. As we would expect, coarse-grained actions whose descriptions employ the same core verb, such as John's singing the "Marseillaise" and his singing loudly, count as one and the same, just like the individual accident that corresponds to both. Conventional actions, too, are easily dealt with: if the convention that makes it possible for Mary to signal a turn by extending her arm has it that doing the latter *counts as* doing the former, then her extending her arm and her signaling a turn must consist in the same dynamic sequence. Finally, as for the case of Smith and George, Smith's jumping six feet three inches is identical with his outjumping George, because in jumping six feet three inches Smith jumped a greater distance than George did. His outjumping George does not include any further events—none, particularly, in which George is involved—because there is no dynamic interaction between Smith and George when Smith outjumps him.[29]

Conclusion

If the approach to the unity of agency I have outlined is correct, terms like *event* and *action* actually refer to two entirely distinct kinds of entity, with different relations to time and different conditions of identity. Is this an exercise in ontological prodigality? I think not. For one thing, the linguistic evidence in favor of a twofold conception is too strong. We do have two types of construction for referring to "events," and they do not behave alike. It may be, therefore, that both conceptions are part and parcel of our conceptual apparatus for comprehending the world, and cannot be

[29] Ginet appears to view this matter differently. See his suggestion that if a person jumps further than she ever has, that act "includes the circumstance" of her never having jumped this far before, a circumstance which in turn includes all her previous jumps. *On Action*, p. 50.

gotten rid of. But the really important question is whether we can understand change better under one of these conceptions alone than we can using both. I do not think we can. To give up abstract particulars in the category of change is equivalent to saying that when events take place nothing ever happens in the true sense, nothing ever truly goes on. That seems to me completely unacceptable. We ourselves are temporally persistent beings, and I do not see how we can conceptualize our experience fully if we relinquish the idea of temporally persistent individual accidents—not to mention the refined understanding of change we are able to achieve by viewing it in fine-grained terms. As for temporally extended events, they may seem more dispensable, but I think they are not. The conception of time as a dimension analogous to space is part and parcel of current science; and even if that were to change it is hard to see how we could form a unified conception of history without the notion of an event that occupies a segment of it. Certainly, it seems to me, we could not produce as satisfying an account of the unity of agency.

I see no reason, then, why ontology should not accommodate both these sorts of entity. In a sense, after all, the parties to the disputes we have considered are all agreed about what goes on in the examples: about what is accomplished, about means-end relationships, and so on. It is only when we try to account for these facts using too limited an ontology that the disputes arise. That is an issue of how change is best conceptualized, and even if we could supplant the conceptualizations reflected in everyday discourse about events, it is not at all obvious that we could improve upon them. If that is right, then the ontology of action should allow a place for both of the types of action considered here.

II

THE FOUNDATIONS OF ACTION

3

Is Raising One's Arm a Basic Action?

It is frequently claimed that certain bodily actions, such as raising an arm or moving a finger, are in most instances of their performance apt candidates for description as "basic actions," "simple actions," or something similar.[1] One reason for the importance of such claims is that it appears that some actions must be fundamental in one or more respects, and whatever these actions are they need to be recognized. More important, however, is the fact that if actions like arm raising have this status, they cannot involve more primitive actions of flexing muscles or willing the movement of the arm. Since traditional treatments of action often suggest one or both of these things might be the case, claims that arm raising is basic have come to be associated with attempts to refute such accounts. But it seems to me that, insofar as they tend to suggest raising an arm is a nonbasic action, the traditional accounts are correct. I shall offer no view here as to what actions are basic, but I shall attempt to show that actions like raising an arm never are. My contention is that these actions involve actions of physical exertion on the part of the agent, the involvement being of a sort generally taken to be excluded by an action's being basic.

---

[1] See, for example, Arthur Danto, "Basic Actions," *American Philosophical Quarterly* 2 (1965), 144, and "What We Can Do," *Journal of Philosophy* 60 (1963), 436; A. I. Melden, *Free Action* (London: Routledge & Kegan Paul, 1961), p. 65; Fredrick Stoutland, "Basic Actions and Causality," *Journal of Philosophy* 65 (1968), 471; and Richard Taylor, *Action and Purpose* (Englewood Cliffs, N.J.: Prentice-Hall, 1966), p. 118.

A Necessary Condition for Basicness

One difficulty about deciding whether an action is basic is that the concept of a basic action is clouded, there being no complete agreement on what conditions must be satisfied for an action to be fully basic.[2] But widespread agreement is approached on one point: most philosophers who speak of basic actions appear to hold that, in order to be basic, an action A of an agent M must satisfy the negative condition that it not involve something B which is also an action of M's and which is related to A, as an action of shooting or poisoning a person might be to that of killing him. An action would be considered nonbasic if it did involve something of this twofold description. Spelling out the requirements of the description will provide a means for evaluating claims that an action is basic, which, though not complete, suffices for present purposes.

The first requirement is that B be an action. What it is for something to be an action is of course a vexed question, but I shall try to avoid further vexing it here. I propose to adopt a list of conditions strong enough so that anything satisfying them would generally be considered to belong in the category of action. I shall say B is an action of M's only if, like shooting or killing a person, B is an occurrence that could ordinarily be correctly described as something M does. I shall further require that M know he does B, that he do B intentionally, and that he would be held responsible for doing B. On this criterion, then, killing would be considered an action only if it were done knowingly, intentionally, and responsibly. I know of no place where anything satisfying all these conditions is treated as less than an action. In any case, if something satisfying them turns out to be related to arm raising in the way about to be described, the claim that arm raising is a basic action would be robbed of its significance, if not its truth.

As to the relation in question, it seems most safely treated as itself twofold in character. Consider a case where Smith performs the action of killing Jones. Here there will be another action of Smith's—say, shooting Jones—related to his act of killing, for actions like killing cannot be performed outright. In such cases, we tend frequently to use the word *by* in describing the relation between the actions: we say Smith kills Jones by shooting him. But in typical cases where this is said, there are actually two important relations between the actions. One can be explicated along lines

---

[2]   For discussions of what a basic action is, see the articles by Danto and Stoutland cited; also Danto, "Causation and Basic Actions," *Inquiry* 13 (1970), 108–25; and Annette Baier, "The Search for Basic Actions," *American Philosophical Quarterly* 8 (1971), 161–70.

suggested by Fredrick Stoutland, in terms of a distinction between results and consequences of actions.[3]

To do something, unless the doing is strictly mental, is to bring about a change or changes in the world, and whether one performs a given action depends in part on what changes one brings about. If Jones does not die, or if he dies but Smith cannot be said to have brought about his death, it follows logically that Smith does not kill him. The change that corresponds to an action in this way—that is, the change the bringing about of which is the action in question—may be called the *result* of the action.[4] Opposed to the result of an action are its *consequences*, which are changes caused by the result of the action. Smith's action of killing Jones might, for example, have it as a consequence that Jones's wife suffers grief; this would be so if her husband's death caused Mrs. Jones sadness. The crucial point is that the same change may be both the result of an action *A* and a consequence of a logically distinct action *B*. That is what obtains when Smith kills Jones by shooting him. Jones's death, the result of Smith's action of killing him, is caused by the entry of a bullet into his body, which is in turn the result of Smith's action of shooting him. When an action *A* is related to an action *B* in this way, I shall say *B* is *causally more basic* than *A*. Thus Smith's shooting Jones is causally more basic than his killing him.

A second relation that obtains, at least in many cases where Smith would be said to kill Jones by shooting him, is that Smith will have performed the act of shooting Jones *as a means* to killing him. This would tend especially to be true in cases where the killing is intentional, as the criterion for action adopted above demands. Now insofar as a person *B*'s as a means to *A*-ing, his action *B* is viewed by him as ancillary to his action *A*: it occupies a place subordinate to *A* in his purposes and is done by him with the intention of *A*-ing. Actions viewed in this way by their agents may be said to be *teleologically more basic* than the action to which they are considered ancillary. In the case at hand, then, Smith's action of shooting Jones is both causally and teleologically more basic than his action of killing Jones.

It seems best to interpret the requirement for basicness cited above as having it that, in order to be basic, an action must involve no other action of the same agent that is both causally and teleologically more basic. For suppose a person knows enough about physiology to be able to describe and pick out precisely the set of muscles that control the upward move-

---

[3] Stoutland, "Basic Actions and Causality," pp. 470–72. Stoutland borrows his terminology from G. H. Von Wright, *Norm and Action* (London: Routledge & Kegan Paul, 1963), pp. 39–41. But Von Wright uses *consequence* to cover only causal consequences, whereas Stoutland uses the term more broadly; here I follow Von Wright.

[4] The word *change* here covers nonchanges also, these being the results of acts of prevention and forbearance.

ment of his arm. It is generally agreed that such a person, because he knows those muscles will be flexed if he raises his arm, is able to perform the action of flexing them. If he does perform this physiological action, it will be causally more basic than his raising his arm, just as Smith's action of shooting Jones is causally more basic than his killing him: the tensing of the muscles will cause the arm to go up. Yet in such a case we may be inclined to say not that the person raises his arm by flexing his muscles, but that he flexes his muscles by raising the arm. That is, we may expect such cases normally to be such that the agent views his act of arm raising as a means, if not of performing the physiological action, at least of seeing that it gets performed, in which case it, rather than the physiological act, would appear to be teleologically more basic. The question is whether in such cases raising an arm is to be viewed as a basic action.[5]

If the only requirement for basicness were that an action not involve any causally more basic action of the same agent, the answer would have to be "No." Arm raising violates that requirement in the case described. But if we insist also that, for one action to be truly more fundamental than another, it must be teleologically more basic, it may yet be possible to accommodate this example. For it is not yet clear that the agent in it does anything teleologically more basic than raising his arm. In effect, then, we make it easier for raising one's arm to count as a basic action if our standard for basicness includes a teleological component. Accordingly, I shall in what follows assume that, in order to be basic, an action A of an agent M must include nothing B that is also an action of M's and is both causally and teleologically more basic than A. This requirement would, I think, be all but universally accepted as a necessary condition for basicness.[6]

There are, of course, cases where arm raising violates this requirement—for example, where a person raises an arm by grasping it with his other hand and lifting it. But this does not normally occur when one raises an arm, and the general opinion is that the requirement is not violated in the normal case. I wish to argue that it is.

Trying to Raise One's Arm

It is helpful in this connection to consider cases where a person tries to raise his arm. For even if not every case of arm raising is best described as

[5] My discussion of this difficulty is heavily indebted to that of Baier, "The Search for Basic Actions," pp. 166–68. She points out that cases like this render some criteria for basicness undesirable, if it be demanded that such criteria select only mere bodily movements as basic.

[6] But not a sufficient condition: numerous further demands can be made, such as that the action have no other action related to it as extending one's arm out a car window might be related to signaling a turn. See Stoutland, "Basic Actions and Causality," p. 474.

one of trying to raise it, actions that normally serve as a means to raising one's arm, if there be such, might be more easily noticed in situations where they count as attempts. Now we generally speak of trying either when someone sets out to perform an action and unexpectedly fails, or when at the time he sets out to perform the action there is doubt that he will succeed. The reason for failure or doubt of success may vary: where a bodily action is attempted, it might be that the agent is paralyzed. I shall have nothing to say about cases of paralysis here; they are important, but they can be better understood if one first understands cases where the agent is of normal physical ability.[7] Here, then, are three cases where an able-bodied person tries to raise his arm:

(1) A man's arm is being held down by his young son, who in a test of strength challenges him to raise it. The father doubts he can, but says he will try. He then tries to raise his arm, and succeeds.

(2) The same as (1), except that the father fails to raise his arm. It does not move the slightest bit.

(3) A man seated at a lecture wishes to ask a question. Unbeknownst to him his sleeve has gotten caught on the arm of his chair. He tries to raise his arm to get the speaker's attention. He fails; the arm does not move at all.

It is at least generally true of attempts that they consist in something a person does, and these cases are no different. If we were to ask the agent in each of them what he did by way of trying to raise his arm, we would be surprised to hear him say that although he tried to raise his arm, there was absolutely nothing he did that constituted his attempt to raise it.[8] Rather, we would expect his reply to be a description of something he did. As to what the doing might be, that could vary. The father, being aware of an obstacle, might by way of trying to raise his arm have jerked upward on it with his free hand. But he need not have behaved in this way (perhaps his son would have considered it cheating), and the man in (3) probably would not have done this, since he anticipated no difficulty. Accordingly, let it be assumed that in none of these cases does the agent's attempt involve the use of some part of his body that does not ordinarily serve as an instrument for raising his arm.

If this be assumed, then in all three cases roughly the same reply would most likely be given to the question what was done by way of trying. We would be told the attempt consisted in putting forth a physical effort to

---

[7] For an analysis of the attempts of paralytics, see "Trying, Paralysis, and Volition," Chapter 5 in this book.

[8] Taylor seems to think something like this might be said when a completely paralyzed man tries to raise his arm and fails; *Action and Purpose*, pp. 84–85. But I think even he would concur that such a statement would be odd when the agent is able-bodied.

raise the arm. The degree of effort and the suddenness with which it was made might vary from case to case: perhaps it was very strenuous and sudden in (1) and (2), for example, but less so in (3). But in most cases like these, this would be the only significant difference. Asked what he did by way of trying to raise his arm, the agent in each case would probably say, "I exerted effort to raise my arm," "I strained to raise it," or something of the sort, and onlookers would give the same type of account. Making a physical effort to raise one's arm can, then, count as an attempt to raise it in cases such as these.

It is important to observe that in all these cases, we treat the agent's attempt as consisting in something he can do and yet fail to raise his arm. It is sometimes said that attempts to perform acts like arm raising consist, in some or all cases, in actually performing the action, or in performing it with a special degree of exertion.[9] Accounts of this kind will not do. In the first place, trying to raise one's arm cannot always include raising it, for then it would be impossible to try to raise one's arm and fail, which quite obviously it is not. But even where the agent tries and succeeds, as in (1), his trying does not include raising his arm. If that were so, what his attempt consists in would depend on whether or not it was successful, and trying never has this characteristic. If it did, we should be able to infer from statements like "He will try to raise his arm, but it is not certain whether he will succeed," a statement such as, "He will try to raise his arm, but it is not certain what his attempt will consist in." Yet no such inferences are ever drawn; in fact, in most cases where the first statement is true, the second is false.

It is a further error to suppose that when trying involves physical exertion, the exertion must be to some special degree. That is often so in cases where the agent is unsure of success, but it is less likely where he anticipates no difficulty. And even where difficulty is anticipated, no special degree of exertion need occur. Thus a person might suspect his sleeve is caught on his chair, try to raise his arm in order to find out, and specifically avoid exerting himself to any extraordinary degree, so that in the event the sleeve is caught it will not be damaged.

Now if in the cases described the agent's attempt consists in making a physical effort to raise his arm, the question arises whether in case (1), where the action of arm raising is successfully performed, the action violates the requirement for basicness cited earlier. I want to argue that it does, but first I want to argue that the normal act of arm raising is much like that which occurs in case (1).

---

[9] For example, Danto, in "What We Can Do," pp. 439–40, holds that "trying to do *B*" is equivalent to "doing *B* with a special effort," and gives the example of moving one's arms against ropes that bind one.

The Normal Act of Raising One's Arm

It often happens that, by way of trying to perform an action A, a person does something of a sort that would normally be involved in A-ing anyway. By way of trying to kill Jones, for example, Smith might shoot him. The above cases of trying to raise an arm are like this. Normally, raising one's arm does not involve straining to raise the arm, but it does involve making an effort to raise it. One way to see this is by noting that the agent in (3) did not know his sleeve was caught, and so had no reason to suppose beforehand that he would fail to raise his arm. This being so, his attempt would not consist in anything very unusual. That is, what the agent in (3) does by way of trying would be nothing *in addition to* what he usually does in raising his arm, except insofar as having once noticed difficulty he might instead of ceasing to try begin to strain. Hence it must be that he, and anyone else, normally makes an effort to raise his arm when he does raise it.

Other considerations lead to the same conclusion. Sometimes attempts to raise an arm do consist in exerting a special degree of force to raise it. But how can we speak of a special degree of exertion in these cases if there is no normal degree of exertion associated with raising an arm? There must be some degree of exertion by comparison with which others are extraordinary. Also, we need to account for the fact that the average person would resist any suggestion that he does not, in normal cases of raising an arm, make an effort to raise it. If the agent in (1), for example, were told his act of arm raising differed from normal in that here he exerted himself to raise his arm, whereas he normally just raises it, he would say that if by "just raises it" we mean he does not normally engage in any exertion at all to raise his arm, the analysis is false. In the normal case too, he would say, he makes an effort; that is one of the differences between cases where one raises his arm and cases where the arm goes up because someone else raises it. One can, of course, say a person "just" raises his arm in the normal case, but to say this is not to say he does nothing else. It is to say the action comes off in the normal way, with no undue complication, as when a practiced and callous murderer says, "There was nothing to it really; I just killed him."

Another point needs to be noted here, one which, though puzzling in some ways, also indicates that the normal act of arm raising involves making an effort to raise the arm. In the above cases of trying it was assumed that the attempt did not involve jerking upward on the arm with one's free hand. Yet someone who did do such a thing could, after all, also be said to have made a physical effort to raise his arm. Now suppose we were to ask one of the agents in cases (1) to (3) how his exertion had differed from that of the man who jerks upward on his arm. Aside from telling us what he had not done—that is, that he had not used his free hand—about the best thing the agent could say would be: that he had exerted himself in the way normally suited to raising the arm, whereas the man who jerks on his arm does not. That is how he would have to go about telling us what he *did* do. More will have to be said below about the necessity for this reply, but the important thing here is that it, too, indicates that the normal act of raising an arm is like that performed in case (1). Hence I conclude that this is so: the typical case of raising one's arm is a case in which one makes a physical effort to raise it.

Making an Effort to Raise One's Arm as Action

I turn now to the question whether the normal act of raising one's arm, and that performed in case (1), violates the condition for basicness set forth above. The crucial business here, as it turns out, is to see that making an effort to raise one's arm, as it occurs in these cases, is an action, and to understand the kind of action it is. Once this is done, it is an easy matter to deal with the other aspects of the necessary condition for basicness. Now it is obvious that the first of the four requirements embodied in the criterion for action I have adopted is satisfied here. Making an effort to raise an arm is clearly something a person can be said to do. It is not difficult to see that the other requirements are satisfied as well.

When a person makes a physical effort to raise his arm, he knows it. The man in case (3) would be surprised, no doubt, that when he set out to raise his arm he failed to raise it. But he would hardly be surprised at having made an effort to raise it. Indeed, it is precisely *because* he knows he made an effort to raise it, and knows the effort generally issues in success, that he would be surprised he did not raise his arm. Equally, he would have known he had made the effort if he had succeeded in raising his arm. No one who performs the typical act of arm raising needs to be told that in so doing he makes an effort to raise the arm. The condition of knowledge is, then, fulfilled.

Making an effort is, in these cases, also something we do intentionally. What a person does is done intentionally provided it is done *with* some intention. Now when a person exerts himself to raise his arm, he exerts himself with the intention of raising his arm. This is signified by the *to* in the description of the doing. "He exerted himself to raise his arm, but did not exert himself with the intention of raising his arm" is self-contradictory. The person might, of course, have had other intentions also, but if he did not make the effort with the intention of raising his arm, then whatever else it may have been, it was not an effort to raise his arm.[10]

Finally, a person's making an effort to raise his arm is in most cases a doing over which he exercises full control and for which he would be considered responsible. The average person would, I submit, say that if when a person raises his arm he is not responsible for exerting himself to raise it, then he is not responsible for raising it either, or for anything he does by raising it. Also, there is the consideration that the agent in case (3) might be blamed for exerting himself to raise his arm. Someone might say, "He had no business even making an effort to raise his arm when he did; the speaker was still in the middle of his talk." To say this is to hold him responsible. But if he is responsible, then anyone who raises his arm in normal circumstances must also be responsible for exerting himself to raise it. For up to and including the point at which the effort is made, what goes on in (3) does not differ in any respect relevant to questions of responsibility from what goes on in the normal act of arm raising.

I conclude that exerting oneself to raise one's arm is, in cases (1) to (3), and in the normal act of arm raising as well, an action. To see just what kind of action it is, it must be decided what its result is; for what sort of action a person performs depends above all on the type of change brought about in performing it. What, then, is the result of this action? It is, of course, the very change a physiologist would describe as the tensing of those muscles that control the upward movement of one's arm. In the cases under discussion, when a person exerts himself to raise his arm he brings about what is in fact this change, and he does so knowingly, intentionally, and responsibly.[11] That is not to say, however, that the action ought to be described as one of flexing muscles. There is a crucial difference between it and the act of muscle flexing earlier seen to raise problems for the concept of basicness. The latter is an action comprehended by its agent in physiological terms; the act of exertion that normally occurs when an arm is raised is comprehended by the way it feels.

It is often deemed erroneous to speak of actions of muscle flexing except in special circumstances, where bringing about an event of an explicitly physiological sort is something the agent understands himself to be doing and intends to do. There is a point to such claims: to describe an action in physiological terms is to suggest that the agent comprehends it as

---

[10] Some authors would deny this. They hold that if the agent is so unsure of success as to believe he will not *A*, then he cannot intend to *A*, although he may still try to *A*. For an argument against this view see "Settled Objectives and Rational Constraints," Chapter 10 in this book.

[11] Lawrence H. Davis argues for this claim in "Individuation of Actions," *Journal of Philosophy* 67 (1970), 527–28.

such, and this suggestion is only rarely in order. But merely to say this is to overlook the fact that a change that has characteristics normally of interest only to physiologists might be comprehended by the average person in terms of entirely different characteristics, and so turn out to be the result of an action that is quite commonplace. That is what obtains regarding the act of exertion normally associated with arm raising. What the physiologist understands as the tensing of certain muscles the ordinary person understands as an event characterized by what he feels when it occurs—that is, tension in a certain part of his body. As so characterized, the tensing of those muscles counts as the result of the act of exertion.

Any able-bodied person knows what it feels like to engage in an act of exertion of the sort that counts as an attempt in cases (1) to (3); indeed, there is little besides the feeling by which to know the action, for no publicly observable event like the movement of an arm need occur for the action to be performed. The event that is the agent's sensing of the exertion is not, however, the result of the act of exerting oneself; if it were, producing the sensation by artificial stimulation of the brain would count as making an effort to raise one's arm, and that is surely false. Rather, the result of the action is the exertion itself, the event characterized by the tension felt when it occurs. But what is this event except the tensing of the muscles that control the upward movement of one's arm? It is where those muscles lie that we would locate the tension felt, and it is felt just when those muscles contract. It must, then, be the tensing of those muscles that is the result of the act of exertion in cases (1) to (3), and the similar act performed in the usual case of raising an arm. It counts as the result, however, not in that it would satisfy some detailed physiological description, but in that it feels just as it does, for it is in the latter respect that it is understood and intended.

It is because its result is understood by the agent in this way that it is misleading to speak of the act of exertion involved in raising one's arm as an act of flexing muscles. But if this sort of description is ruled out, how is the action to be described? Usually, the best alternative is simply to characterize the action in terms of the publicly observable event it is usually associated with: the upward movement of the arm. The reason is that the characteristics in which the act differs from other acts of exertion, and in virtue of which it is intentional, are felt characteristics. They are therefore accessible, in any given case where the action is performed, only to the agent who performs it. Our language is spare in the apparatus it provides for speaking directly of such characteristics, so it is difficult to give precise descriptions of acts of exertion in terms of them. We can speak of bringing about a felt tension and give the rough location of it, but little more. And though this approach might suffice to distinguish making an effort to move an arm from, say, making an effort to move a leg, it is doubtful that

it could be used to make finer distinctions than this, at least without getting into descriptions so complex as to become impractical.

Greater accuracy and speed in making such distinctions can be achieved
by characterizing acts of exertion in terms of overt bodily motions associated with them. This is done when an act of exertion is characterized as
making an effort to raise an arm, or as making an effort of the sort normally
suited to raising it. Part of the role of the first description, and most of that
of the second, is to imply a difference between this and other sorts of exertion. The difference is not, of course, described in terms of characteristics
intrinsic to the act of exertion in question, but accounts like this can be used
to make clear in an indirect way what those characteristics are, provided
the listener is himself able to make an effort of this sort. He will know what
it feels like to make the effort, and that it is normally associated with the
upward movement of one's arm; hence he will understand what is being
talked about.[12] Most of us are in this position with respect to a lot of actions
of physical exertion, thus this way of speaking about them is the most
useful. It does not follow, however, that the only characteristic of the exertion normally suited to raising an arm is that it is so suited, or that this is
the only characteristic we know it to have.[13] It has many other characteristics, many of which we know, but not all of which are suited to effective
communication with others about it. We know how it feels, and most of us
know that the result of this action is in fact the event which is the tensing of
the muscles controlling the upward movement of the arm.

If this last point be doubted, consider again something said earlier: that
the best way for the agent in cases (1) to (3) to distinguish his act of exertion from that of the man who jerks upward on his arm is by saying his
own exertion is of the normal sort. The reasons why this is the best course
should now be obvious; but note it was not claimed that this is what the

---

[12]   Such an account would, of course, be useless to a man who has never been able to perform acts of exertion, but that is not because the account is indirect: any other would be
equally useless. The reason is that acts of exertion must, like colors, be experienced before
words describing them can be understood.

The need for this experience also explains why teaching others to perform bodily acts—
complicated dives, for example—involves little verbal instruction, and much showing and
supervised practice. It is not that such actions are basic, for if that were so there would be
nothing to teach. Rather, it is that the means for performing them need to be felt to be fully
learned.

[13]   This misapprehension could arise if the idea that actions are known and intended by
their agents "under descriptions" is taken too literally. The point should be that actions are
known and intended insofar as their results are understood to have certain characteristics.
There is no harm in making this point by speaking of descriptions, but it should not be
thought that, in the absence of words that stand for the characteristics in virtue of which
something is known, it cannot be known. Such a view would be odd, to say the least: it
suggests that language had to exist before anyone ever came to know anything, including
a language.

agent *would* say, and he might well not have said it. Anyone who has ever discussed these matters with the philosophically uninitiated knows that, as like as not, the first thing he would say is that he had flexed the muscles that raise his arm. We, being initiated, would seek to dislodge him from what this implies, but we should not do so without seeking to understand why he would say this. It is because he, like us, knows the rudiments of physiology, and knows that when he makes the normal physical effort to raise his arm he does in fact flex just those muscles. Being unable to say much about the felt characteristics of the exertion, he seeks to describe the action in this way, even though he cannot name the muscles in question, could not pick them out in an anatomical diagram, could not explain the role of each, and so on. He does so because this, too, is a way of giving the listener some idea of what the result of the action is. Though misleading in some ways, then, this kind of account also can be used for conversing about acts of exertion, and it frequently is.

Raising One's Arm by Making an Effort

It remains only to be observed that the act of exertion normally suited to raising one's arm is both causally and teleologically more basic than the act of raising it. Both points should by now be obvious. As for the first, it is a matter of physiological fact that when a person performs a normal act of arm raising the upward motion of his arm is caused by the tensing of a set of muscles. Since in such cases the event that is the tensing of those muscles is the result of an action of physical exertion on the agent's part, it follows that the upward motion of the arm is a consequence of the act of exertion. But the motion of the arm is the result of the action of raising it. Therefore, making a physical effort to raise one's arm is, in the general case, an action causally more basic than raising it.

It would be useless to object here that the causal relation between the result of the act of exertion and the result of the act of arm raising cannot obtain, because the former action needs to be characterized, in the usual case, by reference to the latter, or because the result of the act of exertion might, for some purposes, need to be characterized as a tensing of a sort associated with the upward movement of one's arm. It is sometimes argued that this sort of descriptive dependence bespeaks a logical relationship between the events so characterized, or at least that it does so where no independent descriptions are available, and that this rules out a causal relationship between the events.[14] Present space does not permit a de-

14   See Melden, *Free Action*, pp. 51–52; and Taylor, *Action and Purpose*, pp. 68–69.

tailed treatment of such arguments, which have in any case come under heavy fire from other quarters.[15] But such a treatment is unnecessary: all that needs to be noted is that such arguments have no force against the view I have set forth, not because, as It turns out, independent physiological descriptions are available for the events I have said are causally related, but because of the simple fact that these events *are* causally related, regardless of how they are or must be described. If this turns out to be incompatible with claims about alleged logical relations between events, then those claims must be abandoned.

Finally, the act of exertion usually involved in raising an arm is teleologically more basic than that of raising it. The action is one of making an effort to raise the arm, and to say this is to say the agent engages in the exertion as a means to raising the arm, hence with the intention of raising it. When an action is performed in this way it is understood by its agent as ancillary to raising his arm, and occupies a place in his purposes subordinate to the latter act. Hence, it is teleologically more basic. In the case where, in raising his arm, the agent also intends to perform the explicitly physiological action of tensing the set of muscles that control the upward movement of his arm, there occurs the interesting phenomenon that the bringing about of precisely the same event counts as an action in two different respects: first as exertion and second as muscle tensing, In the first aspect, it is teleologically more basic than it is in the second. It is worth noting that this sort of thing occurs frequently: signaling a question by raising an arm is such a case, and so is exacting revenge from Jones by killing him.

The claim that exerting oneself to raise one's arm is an action teleologically more basic than that of raising it should not, of course, be taken to imply that in raising an arm we need necessarily give serious thought to the act of exertion, or deliberate over whether to employ it as a means. We might, but this is usually not necessary, just as it is not necessary to give serious thought to actions like raising an arm, when they are done as a means to doing something else. The reason is that for the great majority of agents, physical exertion is the standard means by which acts of arm raising get performed. It is part of our normal plan. And when an action *B* is part of one's normal plan for *A*-ing, to consider *A*-ing *is* to consider *B*-ing. Independent deliberation about *B* thus becomes unnecessary. The same holds for most bodily movements, which is doubtless a large part of the reason why actions of exertion have tended generally to be overlooked.

---

15 See especially Donald Davidson, "Actions, Reasons and Causes," *Journal of Philosophy* 60 (1963), 685–700; and J. J. Valberg, "Some Remarks on Action and Desire," *Journal of Philosophy* 67 (1970), 503–20.

Conclusion

If the considerations I have presented are correct, then the necessary condition for basicness adopted earlier is violated in case (1) and in the normal case of raising an arm. I conclude, therefore, that raising one's arm is not a basic action. Considerations analogous to those raised here apply to other actions that, like raising an arm, have publicly observable motions of the agent's body as their result; so it seems a reasonable conjecture that the entire class of overt bodily movements possesses few, if any, members that are basic.

Naturally, this gives rise to a problem: If, as is frequently argued, the view that all actions are nonbasic gives rise to an unacceptable infinite regress, there must be basic actions.[16] The question thus arises which actions have this status, and that is a question I have not tried to answer. It seems to me that answering it requires giving a satisfactory account of cases where paralytics try to perform bodily actions, and that is a story long in the telling. But first things first: if what has been said here is correct, more has been learned about actions like raising an arm, and that is a gain.[17]

---

[16]   There are several such arguments. See Danto, "Basic Actions," p. 145; Stoutland, "Basic Actions and Causality," p. 467; and Taylor, *Action and Purpose,* p. 118.

[17]   I am indebted to Alan Donagan, to my colleagues Charles E. Harris and Manuel Davenport, and especially to Michael Loux for their many helpful suggestions on the matters discussed here.

4

Volition and Basic Action

The purpose of this chapter is to defend the view that bodily actions typically involve the mental activity of volition or willing and that this activity is, in at least one important sense, the *basic* activity we engage in when we do things like raise an arm, move a finger, or flex a muscle. The defense will be theoretically oriented, concentrating on the advantages of a proper account of volition for solving certain general problems about action, rather than on providing independent evidence that volition occurs.[1] The latter emphasis also deserves development, but both tasks cannot be performed at once, and it is easier to search for something after one knows what one is looking for and what its value is. Knowing these things requires a theoretical development; hence the present task deserves priority.

Since I shall maintain that volition itself counts as action, I cannot argue that it is the key to understanding the nature of action generally. It does, however, provide a solution to what I shall call the *action–result* problem. This is the problem that gives rise to Ludwig Wittgenstein's question, "What is left over if I subtract the fact that my arm goes up from the fact that I raise my arm?"[2] A strong theoretical case for volition will have been made if it can be shown to lay this problem to rest. Along the way, we shall see that a theory of volition sheds considerable light on other important matters as well.

[1] For an argument of this sort, see "Trying, Paralysis, and Volition," Chapter 5 in this book.
[2] Ludwig Wittgenstein, *Philosophical Investigations* (New York: Macmillan, 1953), sec. 621.

Actions and Results

A great many of our actions may be said to consist in bringing about some change. Raising my arm is bringing it about that my arm goes up, and moving a finger is bringing about the finger's motion. In some cases the change brought about is external to the agent: killing Smith is bringing it about that Smith dies. Finally, there may be cases where what I bring about is some "other" action of mine. Convincing examples are hard to find, since they involve the question of free will. But suppose for the sake of argument that I am attached to a machine of such a kind that if I push a certain button, I will perform an *action* of raising my arm. If I then push the button, I will have done an action of *bringing it about that* I raise my arm, as well as one of raising my arm.

When an action is one of bringing about a certain change, that change may be called the *result* of the action in question.[3] The result of raising my arm is that my arm goes up; that of killing Smith is that Smith dies. The result of making myself raise my arm, on the other hand, is my act of raising my arm.

Results have a number of important features, two of which are worthy of special attention here. The first is that they are intrinsically tied to actions. A result is always a change of a sort an instance of which is logically required for an action of the kind in question to have occurred at all. Thus raising my arm requires that my arm go up, and killing Smith requires that Smith die. This feature of results is what distinguishes them from other changes a person might bring about in performing an action. For example, killing Smith might involve causing a bullet to enter his body. But the entry of the bullet would not count as a result of the killing, for killing Smith does not require that an event of this type occur, nor any event with which it might be construed as identical. Events that follow upon the killing—for example, the sorrow that might be caused by Smith's death—do not count as results of killing him either.

Results, then, are events that are necessary for those actions whose results they are. But—and this is the second important feature of results—they are never sufficient for those actions. An event appropriate to serve as the result of an action *A* might occur without *A* occurring at all. If Smith dies someone may have killed him, but no one need have. An upward motion of my arm does not guarantee that I have raised it. And if I do raise

---

[3]   G. H. von Wright distinguishes results and consequences of actions in *Norm and Action* (London: Routledge & Kegan Paul, 1963), pp. 39–41. The usefulness of such a distinction for dealing with basic actions is demonstrated by Fredrick Stoutland in "Basic Actions and Causality," *Journal of Philosophy* 65 (1968), 467–75.

my arm this does not assure that, as in the machine example, I have brought it about that I raise it.[4]

This lack of sufficiency is what made Wittgenstein's question about arm raising possible. We would have at least part of the answer to this question if we could explain what it is when a person raises his arm that makes the motion of the arm the result of an action of arm raising. And of course the same problem can be raised whenever an action has a result. We can fasten on the difference between Smith dying and someone killing him, or between raising one's arm and making oneself raise it, and ask why it is that the former event in each case counts as the result of the action that is the latter event. The general problem of answering such questions I shall call the *action–result* problem: it is the problem of providing an account of how it is, when events and processes qualify as results of human actions, that they do so qualify.[5]

The importance of this problem is indicated by the fact that in ordinary discourse the distinction between action and result is quite strictly observed. We never identify results with the human actions whose results they are.[6] Actions, after all, count as things we do. But if someone kills Smith, the proper response to the question "What did he do?" is "He killed Smith"; it is not "Smith's death." The action is the bringing about of Smith's death, not the death itself. Similarly, the correct answer to the question whether one's arm going up counts as an action of his is always "No." And I take it that this means what it says. It does not mean

[4] An objection might arise here. Perhaps expounding the notion of agency would require saying that a person is always the cause of his actions, so that the mere fact that an action occurred would guarantee the agent caused it. If so, it might be thought that arm raising and every other action would, by the very fact of being an action, count as the result of some action, perhaps as a result of itself. But this would be an error. Put in the language of agency, the point is that an event counts as a result only if it occurs due to an exercise of agency that is not required of necessity by the mere occurrence of the event in question, but rather is a further matter. Hence, whether raising an arm counts as a result depends not on whether it is an action in itself, but on there being an exercise of agency extrinsic to it through which it occurs, as in the machine example. No such thing is guaranteed should it turn out that we always cause our actions, for the kind of causation involved here could not be extrinsic to the action in question. If it were, then for every act we perform there would be an act of bringing it about that was somehow distinct from it, which implies an infinite regress.

[5] Robert A. Jaeger argues that Wittgenstein's question is a bad one, due to problems connected with the assumption that we can simply subtract one fact from another, leaving a kind of logically independent remainder. See his "Action and Subtraction," *Philosophical Review* 82 (1973), 320–29. Whatever the value of these criticisms, they do not apply to the action–result problem as I have formulated it. The problem requires no such assumption, nor would I want to make it.

[6] Interestingly, the matter is different with what are called "acts of God." A tornado, which could at best be the result of a human action, might be described not only as brought about by God but as itself an act of God.

the issue depends on the circumstances—for example, on the agent's intentions, reasons, and so forth. For even where a person raises his arm intentionally, it is still his *bringing about* that result which alone is treated as action. Apparently, then, there is more to these actions than the mere occurrence of the result. Solving the action-result problem would accordingly shed important light on the nature of at least a great many actions.

Causally Basic Actions

Fortunately, it is possible to make some progress toward a solution without difficulty. For besides results, actions can also have *consequences*. Like results, consequences are changes one brings about in performing an act. But unlike results, they are not intrinsically tied to the action. Rather, they are caused by it. Thus an action of moving one's finger might have it as a consequence that a gun fires. Now since the connection between an action and its result is intrinsic, the result of an action A cannot also be a consequence of A. Frequently, though, the result of A counts as a consequence of an action B of the same agent, which is in some sense "other" than A. This fact, when it occurs, generally provides a solution to the action–result problem for A.

The most obvious cases are those like the example of killing, where the agent brings about changes external to himself. I observed above that killing Smith might involve bringing it about that a bullet enters his body. The entry of the bullet could not be the result of the killing, but it could and most probably would be the result of an act of shooting Smith. If Smith dies as a consequence, then the result of the act of killing Smith is caused by the act of shooting him. We would say in such a case that the agent killed Smith *by* shooting him. Similarly, where I bring it about that I raise my arm by pushing a button, the latter act causes my act of raising my arm, which is the result of my act of bringing it about that I raise my arm. Note, however, that shooting Smith does not cause the agent's action of killing him: it causes only the result of that act. And pushing the button causes only the result of my act of bringing it about that I raise my arm.

We are concerned, then, with a pattern of action in which an action B causes the result of an action A of the same agent, but not A itself. Whenever this pattern is exemplified, I shall say A is a *causally nonbasic* action and that B is *causally more basic* than A.[7]

---

[7]   Cf. Stoutland, "Basic Actions and Causality," p. 473; and Arthur Danto, "Causation and Basic Actions," *Inquiry* 13 (1970), 114.

This is only one of a number of patterns in which a person does one thing by doing another or others, and in terms of which elaborate and complicated actions can be analyzed as based on more fundamental ones.[8] Unlike other patterns, though, the causal pattern is especially useful for dealing with the action–result problem, since it allows us to explain how the result of the less basic action *A* came to occur at all, and to explain it in terms of action on the part of the agent. Thus if killing Smith involves a causally more basic act of shooting him, we can appeal to the shooting to explain Smith's death. And since the cause is an action, the explanation places the death in an action context. Besides merely accounting for the death, it shows why it qualifies as the result of an act of killing, for the explanation amounts to a description of how the agent brought about Smith's death, and bringing about this result *is* the action of killing Smith. Thus when an action *A* involves a causally more basic action, the fact that it does provides a solution to the action-result problem for *A*. The result of *A* qualifies as a result because it is brought about by performing the causally more basic action *B*.

But now suppose *B* also has a result, as shooting Smith has its result in the bullet entering his body. If so, we must face the question how this event qualifies as a result. And if answering this question involves pointing to an action that is causally still more basic, in this case firing a gun, then we are clearly on a path that must have an end. For if every action encountered in this type of analysis involves both a result and a causally more basic action, one would have to bring about an infinite series of further changes in order to bring about any change or set of changes at all. Humans cannot do this, but they perform actions with results all the time. Hence the analysis of such actions in terms of the causal pattern must eventually terminate in an action that does not involve such a sequence.

Such actions are *causally basic*, and concerning them we may agree that if such an action has a result, that result does not occur as a consequence of a causally more basic action. But the crucial question is: Can a causally basic action have a result at all? Suppose that, as many recent philosophers have believed, the causally basic action in the case of killing Smith is one of moving a finger, a consequence of which is that the trigger of the gun is depressed. If so, we can use the causal pattern to analyze what the agent does down to this level. But we have not yet escaped the action–result problem, for bodily actions like moving a finger always have

---

[8]   For treatments of other patterns, see especially Annette Baier, "The Search for Basic Actions," *American Philosophical Quarterly* 8 (1971), 161–70; and Alvin I. Goldman, *A Theory of Human Action* (Englewood Cliffs, N.J.: 1970), chap. 2.

results: that of moving a finger is that the finger moves, that of raising an arm is that the arm goes up. And if the appeal to causally more basic actions is ruled out, we must solve the action–result problem in these cases by different means.

The situation is not essentially different if, as I have elsewhere urged,[9] we admit still more basic actions of physical exertion, these being understood to serve as causal means to acts like arm raising. For here too we are dealing with actions that have results—namely, the tensing of muscles—and here too the gap between action and result needs to be bridged. No action that consists in bringing about a bodily change can be causally basic unless we have an alternative device for solving the action–result problem.

Actions, Results, and Reasons

Undaunted by the potential difficulty of locating such a device, most recent philosophers have treated acts like raising an arm or moving a finger as usually "basic," where this is understood to include causal basicness at least. And it seems to be widely believed that light may be shed on the action–result problem as it applies to these actions by considering the role of intentions and reasons in action. There is merit in this idea, for while there certainly are unintentional actions, it is nevertheless true that a common difference between cases where a bodily action is performed and cases where some part of one's body moves as a mere response is that in the latter what occurs will be unintended and involuntary, whereas in the former an intentional action will have occurred. But it may be questioned whether any analysis of intentionality can solve the action–result problem without appealing to mental acts. My own view is that unless this is done we cannot understand what it is to bring about a result intentionally.

Following Donald Davidson, we may understand a person's reason for performing an action to consist in a desire and belief of his, either or both of which might be cited as explaining his action.[10] Thus one's reason for moving a finger one has placed on the trigger of a gun might be a desire to kill Smith, coupled with a belief that one will do so if one moves the finger. To move the finger *for* this reason is to move it with the intention of killing Smith. What is it, then, to bring about the motion of one's finger for a reason?

---

[9] "Is Raising One's Arm a Basic Action?," Chapter 3 in this book. See also Lawrence H. Davis, "Individuation of Actions," *Journal of Philosophy* 67 (1970), 527–28. Davis suggests too (p. 530) that volition is the starting point for the performance of complicated actions.
[10] Donald Davidson, "Actions, Reasons and Causes," *Journal of Philosophy* 60 (1963), p. 686.

Some have tried to handle this question in a way that avoids not only an appeal to mental acts, but also the claim that reasons function as causes. But this approach yields little success, for if causality is renounced along with mental acts, the relationship between reasons and actions that makes the latter intentional tends to be assumed rather than explicated. Not that there is no value at all in this approach: it is still possible to say something about how *citing a reason* deepens our understanding when in fact the relevant tie with action does obtain. In the case of killing Smith, for example, we can point out that citing the reason tells us more about what the agent thought he was accomplishing in moving his finger, and the place the movement held in the general scheme of his goals and purposes. There is no explicit appeal to causation in saying only this much, and information of this kind often satisfies us that we know why an action was performed.

Unhappily, however, the information can be relied on only if we *presuppose* that the agent acted for the reason in question. He might, after all, have had the reason and not acted on it.[11] He could have moved his finger only to obey the order of someone he feared who cried "Shoot!" If so, the desire to kill Smith and the accompanying belief about the appropriate means will indeed have been present, but will explain nothing. Treatments of reasons that avoid both causality and mental acts can, then, tell us something about how reasons explain action: they can describe some of the sorts of valuable information reason explanations are able to convey. But they do not tell us *why* reasons explain action, in the sense of spelling out the relationship between reason and action that allows such explanations to be given at all. It is the latter task that must be accomplished if we are to understand what it *is* to act for a reason.

The lesson to be drawn here is clear: if appealing to the role of reasons is to help us solve the action–result problem for bodily movements, we cannot treat the agent's reason as merely accompanying the act in question. Unless we can see how reasons figure in the actual process by which bodily results are produced, we will not have understood what it is to produce such results intentionally. A fortiori, we will have shed no light on what it is to bring about a bodily result *sans phrase*. It is at this point that many philosophers have found causal accounts of reasons attractive, for it might be thought that such an account could solve both problems. Perhaps postulating a suitable causal role for desires and beliefs in leading to behavior is the key both to a correct understanding of intentionality, and to a solution to the action–result problem that will preserve the claim that actions with bodily results are causally basic. Here, however, a choice must be made: it

---

[11]   Davidson, "Actions, Reasons, and Causes," p. 691; Goldman, *A Theory of Human Action*, pp. 54–55.

must be decided whether we are to say that reasons cause actions or only the results of actions. And neither choice leads to a satisfactory outcome.

Suppose it is said that reasons cause actions. There is something to be said for this move, for in ordinary usage it is actions that reasons are primarily cited to explain. And it provides at least a promising start at an account of intentionality. We can say that a reason explains an action only if it causes it, thus getting around the chief objection to noncausal accounts, and that an action is intentional only if the reason causing it is one in which it is viewed (under the appropriate description) as a suitable means to a desired end, or as an end in itself.

Obviously, though, to say that reasons cause *actions* is to leave the action–result problem untouched, while at the same time moving to dispose of the notion of intentionality, which it was hoped would provide the solution. All that has been said so far is that when a person moves his finger or raises his arm intentionally, *his moving his finger* or *his raising his arm* is caused by an appropriate reason. And whether or not this is true, it says nothing about the action–result problem, for the gap between the two is already assumed to be bridged in this formulation. No doubt, if a reason causes me to raise my arm it also causes my arm to rise. But this no more helps us understand the difference between raising my arm and the arm going up than it helps us understand the difference between ballgames and innings to say that ballgames, and hence their innings, are played. Thus if we must be content with an account of intentionality that has reasons causing actions, and only thereby the results of actions, and if we still insist that actions with bodily results can be causally basic, we threaten to leave more obscure than ever the question how the results of these actions qualify as such.

Well, then, what about the alternative formulation? Theories of reasons as causes commit us to the claim that reasons cause results of actions anyway, and perhaps this is the key to the action–result problem. Maybe an event like the motion of one's finger or the rising of one's arm qualifies as the result of an action whenever it is caused by a desire and belief of that person, and the action in question is intentional provided it is just such an act he desires to perform or views as a suitable means to doing something else he wants to do. This approach promises a solution to the action–result problem as well as an account of intentionality, without speaking of mental acts.

It is well known, however, that at least as it stands this view is demonstrably false. It is easy to imagine cases in which bodily changes are caused by an appropriate reason but where it is hard to see that any action at all is performed, much less an intentional one. Suppose a man zealously believes it is possible to exert voluntary control over bodily changes that normally occur only as autonomic responses. While undergoing a physical examination, he suddenly conceives a strong desire to demonstrate this power to the physician, and believes he will if he speeds up his heartbeat. As a consequence he becomes excited, so that his heartbeat speeds up quite involuntarily, without his *doing* anything to speed it up. Here an appropriate desire and belief cause just the sort of change required as the result of an act of speeding up one's heartbeat. But the man could hardly claim to have done so intentionally. Indeed, it is hard to see how one could argue that any bodily *action* at all is performed here; in any case, it would hardly be a paradigm of such action.

Here is where the problem endemic to causal theories of reasons emerges: just where we are most certain reasons cause physical responses in people, an essential element of action is lost. The thesis that reasons are causes is, after all, a matter of debate. But it is not debatable that they act as causes in cases like the above, where no bodily action seems to be performed. Nor does the difficulty apply only to the claim that reasons cause *results* of actions. Similar examples have been offered where a reason causes what would ordinarily be called a "doing," but where the doing seems to come to less than action.[12] In these cases, too, an essential element of action is lost, and this invites the conclusion that it is lost precisely *because* the reason functions as a cause.

The missing element is, of course, the agent's voluntary control over the changes that are going on. And it is precisely this that is essential to the difference between bodily actions and mere responses: what makes a change count as the result of an action is that it is brought about through the voluntary control of the agent. The absence of control in cases like the heartbeat example is what distinguishes them from cases where one clearly does perform an action of raising an arm, moving a finger, or even altering his pulse rate voluntarily, which can be done by consciously influencing one's autonomic responses. Rather than shedding light on the action–result problem, therefore, existing theories of reasons as causes tend to run afoul of it. Any theory of intentionality will fail unless the role it assigns to reasons is such that voluntary control can still be seen to be present. And it will shed no light on the action–result problem unless it helps us see *how* it is that this control over the results of actions ultimately is exercised.

We should not, of course, give up too soon. It will be protested that in the case of the causal theory especially, some kind of supplementation is liable to provide for the element of control. But voluntary control over an

---

[12]   Goldman, *A Theory of Human Action*, pp. 60–61; Richard Taylor, *Action and Purpose* (Englewood Cliffs, N.J.: Prentice-Hall, 1966), p. 249; and Roderick Chisholm, "Freedom and Action," in Keith Lehrer, ed., *Freedom and Determinism* (New York: Random House, 1966), p. 30.

event that is not an action is usually exercised through an action which causes it, and I see no way of accounting for the control bodily acts exhibit unless we appeal to a mental activity that has just this function. Certainly the usual alternative maneuvers will not suffice. It will not do, for example, to say that control, where it exists, consists in its being the case that if the agent had had a strong enough reason for doing something else some other response would have ensued, or that it lies in the agent's knowing or having learned how to perform bodily acts of the kind in question.[13] Assuming reasons are causes, the heartbeat example can easily be modified to accommodate these claims. We need only assume that the agent has indeed learned to control his pulse voluntarily. But this would not make the change in his heart rate controlled. It is involuntary regardless of what would have happened in cases where other reasons were operating, and regardless of what he knows how to do. Voluntary control cannot consist in such peripheral facts. It is something that is *exercised*, and that is a matter of what *happens* when an act is performed.

Nor, finally, will it do to grant this last point but then place the burden of describing what happens on the science of physiology. This is the strategy of Alvin Goldman, who claims intentional action requires that reasons cause behavior "in a certain characteristic way," but that it is unfair to expect philosophical analysis to specify exactly what the causal process consists in. As he sees it, doing this would require extensive neurophysiological information, which cannot be gotten from common-sense knowledge.[14] But this fails to do justice to the fact that whereas at present no one, physiologist or not, has the scientific information Goldman calls for, we all usually *know* when changes that occur in our bodies count as results of intentional actions on our part, and when they occur as mere involuntary responses. Indeed, this is the only way examples like the heartbeat case could have any force to begin with. Now barring an epiphany of a sort even volitionists would find objectionable, there must be something going on when intentional action occurs that serves as a basis for this knowledge. And it is not unfair to demand of philosophy that it give an account of *this* process, for even if it turns out to be identical with some physiological process, the terms in which it is known clearly cannot be physiological. The philosophical problems we have been considering cannot, then, be made hostage to physiology in this way. They must be solved on their own ground, and we have yet to see how this is to be done.[15]

---

[13]   For these suggestions see Kurt Baier, "Responsibility and Action," in Myles Brand, ed., *The Nature of Human Action* (Glenview, Ill.: Scott Foresman, 1970), pp. 100–16, esp. pp. 114–15.
[14]   Goldman, *A Theory of Human Action*, p. 62.
[15]   For further discussion of this issue see "Agency and the Problem of Causal Deviance," Chapter 6 in this book.

Thinking

There is no denying that a full understanding of action requires settling the question whether reasons cause it.[16] On reflection, however, it does not appear that it should be necessary to do this in order to solve the action–result problem, or indeed to shed considerable light on the nature of intentionality. For even people who are honestly uncertain whether reasons cause actions have no such difficulty about whether some bodily change counts as a result of an action on their part, or whether the act was intentional. In my view, the correct approach to both issues is in terms of the causal pattern of action, where the causally basic action is a type of thinking. Caution is necessary here, since it may be questioned whether thinking counts as action. There is, however, a strong case to be made that certain types of thinking are characteristically actional. If such a view is correct, it holds a number of benefits for the philosophy of action. A principal one is that it makes possible a solution of the action–result problem, for this problem does not arise about thoughts. Unlike acts of moving a finger or flexing a muscle, thoughts do not have results.[17]

This may be seen by considering a relatively neutral example. Suppose you ask me to think of a single-digit number, and I comply by thinking of the number 1. Since I think of the number in response to your request and am in principle responsible for doing so, there is reason to think something actional is going on here. But there is no event I bring about which is both logically required for the act's occurrence yet not sufficient for it, as the motion of my finger is in the case where I move it. Of course the *content* of my thought—that is, the number 1—is distinguishable from my thinking of it. But one is not an event at all, let alone an event I bring about in thinking of 1. Nor, obviously, can my act of thinking of 1 be considered its own result. Results cannot be sufficient for the occurrence of the actions whose results they are, but thinking of 1 is sufficient for thinking of 1. To think of the number 1, then, is not to bring about any result at all. The same applies to all thinking, actional or not.

There is an objection to consider here. Even if thinking of a number can count as action, it might be argued, there is still a distinction between cases where a thought simply occurs to me by happenstance and cases where I think of something deliberately.[18] For example, the thought of the number 1 might occur to me as part of a reverie about my first day in school as a boy. There does not seem to be anything very actional about

---

[16] The way in which reasons and intentions enter into decision and action is the subject of the papers in Part III of this book.
[17] This point was made clear to me by Richard McKeon.
[18] Cf. Richard Taylor, "Thought and Purpose," *Inquiry* 12 (1969), 157.

that. And in any event this case appears to exhibit less control than the one above, where I seem to call up the thought of 1 rather than just have it occur. Might not the difference be that in the first example I bring about the thought as a result, whereas in the second it occurs from different causes? And if so, then the action–result problem applies as much to thinking as to any kind of action.

These examples illustrate the need for a distinction, but it is not one between thoughts that consist in bringing about a result and thoughts that do not. The word *thought* is ambiguous: it can mean either the actual process of thinking of some content, or the content itself. Now since the content is not an event and so cannot be brought about, the only sense that can be attached to the claim that I bring about my thought of 1 in the first example is that in this case I bring about *my thinking of 1*. But if this is true at all, it is certainly not true that what is "brought about" here is an event distinguishable from my act of thinking of 1 in the way characteristic of results; rather, what is brought about can only be the act itself.[19] And if this is so, these examples do not show that this action can be analyzed as involving a result. It is possible, as we shall see, that by engaging in volitional thinking I might bring about the results of other actions, to which volition is a means. But no act of thinking ever *consists* in bringing about a result.

To see what distinction is needed here, we need to realize that our two examples do not differ as radically as might at first be supposed. It is true that the first appearance of content before the mind is not actional; the example of reverie illustrates that. But it is a mistake to think that in the case where you ask me to think of a number, I call the thought of 1 to mind directly—as if by some sort of command. To do that I would have to be aware already of what content I need to call forth, and then the command would be unnecessary. Rather, I think, the first appearance of the number 1 in my consciousness is as passive in this case as in that of reverie. No doubt, it is prompted by association with some aspect of the content of your request. What is fully actional is only what occurs after that— namely, my attending to or dwelling on that content. It is this selective direction of attention on my part that constitutes my act of complying with your request. It alone counts as my voluntarily thinking of the number 1. But neither it nor my first thinking of the number has a result, in the sense we have defined.[20]

---

[19]   The "bringing about" called for by this objection can only, I think, be so-called agent causation, which does not involve a result (see note 4, above).

[20]   I can, of course, bring about a thought as a consequence of another thought: causing myself to remember a license number by some mnemonic device is an example. But neither my remembering nor the thought that caused it would have a result. My act of *making myself remember* would have a result—that is, my remembering. Interestingly, though, making myself remember is not a thought, though it certainly can be called a mental action.

That acts of thinking do not have results means there can be no action-result problem about thinking. If there is no result to be distinguished from an action, there can be no question as to what makes it a result. It follows that *all acts of thinking must be causally basic.* This is not to say, of course, that acts of thinking cannot be caused. That may or may not be true, but it is in no way relevant here. Whether an act is causally basic is a matter not of whether it itself is caused, but of whether it involves a causal sequence wherein its result is caused by a more fundamental action. Obviously, such a sequence can exist only in the case of actions that have a result to begin with, which acts of thinking do not. There is, then, no case where an act of thought is anything but causally basic.

This makes acts of thinking peculiarly suitable for providing a solution to the problem of the threatened regress that arises if all actions that do have results are analyzed in terms of the causal pattern. Suppose, for example, that I am attached to a highly advanced electroencephalograph that displays a characteristic pattern whenever I think of a one-digit number. An examiner asks me to produce the pattern, which I do by concentrating on the number 1. Here my act of producing the pattern is causally nonbasic, since the occurrence of the pattern is caused by my mental activity. The latter, however, is necessarily causally basic. We could then say how the occurrence of the pattern qualifies as the result of my action of producing it, without analyzing my producing it in terms of any act about which the action–result problem arises.

Volition

The main point of theoretical importance about volition should now be obvious. For volition, too, is thought and hence not possessed of a result. Contrary to the suggestion of A. I. Melden,[21] therefore, there is no difference between an act of volition occurring on my part and my performing such an act, any more than there is a difference between an act of arm raising occurring on my part and my raising my arm. And unlike raising an arm, volition involves no event about which such a question can sensibly be raised. Consequently, volition must be causally basic if it occurs at all. Supposing, therefore, that in the usual case where an action that has a result is performed, the agent's causally basic activity consists in volition, the action–result problem would be solved.

Nor is this the only advantage a theory of volition would afford. More emerges once it is seen what the nature of volition would have to be. The

---

[21] A. I. Melden, *Free Action* (London: Routledge & Kegan Paul, 1961), p. 45.

first important thing to remember here is that when a bodily change is brought about by engaging mental activity, that activity serves as the means by which voluntary control over the change is exerted. It thus constitutes the exercise of agency through which the bodily change and its consequences come to qualify as results of actions. Accordingly, volition cannot be conceived as merely accompanying the actions performed by means of it. Rather, it is essential to them, being the key element in the process necessary for the results of those actions to count at all as changes brought about by the agent.

Bearing this in mind, it can be seen that the content of volition—that is, what the agent wills—cannot be that an *action* of the envisioned sort occur. If in raising one's arm one generally engages in willing, one does not will *to raise one's arm*. That would lead to an infinite regress: since volition is essential to the very process of raising one's arm, to will to raise it would be to will to will to raise it, and so forth.[22] Rather, what is willed must be the nonactional changes that will set in motion the sequence of events the agent intends to bring about through his volitional activity. Specifically, the agent needs to will in sequence, and for as long as they are required, the exertional changes necessary for whatever bodily movements he intends to make. These would be the projected *results* of the acts of physical exertion by which he will make those movements.[23] So if an intentional act of raising an arm or moving a finger is done by engaging in volition, the primary content of the agent's volitional activity would be that the exertion needed to make the arm rise or the finger move take place. Now in practice those exertional changes are not easily distinguished from the movement of the arm itself, for we comprehend physical actions by how it *feels* to perform them. For convenience, therefore, we may say the agent wills that the arm rise or that the finger move. It should be borne in mind, however, that the agent's volitional activity needs to go on as long as physical exertion is needed to accomplish whatever deed he undertakes. Exertion is not just initiated but also sustained by volition. For complex physical activities, that can mean an extended sequence of mental activity, whose content parallels that of the physical changes being produced.[24]

Note, however, that in no case can the content of volition be physical change itself. The content of a thought cannot be an event. Rather, it is

[22]   This is the regress noted by H. A. Prichard in "Acting, Willing, Desiring," in Prichard, *Moral Obligation* (Oxford: Clarendon Press, 1949), p. 192.
[23]   For more on the role of physical exertion in bodily movement, see "Is Raising One's Arm a Basic Action?," Chapter 3 in this book.
[24]   Cf. Wilfrid Sellars, "Fatalism and Determinism," in Lehrer, ed., *Freedom and Determinism*, 159. This point renders futile the objection of Gilbert Ryle that it is unclear how we are to "count volitions" or give a ready answer to the question how many it takes to recite "Little Miss Muffet" backwards. Ryle, *The Concept of Mind* (London: Hutchinson, 1949),

conceptual or proposition-like. Indeed, the envisioned result need not occur at all in order for willing to take place. The volitional activity involved in an action and the result of the action are quite distinct as events. That is what makes it possible for the volition to cause the result willed.[25] It is also why, when an action is of a type that has a result, it is always possible to try to perform it and fail.

Thinking and content, on the other hand, are not separate events. The only thing that can count as a process or event when volition takes place is the volitional doing itself. The content is not an event, nor is what there is to volition besides the content. For as with all thinking, there is in addition to the content the *mode* or manner of the thought. I can think of no more succinct way of describing the modality in this case than simply to call it *willing* the content. It is doubtless this aspect of volition that many philosophers have thought of as *sui generis,* and I would agree that no other mode of thought is quite like it. But it does not follow that nothing informative can be said about it, and it does not matter what we call it as long as we understand what it is. The main thing to remember here is that the modality of volition is what makes it *practical* thought, rather than speculative, assertive, desiderative, or wishful. To will the occurrence of a change is not, therefore, merely to want it to occur. Nor is it exactly like commanding, for commands await execution by other agents. Volition *is* execution: to will the occurrence of a change is to enter upon the act of bringing it about.

The value of volition for dealing with problems about intentionality emerges at this point. Unlike volition, both intentions and the desires most relevant to action have as their primary content my doing something. When I am in these states, I intend or desire *to perform an action* of a certain sort. Suppose, then, that deeds of the sort in question have results, and that willing the result or an appropriate causal antecedent of it is the standard means for performing such actions. If so, volition serves as a conscious, executive activity with respect to intention and desire. In it, what is intended begins to come to pass, in that volition constitutes the first step in the process of the action's occurrence. And the main element of the action that does not occur with volition—that is, the result—is ei-

---

p. 65. The answer to such a question would depend on the speaker's proficiency and the way in which it is decided we will chop up the mental activity. Precisely the same difficulty can be raised about the number of public events that occur when the recitation takes place.
[25] This *pace* Melden, *Free Action,* p. 53, and others who have claimed volition is "logically related" to its effect. The arguments against this position are given by Davidson, "Actions, Reasons, and Causes," pp. 695–97; Goldman, *A Theory of Human Action,* pp. 109–12; and many others.

ther projected in the content of the volitional activity or intended as a consequence. What is willed, then, is a change of just the kind needed for an action of the intended sort to occur. If it leads to the expected outcome, the activity of willing will have served as the causally basic doing by means of which the intended action is performed. It will therefore both belong to the process of the action's occurrence and be the conscious activation of the agent's intention or desire.

This account neatly fills the gap between the mere having of reasons and intentions, and the occurrence of changes that are results of actions. If it is correct, the connection between the two is through the agent's executive thought. This provides a role for intention and reason, as guides for conscious action. And although the causal question remains to be considered, the account thus far does not do any violence to the voluntary control that, in acting, an agent exerts over the changes that occur in his body. For it would be through the activity of willing that the control is exercised. So treating actions with results as founded in volition gives insight into intentionality, while avoiding problems that undermine other approaches to the subject. Actions with results would be fully intentional on this account, provided the result was intended and was caused by the agent's volitional activity in the anticipated way. Cases where the action is unintentional or not fully so could be accounted for by the result being caused by the volitional activity but not intended, or by its coming to pass in an unexpected manner. Mere responses would be changes that, whether caused by reasons or not, are neither willed nor caused by any other act calculated to make them occur.[26]

Finally, the position sketched above would help us see how it is that a person knows when he is performing an intentional action, or at least trying to. It is often remarked that this knowledge is noninferential, the emphasis being on the point that in order to have it, the agent need not receive sensory information about his behavior. Equally important, however, is the fact that neither can such knowledge be based on the mere having of an intention or desire. For even if one is directly aware of these, they at best *imply* that he will act. They do not themselves belong to the action, for they are not events, and any number of interfering factors might prevent them from issuing in action even at the moment it was to occur. Still less is it the case that one deduces he is trying to A from his knowledge of such states—for example, that knowing he intends to A at t, and that it is now t, he concludes he is (probably) trying to A. The only reasonable alternative seems to me to be volition. This is something the agent can be immediately aware of, since it is thought. It is also the initiation of

---

[26] See Chisholm, "Freedom and Action, pp. 36–38.

the intended action, and has the content that exertion intended to produce the appropriate result occur. Thus a person who engages in volition can know directly that he is acting, and what it is he is trying to do.

Volition as Action

The advantages of a volitional theory of action should now be obvious. And it is to be noted that these advantages do indeed accrue without our settling the question whether reasons cause actions, which is as it should be. In itself, the explanatory power of this kind of theory, a power not even approached by the alternatives usually offered, gives good reason for believing volition does indeed constitute the causally basic activity occurring when actions that have results are performed. The subject cannot be pursued here, but evidence for the existence of volition can be gotten from other sources also. Especially useful is the testimony of victims of paralysis as to what they do in trying to perform bodily movements.[27] Such attempts appear to consist in volition, in which case a volitional theory is the key to solving this puzzle about action also.

But volition does not, in my view, enable us to analyze action in general. Recognizing its existence can only set the stage for such an analysis, for volition is itself to be considered action. Like selective direction of attention, volition is always focused on content that is already before the mind, in the plans for action represented in our intentions and reasons. So there is no chance of an agent willing something unexpected, or that the content of his volitional activity will suddenly befall or "occur to him." And volition has all the other features usually associated with full-fledged action, with the single exception that it lacks a result. For suppose a person engages in the act of willing the appropriate exertion to make his arm rise. Besides constituting a conscious endeavor in which he can know he engages, I think it is perfectly natural to say this activity is undertaken by the agent *in order to* raise his arm, and that in normal circumstances he would be responsible for engaging in it. To be sure, such features are usually imputed mainly to the actions I hold are performed by means of willing. But suppose the arm does *not* go up, as it surely would not in a case of paralysis. It hardly follows that the agent has failed to act intentionally and responsibly. Indeed, he would surely be held responsible if, as is sometimes the case, the activity was meant to constitute a test for paralysis. And if the agent is paralyzed, then only the volitional activity would occur: hence it

---

[27] See, for example, E. Hodgins, *Episode: Report on the Accident Inside My Skull* (New York: Atheneum, 1964), *passim*, esp. p. 27.

alone could have these properties. Indeed, it is hard to see how volition could fail to be at least intentional. It is just like attending to one's thought of the number 1, where this is done to produce a wave pattern.[28]

It may be thought unusual for activity that occurs only in the mind to constitute responsible behavior. But, in fact, moral experience is replete with cases wherein people are held responsible for thoughts. We are responsible above all for our decisions and the intentions formed by them. But we can also be praised or blamed for the subjects to which we attend—the content we dwell on and that which we ignore. The example of the paralytic indicates that volition, too, counts as responsible behavior, and hence displays the control typical of human agency. For here as always, responsibility implies that the agent can do otherwise. We must, then, think of volition as under the agent's control. Moreover, doing so does not in the least commit us to postulating some further act of will by which control is exerted. To suppose that if volition provides the element of control in actions like raising one's arm volition can itself exhibit control only through further volitional activity is rather like supposing that if we explain the wetness of a wet street by saying there is water on it we must explain the wetness of water by postulating further water. Volition can be voluntary in the way water is wet—that is, essentially, in a way that does not require some means as explanation.

Volition, then, has all the features of the normal, intentional action of raising one's arm or moving a finger, except that it lacks a result. And this, after all, is what we should expect to find, for the fact that the results of most bodily acts do not themselves constitute action indicates that the essential qualities of action must be located in the means by which they are brought about. Whether we choose to *speak* of volition as action is, of course, partly a matter of stipulation. Some might prefer to speak of it, along with other actional thinking, as a mental act or activity, and reserve the term *action* for the deeds that consist in bringing about a result.[29] There is no harm in this, provided it is understood to imply no more than that actional thinking does not have a result. But the danger is that it would be taken to imply much more: that volition is not truly conduct, that it is not intentional, that we are not responsible for it, or that it is not under the agent's control. But volition is conduct in every important sense, and apart from lacking a result it has all the characteristics usually taken as

---

[28]   Sellars portrays volition as itself an "act of intending," "Fatalism and Determinism," p. 155. But this seems to me to obscure too many differences. Intending, properly so called, is a mental state, whereas volition is a mental activity, and the conceptual content of the two is different. Moreover, the state of intending is not itself intentional at all, a point I owe to Alan Donagan. Volition, on the other hand, seems always to be so.
[29]   Compare the suggestion of Sellars, "Fatalism and Determinism," pp. 151–53.

crucial to action. Hence I prefer to speak of it as such. If terminology is needed to distinguish those doings that have results from those that do not, Roderick Chisholm suggests we use the terms *transeunt* and *immanent*, which in traditional philosophy marked a distinction at least very close to this one.[30]

Such terminology would help us remain aware that volition is not sufficient in itself to provide a solution to all the problems about action. In fact, I suspect a great deal of the offensiveness many philosophers have found in the concept stems from many of the older volitionists' having thought they could accomplish far more with the concept than was feasible. One can indeed accomplish a great deal with it, as has been shown. But the great problems about action remain. They are, of course, the free will problem, and the related problems of the nature of agency (of which the action–result problem is only a relatively insignificant part), and whether desires and beliefs cause action. I see no decisive solution to any of them in what I have said here, largely because volition has primarily to do with the execution of intention, whereas the free will problem is mainly concerned with its formation. But both the formation and execution of intention are functions of mental agency, and both can be carried out in the same act, so perhaps what has been said here will help lead us in a more fruitful direction than some that philosophers have followed. For the most important thing about the free will problem is that it is a problem about the will.[31]

---

[30]   Chisholm, "Freedom and Action," p. 17. Cf. St. Thomas Aquinas, *Summa Theologica*, I, 54, 2.

[31]   I am indebted to my colleagues at Texas A&M University for their comments on an earlier version of this chapter, and to the many helpful suggestions of Robert Audi and Alan Donagan.

5

Trying, Paralysis, and Volition

"Watch what I'm doing: I'm touching each of my fingertips against my thumb, one-two-three-four, just as fast as I can. Let me see how well you can do that with your left hand."

I could scarcely do it at all. When I ordered the index finger down, the middle finger, perhaps, wavered toward the thumb. Successive attempts made it apparent that my left-hand fingers and my wishes for them were at odds.[1]

This is an autobiographical account of a test for coordination undergone by a man suffering from hemiplegia following a stroke. It opens with the examiner's instructions, following which the subject, whose paralysis is not complete, *tries* to perform a bodily movement. And according to the testimony of the subject, who is not a philosopher but a writer, the attempt consists in something that sounds suspiciously like volition.

The implications of this example for the philosophy of action are, of course, important: at the very least, it casts serious doubt on the often heard claim that the notion of volition is a mere invention of philosophers, having no use outside philosophical contexts. It is, then, worthy of study. But many philosophers have paid practically no attention to actual cases of paralysis. Instead, they have preferred to deal a priori with the possibility of a paralytic trying to perform a bodily movement, and to deal with it in such a way that the occurrence of acts of volition, to which they have theoretical objections, need not be admitted in the theory of action. I have undertaken a theoretical defense of volition elsewhere[2] and so shall deal little with such objections here. Instead, I want to focus on the subject of trying, and especially on attempts like that described above, which are often badly misunderstood. It will be my contention that trying is gener-

---

[1] F. Hodgins, *Episode: Report on the Accident Inside My Skull* (New York: Atheneum, 1964), p. 27.
[2] "Volition and Basic Action," Chapter 4 in this book.

ally present in intentional, overt action, that in cases of paralysis trying has substantially the same features it has in relatively uncontroversial cases, and that the attempts of paralytics constitute sound evidence that the activity of volition occurs typically when bodily movements are performed.

The Ubiquity of Trying

It is a mistake to assert, as Ludwig Wittgenstein once did, that, "When I raise my arm I do not usually try to raise it."[3] For if the act was intentional, then I will have tried. In some ways, the error need not be especially harmful, for even in clear-cut cases of attempts, actions done by way of trying often count as normal means for accomplishing the attempted goal, as when shooting a person is done in an effort to kill him. Thus an examination of what all would agree are attempts to perform actions such as raising an arm could turn out to disclose the normal structure of bodily movement, regardless of whether it is true that trying occurs whenever that structure is displayed. It is easier, however, to see that we normally engage in volition in performing intentional movements if it is first seen that we always try to perform them.

There are, of course, reasons for thinking differently. Usually, we speak of trying when a person has already failed in an undertaking, or where he sets out to perform an act in which we think he might fail. Perhaps some obstacle is present, or at least is thought to be, so that difficulty is anticipated or a special effort required. In the absence of such circumstances, we do not often speak of a person as trying, hence it might seem false to do so. Furthermore, what appear to be denials that one will try are often given where no difficulty is thought to be involved in an action. Asked whether he can do a back flip off a diving board, someone proud of his skill might say, "Oh sure, I can do that without trying." This seems to run directly counter to the claim that anyone who intentionally performs a bodily movement tries to perform it.

But these considerations are not nearly as convincing as they might appear. It is true that our usual concern in speaking of trying is with failure or the possibility of it, though it will be seen shortly that this is not always so. But even if it were, this could at best generate a requirement for *talk* of trying, not for trying itself. Certainly actual failure is not required for trying, since many attempts succeed. Nor could the presence of a significant obstacle be demanded, for if he only anticipates difficulty a person can

---

[3] Ludwig Wittgenstein, *Philosophical Investigations* (New York: Macmillan, 1953), sec. 622.

correctly assert that he will try, say, to do a cartwheel, and then experience no difficulty at all in doing it. Doubt at the time of an attempt could not alone be a requirement either, since many attempts fail precisely because difficulty is not sufficiently anticipated. Nor, finally, does a disjunctive requirement seem indicated here—for example, that one tries only if he sets out and fails, or an obstacle is present, or there is doubt of success. The trouble with this is that the third disjunct can be satisfied in an onlooker, who has nothing to do with the attempt. If I am the only one who doubts that you can touch your toes, I can correctly say you will try to do so. But *you* are the one who tries; trying is something you *do*. And what an agent does cannot be a function of how a mere onlooker happens to view the proceedings.[4] It is unreasonable, then, to suppose circumstances of doubt or difficulty constitute requirements for trying to perform bodily movements.

As for the case of the diver, to treat his talk of doing without trying as anything but hyperbole would be a misreading. For in any case like this it is also correct to say, "I can do it *almost* without trying," which indicates an attempt would be made after all.[5] Imagine, to continue the story, the ridicule that would greet even a professional diver's insistence that when he does a simple back flip, it is false that he does it almost without trying, that the correct account is that he does not try at all. Exaggeration is one thing, but this would be gross vanity. And vanity notwithstanding, it is very unlikely that a professional diver would make either of these statements. The realization that failure is possible even in simple things is part of what professionalism is all about. It is the easy, simple acts that are the professional's enemy: if they never went wrong, nothing else would either.

But now it begins to appear that we *do* try when we make intentional movements, and that the matter of doubt or difficulty is really quite secondary. I think this is in fact the case. In many instances where we speak of trying there is no serious doubt or difficulty. To say of a good swimmer that he did not even try to rescue a drowning child is perhaps to allow for the general unpredictability of human endeavors, but it is mainly to point out that appropriate steps were not taken. The steps would have constituted an attempt, quite apart from any dubiety about the outcome. Similarly, the sportscaster at a dull track meet who speaks of an expert high-jumper as trying to clear six feet need not presuppose any serious doubt on anyone's part about the outcome. He talks of trying to generate suspense, not as a product of it.

Moreover, there are cases where matters like doubt and difficulty have no bearing at all on talk of trying. Suppose that in the act of ducking a

4   Brian O'Shaughnessy, "Trying (as the Mental 'Pineal Gland')," *Journal of Philosophy* 70 (1973), 365.
5   M. R. Ayers, *The Refutation of Determinism* (London: Methuen, 1968), p. 130.

snowball a man touches his toes. Someone might ask him, "Were you trying to do that?" The question here is simply whether he intended to do it. He can answer "Yes" or "No," depending entirely on what his intention was.[6] In the latter case, the deed will have been done without trying. But a "Yes" indicates he did try. And he will have tried whether the act was easy or difficult, and regardless of what anyone thought of his chances for success when he did so.

Note also that in such cases we tend to use the past progressive tense rather than the simple past. We ask, "Were you trying to do that?" rather than, "Did you try?" I suggest this is because the simple past is more suggestive of no effort toward any end having been made, a suggestion unsuitable at least in most cases where we know action occurred. The past progressive differs slightly: it implies that while you may not have been trying to perform the act in question, still you *were* trying to do *something*. And this is in order only if we usually try to do those things we do with intent. The man in our example, furthermore, might not have intended to touch his toes, and yet have done what he did intend. If so, he might reply, "No, I was only trying to get out of the way of that thing," providing a description of what he did intentionally.

Needless to say, the above considerations apply to the actions we perform *by* making bodily movements, also. And although some of the movements mentioned in the above examples tend toward the elaborate, it would not be hard to produce cases involving acts as easy for most of us as arm raising about which the same things could be said. To be sure, it would ordinarily be odd to *say* of a man who performed a typical act of arm raising that he had tried to raise his arm, for that suggests doubt or difficulty. But it would be just as odd to say he did not try. For in ordinary circumstances, "He did it, but he did not try to do it" means the same as, "He did it, but he did not intend to." And in the usual case where a person raises his arm, he intends to raise it.

I would conclude that when someone makes a bodily movement intentionally, he tries to make it. Conditions of doubt or difficultly can at best form part of a limitation on talk of trying, not on trying itself. And this is what we should expect to find. For, unlike what might be deduced from many analyses of the concept of trying, the fact is that we do at times say things like, "The best one can ever do is try." Such bits of homespun philosophy are not meant to suggest we never succeed, or even that it is wise always to consider seriously that the act we are about to undertake might fail. They do suggest, however, that it is *sometimes* wise to consider the possibility that *any* act might fail. And of course it *is* wise, as a reminder

[6]   Ibid. Ayers thinks, mistakenly in my view, that this is a misleading point.

that most if not all of what we do depends on many factors over which we have no control.[7] A worthwhile theory of action must account for this type of talk too, along with the other uses of *try* we have considered. Accounting for them all requires treating trying as present in at least any action that could fail or be unintentional. This includes all intentional bodily movements, so all such acts involve trying.

Trying and Paralysis

It is in this connection that any attempt at overt action a paralytic could make promises to be informative, for paralysis consists in an inability to carry out movements successfully. Thus such an attempt is likely to display, in a setting uncluttered by its consequences, a minimal means for performing overt actions. Yet precisely because paralysis consists in an incapacity for movement, it might be thought to preclude the ability to try as well as the ability to do. After all, even if successful overt action always involves trying, the trying could consist in something opponents of volition would deem relatively harmless—physical effort or exertion, perhaps. But even muscular exertion is ruled out in advanced stages of paralysis. Someone might therefore wish to claim that a person with, say, a completely paralyzed limb would lack the ability even to try to move it.

Many philosophers have tended to think something like this is the case, for they have viewed one's moving a limb as normally a basic or simple action whose performance involves no instrumental means. On this type of view, someone deprived of the ability to raise his arm would have no capacity at all relative to the normal performance of such actions. He cannot, if his arm is paralyzed, take steps toward the normal act of raising it, for there are no steps to be taken. He might use an unafflicted limb to move the afflicted one, but the very use of such means is indicative that he lacks normal capacity, and success in this type of attempt would not give him the capacity. Once that is gone, he cannot make the normal movement, and he cannot try to make it either.[8]

But this claim is in conflict with empirical evidence. Even a cursory look at the medical literature on testing for deficiencies in the power of movement indicates that a paralytic can try to make what appear to be normal movements. Certainly there is no indication that those involved in such testing understand the trying to involve extraordinary means. Such tests

---

[7]   Cf. O'Shaughnessy, "Trying (as the Mental 'Pineal Gland')," p. 366.

[8]   See Arthur Danto, *Analytical Philosophy of Action* (Cambridge: Cambridge University Press, 1973), pp. 133–37, for this view; also Richard Taylor, *Action and Purpose* (Englewood Cliffs, N.J.: Prentice Hall, 1966), p. 83.

usually follow the lines of the example at the beginning of this paper. They are carried out by asking the patient to perform some movement, often against resistance exerted by the examiner. But sometimes gravity provides the only resistance, and there are even cases where the examiner assists in the movement. The patient is said to *attempt* to perform the requested movement, and his success is measured in terms of the degree to which he is able to contract the relevant muscles. A grade of zero indicates no contraction at all. If the claim that a paralytic cannot try to make a normal movement is understood to rule out this sort of test, then, it is clearly wrong.[9]

More abstract considerations are also helpful here. There is no denying that a person can be paralyzed and not know it. Such a person has to be able to *find out* he is paralyzed. And how could he find out if he could not try to move—indeed, if he could not try to make a *normal* movement? Surely it is not by some sort of mental epiphany peculiar to such cases, wherein one simply becomes informed of his disability. And failing this there is ultimately nothing but trying that could provide the information. To be sure, one might be told he is now paralyzed by a physician who has just severed a certain nerve. But he could then try to move in order to see if it was so, and very probably would do exactly that. Indeed, we would not know that severing some nerves results in inability to make normal movements unless people with severed nerves could try to make them and fail.

Nor should it be thought that a paralytic finds out he cannot move simply by knowing he intends to raise his arm at a certain time, knowing the time has come, and then observing that the arm does not move.[10] As it stands, this would not be an adequate test of the ability to make the movement, for such tests require some step to execute the intention. They require it because if an intention, so to speak, "executed itself," through a pathological nervous reaction of some kind, or through the intervention of a machine constructed for the purpose and attached to the unknowing subject's brain and limbs, no action would be performed anyway, hence no ability tested. Moreover, this type of view misrepresents our usual knowledge of what we are doing when we act. Even if there were no such things as changing one's mind, weakness of will, and mental blocks, so that having an intention guaranteed one's moving to execute it,[11] still an intention is not its own execution. Knowledge of one's intentions could at

---

[9] Corroboration of these points can be gotten from any good text on neurological testing. See especially R. N. DeJong, *The Neurologic Examination*, 3d ed. (New York: Harper & Row, 1967), chap. 27, esp. pp. 447–53.

[10] See the suggestion of Mary Warnock in D. F. Pears, ed., *Freedom and the Will* (New York: St. Martin's Press, 1966), p. 23.

[11] It is sometimes suggested that the notion of intention can be spelled out by observing that, given a suitable *ceteris paribus* clause, a person's intending to A at t entails his trying

best make possible a *deduction* that one is now engaged in action. Yet the knowledge we have of what doings we are about is usually no more inferential in this way than it is inferred from observing how our bodies move. We are able to know directly what we are about. And to have such knowledge is to know we are trying.

Finally, it will not do to say a paralytic finds out he is paralyzed by finding out he cannot *try* to move. For then the question is: How does he find *that* out? Not by trying to try, surely, and not simply from the alleged fact that he does not try. For given that such things as weakness of will do exist, that proves nothing. In short, it seems hopeless to deny that a paralytic can try to perform a normal bodily movement. It does not fit the facts, and it generates mysteries instead of clearing them up. It is far more reasonable to think paralytics are as much able to try to perform bodily movements as the rest of us.

Trying as Intentional Action . . .

We have next to see that to try is to engage in action, and indeed in action that must be intentional. Trying is, first of all, an event; attempts either take place or they do not exist at all. But trying is not a passive occurrence. Rather, it is something we *do,* and generally know we do. In fact, our knowledge of what we are trying to do is precisely the special kind of knowledge that is normal for an agent engaging in intentional, overt action. If his arm is anesthetized, a person's sincere avowal that he is raising it might be wrong for the simple reason that, unbeknownst to him, it is being held down. But his claim that he is *trying* to raise it is not corrigible in this way. Also, trying is something we are held responsible for doing or not doing, where a reasonable excuse is lacking. That is why "He did not even try" carries a note of disapproval in cases where one fails to perform an act considered obligatory.

All of this applies to cases of paralysis as much as to other attempts. In them, too, trying is something the agent does, knows he does, and is responsible for. In fact, this is the only way tests for paralysis can constitute tests at all. The paralytic must *cooperate* in the test by trying to perform the

---

to *A* at *t*. This is bad first because, as we shall see below, intending is in turn essential to trying. Second, given a suitable *ceteris paribus* clause, anything entails anything. In this case the entailment can be purchased only at the expense of vacuity, for part of what must be put in the clause is that the agent not change his mind or abandon the attempt at the moment of action. This involves a further reference to intention, which must in turn be analyzed, so that in the end what the claim comes to is that intending entails that the agent tries, unless of course he doesn't.

requested movement. If he does not, if out of boredom, despair, or a desire to collect insurance money he ignores the instruction, no test will take place. He is then subject to blame for not trying.[12]

Finally, and perhaps most important, trying is always intentional. This is evidenced first in the use of the question, "Were you trying to do that?" for discerning the agent's intention. This usage is possible because an agent who tries always acts with the intention of doing what he is said to try to do. In fact, it is impossible to engage in an attempt of any kind accidentally, or without the precise purpose of doing what one attempts. For it is self-contradictory to say anything of the form, "He is trying to *A*, but he is not acting with the intention of *A*-ing."[13] To try is always to try *to* do something, and the main job of the *to*-phrases in descriptions of attempts is to specify the intention with which the agent is acting. In this respect, their use is like that in, "He got up to open the door." No one who gets up to open the door does so without the intention of opening the door, and neither does anyone who tries to do something act without the intention of doing it.[14]

But if all this is true, then trying has all the earmarks of intentional action. Hence we can only conclude that even in cases of paralysis, to try is to act intentionally. Now this, together with the fact that trying seems to attend at least all overt action, might suggest that there is some special activity of trying which is the fundamental means for performing such actions, the basic act on which bodily actions are founded. Such a view is not all that far from the truth, but there are good reasons for not holding it. For while to try is always to act intentionally, trying is never a *kind* of action at all, if by that is meant a distinctive species of behavior, perhaps mental in

[12] Cases like this present a considerable clinical problem. DeJong, *The Neurologic Examination* devotes an entire chapter to the difficulties of neurological testing in cases of suspected malingering and hysteria.

[13] Suzanne McCormick and Irving Thalberg, "Trying," *Dialogue* 6 (1967–68), 40. Robert Audi suggests that a person who tries to *A*, believing his attempt has only a minimal chance of success, can be said only to hope to *A*, not to intend to. See his "Intending," *Journal of Philosophy* 70 (1973), 387–88. I believe the difficulty here stems from the fact that "I intend to *A*," said before acting, carries a note of confidence of success that admittedly is inappropriate for such cases. Nevertheless, I would want to hold that such a person does intend to *A*. He could, after all, say as he engages in the attempt, "I intend to *A* if I can." Now since he is already involved in the attempt, this cannot mean he plans to wait to find out whether he can before he tries; rather, the *if* here has to be taken as one of J. L. Austin's nonconditional ones. That is, the statement would imply that he intends to *A* whether he can or not. Austin, "Ifs and Cans," in his *Philosophical Papers*, ed. J. O. Urmson and G. J. Warnock (Oxford: Clarendon Press, 1961), pp. 153–80. For further discussion of whether an intention to *A* is possible when success is considered unlikely, see "Settled Objectives and Rational Constraints," Chapter 10 in this book.

[14] By contrast, the *to*-phrase in "He intends to open the door" specifies only an intention one has and need not be acting on. This points up some of the differences between intending and trying: trying is always action, and always intentional. Intending is not even an event; it is a mental state that can exist when one is not engaged in action of any kind.

nature, that is logically distinct from all others and on an equal footing with, say, the act of thinking of a certain number.

. . . But Not a Species of Action

It is easy to see how one might be misled here. Suppose a would-be murderer says he will try to kill someone, believing he will take a shot at the fellow and hoping it will strike home. But when the time comes he does not even get that far: he forgets to load the gun, and when he pulls the trigger no shot is fired. Nevertheless, he *has* tried to kill the victim, and would have tried if he had done much less still—even if, to take the extreme case, he had at the moment of action suddenly been afflicted with paralysis. Perhaps, then, there occurs here an act of trying that is not to be identified with any overt action, but rather is a special mental deed the role of which is to initiate overt performances, and which constitutes the minimum that can be done toward accomplishing them.

In addition, there is the point that the privileged knowledge of one's own intentional, overt acts is precisely the knowledge that one is trying to perform them. This type of knowledge is typical with regard to mental states and events, and indeed seems to have a place only when one is in a relevant mental state, or going through a conscious process, of which he can be directly aware. Since, then, trying is not a state but an action, it seems there must be a peculiar sort of conscious process, a special kind of mental activity of trying.

It is unwise, however, to insist that trying is never anything more than a mental activity. We frequently treat attempts as consisting in perfectly ordinary actions. In cases where there is doubt of success, this move has the effect of informing the hearer of the locus of doubt. Thus before his attempt the would-be murderer might say his trying would consist in firing at the victim. And even though he fails to do even this, such talk would not be a logical misuse of *try*. After a failure, on the other hand, attempts are often described as consisting in all one *did* accomplish intentionally, especially if it is less than was expected. So there would be nothing wrong with our man saying afterward that his attempt consisted in pulling the trigger of the gun aimed at the victim.

Nor does trying always consist in actions conceived as causal means to success. Someone ignorant of the conventions for signaling turns in the locality where she is driving might extend her arm by way of trying to signal.[15] There are even cases where, by way of trying, agents are de-

---

[15]   Cf. McCormick and Thalberg, "Trying," pp. 31–32.

scribed as actually engaging in the action they are trying to perform. Thus, someone trying to climb a mountain can be said simply to be climbing upward on it by way of trying. In fact, ordinary usage seems prepared to allow any type of action to count as an attempt, provided the agent might conceive it as a pathway to success.

But even when, as in cases of paralysis, trying consists in mental activity, the best description for that activity is not "trying." This only leads to an infinite regress. For if trying is a particular mode of thinking, then its content has to be that some action occur, since to try is always to try to *do* something. Now on one approach to the individuation of action, trying is not distinct from those actions accomplished by means of it. Rather, when a person tries to A and succeeds, his trying *belongs* to A, as part of the process which *is* A's performance.[16] And even if we choose not to individuate actions in this way, for an agent to perform an action like moving a finger is not simply for the finger to move. Rather, the agent must *bring about* the finger's motion, which on the present view inevitably involves trying. Now if this is so, and if the content of trying to A is always that A occur, then anyone who correctly understands what A consists in must, in trying to A, also be trying to try to A, trying to try to try to A, and so on *ad infinitum*.

The mere fact of this infinite regress is, of course, the first thing wrong here.[17] If this must obtain for the alleged act of trying to occur, no such act does occur. Our thoughts are not, and cannot be, this complicated. Second, the regress is one of tryings to try. Yet this is something we do not and need not do. If there was ever a case of trying to try, it is that of the man who, thinking he will fire the gun, only pulls the trigger. Yet he does not try to try to kill his victim; he only tries to kill him. This is a point the theory of action must accommodate, not obliterate. Finally, if this is what usually goes on when we act, we could not analyze causally complicated actions like killing, or even raising an arm, as based on more fundamental acts that serve as causal means. For the causally most primitive act would now be one in which the notion of killing or arm raising reappeared as the conceptual content of not just one mental act of trying, but an infinite number of them, each of which we must apparently suppose to have occurred when the agent successfully killed his victim or raised his arm. I think this is too high a price to pay for claiming there is a distinct sort of mental act of trying on which movements and other overt actions are based.

---

[16] For a defense of this approach to individuating actions, see "The Individuation of Action and the Unity of Agency," Chapter 2 in this book.

[17] It is a version of the regress noted by H. A. Prichard. "Acting, Willing, Desiring," in Prichard, *Moral Obligation* (Oxford: Clarendon Press, 1949), p. 192.

What, then, is trying? And how are we to account for the agent's privileged knowledge of what he is trying to do when he acts overtly, and for the fact that he can try no matter how little he does toward what he tries to do? The answer, I think, is twofold. We can account for the second of these things if we realize that *trying* never names a unique species of action, but rather functions always as a general name for the business of *going about* the intentional performance of action, a name as broad in its application as the phrase *intentional action* itself. We speak of trying only when we have occasion to distinguish this business from the actual, complete performance of an act, either intentionally or unintentionally. But it is present wherever action is undertaken: we try to do what, in acting, we are undertaking to do. And however little is accomplished toward the attempted goal, the agent will have tried provided he does not voluntarily abandon the performance too soon.[18] Hence the would-be murderer does not try to try: he simply tries, even though he accomplishes less than expected.

The other point—that there is privileged knowledge of what we are trying to do—is to be accounted for by the fact that while trying is not itself a kind of mental action, all action involves a mental element. In the case of overt action this element is the mental activity of volition. Volition is intentional: it counts as the basic move on the agent's part to execute what he plans to do. It thereby constitutes in itself an *instance* of what is called trying.[19] And where success in overt action is achieved, volition is the fundamental causal means that leads to it.

The Attempts of Paralytics

This is the point at which examples like that cited at the beginning of this paper are most informative for the philosophy of action. In them, trying has the same general features it has elsewhere: it has all the earmarks of action, yet is not itself a species of action. It must, then, *consist* in action. And according to the testimony in the case cited, it consists in what is called commanding or ordering a motion of the part of the body that is paralyzed.

---

[18] When this happens, it is correct to say the agent *was* trying, but we hesitate to say he tried. This is because the latter signifies a kind of completeness that applies to attempts: they are complete when the agent has done as much as he reasonably can of what in his plan of action was viewed as a putative pathway to success.

[19] The distinction between the alleged mental activity of trying and willing is sometimes simply elided. O'Shaughnessy, for example, suggests that we might as well call trying "willing." "Trying (as the Mental 'Pineal Gland')," p. 367. I think this is very close to being correct, but I would argue that trying and willing are always conceptually distinct, even when trying consists in willing alone.

It is worth noting first that the description here is of a mental act, despite the fact that the subject in this case is not completely paralyzed. It might be thought that this is excessive: perhaps trying must consist in mental activity where paralysis is complete, for then the agent cannot even tense the muscles controlling the afflicted part of the body, much less perform an actual movement. But why treat the present case this way? Why not say, for example, that the attempt consists in the botched performance, in "wavering" the middle finger toward the thumb? Or, where such attempts are successful or at least partly so, why not treat them as consisting in doing what one was told, in moving the afflicted member, perhaps with effort?

Several philosophers have thought one or the other of these types of description might at times appropriately characterize attempts.[20] But neither can: the first fails to do justice to the intentionality of trying, and the second to the distinction between *going about* doing something and doing it, successfully and completely. The trouble with botched performances is that to the extent they are botched, they are not intended. Yet trying is always intentional, and this requires that it consist in intentional action. Otherwise, since it is not itself a species of action, to call it intentional action would be rather like saying there are some trees that are neither oaks nor maples nor any other kind of tree, but rather just trees. Trying must, then, consist in action that is fully intentional on the part of the agent, not in an abortion of his intention, as the botched act of wavering is in this case.

It is also a mistake to think trying ever consists in doing just what one is said to try to do, or in doing it with effort. The whole point of talk of trying is to draw attention to the fact of *something* being done intentionally, but not necessarily all that was hoped, or all that in fact was done. If this is the contrast the word *try* marks, it is misleading ever to treat attempts as consisting in or even including precisely what one was said to try to do. Rather, it consists in action the intentional doing of which was assured; otherwise, the description of the attempt must conflict with one's reason for speaking of it to begin with. Now in a case of mild paresis, there might be reasonable assurance that the subject in a coordination test can perform an instructed movement. But then we might not speak of trying at all, or of trying simply to perform the movement in question, with no added requirement as to expertise or efficiency. In any event, the case cited here is quite different: in it, the question is whether the subject is capable of *anything* that would constitute success in the required exercise. This uncertainty stems in turn from uncertainty as to whether he is capable of ex-

[20]   See Ayers, *The Refutation of Determinism*, pp. 144–45; and Danto, *Analytical Philosophy of Action*, pp. 136–37.

erting himself in the appropriate way. All that is assured here is the mental doing, hence it constitutes the attempt, even though in this case the paralysis is less than complete.

Turning now to the mental doing that is reported in our example, consider first the modality of it, which in the subject's description is characterized as "ordering." The indication here is that willing or volition constitutes a kind of command. Yet this should not perhaps be taken too literally, for commands in the usual sense commonly await execution by another agency. Here, the subject must be the agency, and if his agency is to be exercised in volition, volition cannot consist merely in saying to oneself, however determinedly, "Down, index finger." Rather, whatever there is of a person's ability to be creative with regard to states of affairs beyond his brain must be exercised in this act. The modality of volition has therefore to be fundamentally executive, an exercise of the agent's general power consciously to cause, and aimed at causing what is willed. The exact nature of this power is, of course, problematic, perhaps even mysterious. Hence it is no doubt this aspect of volition that philosophers have had in mind in speaking of it as *sui generis*. But human agency is problematic on any view, and *sui generis* does not mean incapable of being understood. Rather, it signifies uniqueness. And a similar uniqueness applies, I think, to other modalities of thought also. In this case, the uniqueness consists in the fact that volition is an exercise of power. Words like *ordering* capture the executive aspect of this, hence they are not all that bad. Or, we might just settle on *willing*.

Because volition has this character, a person who engages in it thereby gives himself over to the performance of an action. That is, volition is a mental activity that can be engaged in only with the intention of bringing about that which is willed. Of itself, therefore, it constitutes an attempt at bringing about the willed event. And agents who engage in it can know directly that they are trying, and what they are trying to do. Of course, the attempt need not succeed, for not all exercises of power have the intended outcome. And we can be surprised at times to learn we are unable to do what we thought we could, or that we are able to do what we thought we could not. It is worth noting, though, that even when agents are surprised at their success in acting, they are not surprised to find that volition is the way to success. The fact that the modality of volition involves a fundamental exercise of power implies that it is *the* way to success, where success is possible.[21]

---

[21] O'Shaughnessy is especially enlightening on what is essentially this point. "Trying (as the Mental 'Pineal Gland')," pp. 377–78. It is important because it helps lay to rest the objection that we must somehow have been amazed on first learning that willing a change is the means to success in bringing it about.

But now if to will is always to try to bring about what is willed, how does volition differ from the alleged mental act of trying, rejected earlier? The key here is to attend to the conceptual content of the volitional act described in our example: it is not that an *action* of moving the finger occur, but rather that the finger move. This is a nonactional change that takes place in the body, a change which, should it ensue, will mark success in what the agent tries to do. And this is all the difference in the world. If what is ordered in volition were action, it would involve the same kind of infinite regress we have seen applies to the alleged mental act of trying, and would consequently be equally useless.[22] The only way volition could possibly constitute a suitable basis for overt actions is that what is willed be that the kinds of bodily and other events occur that are needed for an action of the intended sort to be performed. With this as the content of volition, the sort of regress that affects the alleged act of trying does not occur, for no willing is willed.

We should expect, moreover, that the willing involved in bodily action should have as its content only that the necessary nonactional bodily changes occur. Willing is not needed as a causal means of bringing about *action*, for it is itself action. If it causes a change of some kind, an act of bringing about that change will have been performed by the person who wills, as surely as he will have performed an act of killing someone if his firing a gun causes someone's death. The paralytic's case is helpful here also. His problem is, so to speak, not with himself but with his hand and the muscles that control it. He has no problem getting himself simply to act. The question is whether he can perform an action of the kind requested. There is, then, no need for him to command himself to do something. His attention need only be directed to the parts of his body he must operate. At most, then, what needs to be willed is that the relevant parts of the body behave in the relevant way.

I would suggest, however, that our subject's report of the content of his willing is somewhat misleading. When we perform movements, we do so by engaging in exertional activity—that is, in what amounts to tensing the muscles that control the relevant parts of the body. Such activity cannot, of course, be intended under a physiological description, at least by most of us; rather, it has to be intended by how it feels. Still, the appropriate content for our subject's volitional activity is the sort of felt exertional change that is appropriate for causing his finger to move downward. We have little language for describing exertion, since the sensations through which it is comprehended are subjective. Moreover, since attempts at bodily move-

---

[22] Sometimes *willing* is simply a synonym for desiring. When that is so what is willed can of course be action. This does no harm, because unlike volition desire is not the initiation of action; in fact, it is not an event at all.

ments are usually successful, we do not often distinguish the exertion felt when we cause motion from the motion itself. It is appropriate, therefore, that the subject in our example should report the content of his volitional activity as he does. But a more accurate description would proceed in terms of the exertional effort needed to get the movement accomplished.[23]

Normal Movement

Assume now that in a case of suspected paralysis, volition does cause a bodily change of the type willed, and causes it through the usual neural and muscular apparatus. Since the intentional act of willing has had the appropriate effect, we can only conclude that an intentional bodily act has been performed. The only question is whether a wholly *normal* bodily action has been performed, for it is on this that the claim that volition constitutes the normal means for performing overt acts must turn.

It is fair to say this act would be unusual in one respect, namely that the agent in such a case would be far more attentive in the act, and hence far more aware that it is going on, than we normally are in performing bodily actions. This, I think, is why paralytics, unlike others, tend to be especially aware of volition as such. There is no reason to suppose a volitional theory of action commits one to the view that willing is always a central object of our awareness. In most normal circumstances, even intentional bodily movements are performed with only minimal awareness. If anything, we attend carefully only to what we hope to accomplish by them. And even this can be seen to be the exception if it be considered how, preoccupied with thoughts about almost anything but what we are doing, we nevertheless spend our waking hours in almost constant motion. Furthermore, it must be remembered that in volition we are not *willing to will*—that is, the modality of volition is not part of volition's content. So to the extent that we need devote much of our attentive capacity to volition, it is to the content that we need to attend, since that determines what will be accomplished. We should not expect, then, that the modality of willing should be constantly before our minds, as a central focus of attention.[24]

Yet volition does occur, and it *is* the normal means for performing bodily acts. One way to see this is to consider whether, in a case where a

---

[23] For further discussion of the role of physical exertion in bodily movement, see "Is Raising One's Arm a Basic Action?," Chapter 3 in this book.

[24] I suspect, moreover, that the modality *cannot* be "before" our minds when volition occurs, except in a secondary way. That would be rather like being a spectator at our own actions. Compare Danto, *Analytical Philosophy of Action*, p. 49, where he draws a very helpful analogy between perceiving and what he calls "doing," which is not at all unlike volition.

suspected hemiplegic's volitional activity leads to success, the examiner would then say, "Fine, now let me see you do it the normal way." Obviously, he would not. In this respect, the paralytic's act of volitional activity is nothing special. Hemiplegia is not a hysterical inability to act, so that its victim must somehow operate on his own power of agency in trying to move. And indeed, a hemiplegic can easily move an afflicted member: he need only use an unafflicted one to do it. The question is whether he can perform the movement in the normal way, and extraordinary means are irrelevant to that. It is, then, the ability to perform a *normal* bodily act that is being tested in cases like our example. Otherwise, once again, the test would be worthless. If the suspected paralytic's attempt succeeds, he *has* performed a normal movement, in all respects except that of attentiveness. There is nothing more to be tested. It must be the case, therefore, that what constitutes his attempt is what normally is done as a means to making bodily movements of the type he was instructed to perform.

Theoretical considerations lead to the same conclusion. We have seen already that trying attends all intentional, overt action, and that when we act intentionally we can have direct knowledge that we are trying. And how else could this knowledge be had, except through our awareness, however dim, of a mental process that constitutes the attempt? There is, I think, no other way. And although the case cited at the outset of this chapter indicates volition is anything but a philosopher's invention, anything we were smart enough to invent to occupy its position would have to have all the characteristics volition does.

It is, of course, too much to assert that the foregoing discussion demonstrates for good and all the essential correctness of a volitional theory of overt action. I think, though, that it should help increase conviction on the matter. The hemiplegic is only one case, and an unusually clear and well elaborated one. Taken by itself, it proves very little. What makes it telling is to treat it in the context of an effort to analyze correctly the notion of trying. I think we can have nothing but a perverted notion of trying, as it occurs in cases of paralysis, if we insist first that volition is a myth, and then set out to save the phenomena. What makes the case with which this chapter began good inductive evidence is not just that what is reported in it does occur, but that it is just what *should* occur, and what we can see should occur, if we understand trying correctly.

6

Agency and the Problem of Causal Deviance

What differentiates actions from other occurrences is the phenomenon of agency. Some events in which humans are involved, such as being struck by a snowball or poisoned by tainted food, are not even things we do. They are things that happen to us, events in which we are acted on by other entities. And even among things we can be said to do, not all are actions. In sneezing, perspiring, or digesting I may be active as a biological entity; but I am not an agent in the sense of exerting voluntary control over anything, in the sense associated with my being responsible for what goes on. One is an agent, though, when one drives a car or turns on a stereo, and Booth was an agent when he killed Lincoln. These are actions in the full sense. What makes them so?

It is a hard question, and a fully satisfactory answer may not be available—especially if one thinks a satisfactory answer must reduce agency to some more or less unremarkable process in a supposedly familiar causal order. The view I prefer does not even attempt to do that; rather, it grounds overt behavior in the mental activity of volition, which is itself intrinsically actional and which confers the properties of action on deeds accomplished by means of it. The most popular alternative is the causal theory of action. As usually formulated, this theory is reductive: it finds overt actions to consist in perfectly ordinary bodily events like the motion of an arm or finger, and it holds that such events count as actions when they have a distinctive causal history, originating in the motivational states of the agent. But the causal theory faces two major problems. One I have discussed at length elsewhere: there are good reasons for thinking we enter the causal stream as agents well in advance of such events as the motion of a limb or finger.[1] The other, which I wish to dwell on here, is causal deviance: the fact that bodily events with the kind of history the causal theory claims definitive of action can in principle occur without any action taking place. My aim is to say something about how the problem arises, evaluate efforts to deal with it, and assess its significance for the causal theory.

The Causal Theory of Action

Nearly all overt actions consist in bringing about some nonactional change. When Booth killed Lincoln, he brought about the nonactional change that was Lincoln's death, and when I turn on the stereo, I bring it about that the stereo goes on. When the nonactional change is at any distance from the agent, causal means have to be employed. Booth killed Lincoln by virtue of the fact that he shot him, and that act caused Lincoln to die; I turn on the stereo by pressing a button, which causes it to go on. In each case, the nonactional change is brought about by the agent in virtue of being caused by something else the agent did, by another action of his. If that action, too, is the bringing about of a nonactional change—for example, that a bullet enters Lincoln's body or that a button is depressed, causal means may again be in order. As a result, actions often form a sequence in which the agent stands as the initiator of a series of causally related changes in the world, each such that the bringing about of it was one of the actions in question. Thus Booth killed Lincoln by shooting him, which was accomplished by firing a gun, which was done by pulling a trigger, and so on. And the question is simply: What action initiates the sequence?

The controversy here has centered on overt bodily movements: actions such as raising an arm or moving a finger. For the volitional theory, these are no different from the examples we have already seen. To raise an arm is to bring it about that the arm goes up, and to move a finger is to bring about the finger's motion. And as to how these acts are accomplished, the volitional theory simply continues the causal analysis. One performs movements by engaging in acts of physical exertion, in which one brings about the tensing of the muscles that causes the limb or digit to move. As for exertional acts, the causal means to them is the activity of volition— which presumably is related to events in the central nervous system in

---

[1] See "Is Raising One's Arm a Basic Action?" and "Trying, Paralysis, and Volition," Chapters 3 and 5 in this book.

whatever way a correct solution to the mind–body problem would prescribe, and so is able to cause exertional change via nerve impulses. Volition, however, is not like the other actions we have considered. First, it is intrinsically actional: by its very nature, it exhibits the sort of intentional control essential to agency. Second, because it is a kind of thinking, volition does not consist in bringing about any nonactional change. To will the exertional changes necessary to raise an arm or move a finger is to frame the relevant conceptual content in a uniquely executive modality of thought, not to produce some nonactional event.[2]

Because volition has these features, the volitional theory of action offers a rather tidy solution to what otherwise threatens to be an intractable problem. It grounds actions that consist in bringing about nonactional changes in an activity that does not have this character, and so can plausibly be taken to be "basic," closing off the regress that would result if causal means had to be employed *ad infinitum.* Yet many philosophers have resisted this theory—chiefly, I think, because it has not seemed in keeping with an appropriately scientific understanding of human behavior. In itself, the postulation of nonovert actions was objectionable to many philosophers of a generation ago, imbued as they were with the idea that an appropriately scientific philosophy of action must be behavioristic.[3] And if this attitude has displayed little staying power, there is a second and much more fundamental objection. Acts of will carry overtones of a peculiar autonomy reserved to human agents—of the idea that the mind serves as a locus of events that begin outside the causal stream of the world and enable their agents to redirect that stream in novel and unforeseeable ways.

Even philosophers prepared to accept psychological states and events in the etiology of action have opposed this idea, preferring instead to understand action simply as a product of natural causation. Thus they have tended to claim that overt movements are usually basic or simple actions—that is, roughly, actions that are not performed *by* performing others.[4] And as to what such actions consist in, the standard view simply identifies them with the seemingly nonactional changes that are brought

---

[2]   These claims are defended at length in "Volition and Basic Action," Chapter 4 in this book.

[3]   The classic statement of this kind of position is Gilbert Ryle, *The Concept of Mind* (London: Hutchinson, 1949), chap. 3.

[4]   Among the many authors who claim overt bodily movements are generally basic or primitive actions are Arthur Danto, "Basic Actions," *American Philosophical Quarterly* 2 (1965), 436; Alvin I. Goldman, *A Theory of Human Action* (Englewood Cliffs, N.J.: Prentice-Hall, 1970), pp. 23–24; Donald Davidson, "Agency," in Robert Binkley, Richard Bronaugh, and Ausonio Marras, eds., *Agent, Action, and Reason* (Toronto: University of Toronto Press, 1971), p. 11; Robert Audi, "Volition and Agency," in Audi, *Action, Intention, and Reason* (Ithaca: Cornell University Press, 1993), p. 105; and John Bishop, whose *Natural Agency* (New York: Cambridge University Press, 1989) may be viewed as an extended defense of the thesis.

about when they occur. That is, when I raise my arm or move my finger as a basic action,[5] the action just *is* the motion of the arm or finger.[6] It should be noted from the outset that this is not a very plausible claim. When I raise my arm, the upward motion of my arm is not, as such, predicated of me; it is predicated of my arm. Nor do we ever answer the question, "What did he do?" by replying, "The motion of his arm," or "The bending of his finger." As for nonbodily deeds, it is not likely that Lincoln's death would be mistaken for an action of Booth's, nor do we treat the stereo's going on as my act of turning it on. Why, then, think the opposite in the case of bodily movements?

The answer is that there is really no alternative. If the volitional theory is accepted, there is an approach to the individuation of action that would allow us to treat my arm's moving upward as a *part* of my action of raising it—an action which begins with my willing.[7] Then, the event of the arm moving need not itself have actional features, since the entire action gains them from my volition, to which they belong essentially. Once mental acts are rejected, however, the motion of the arm must stand alone. And since it does not have actional features of itself, a way has to be found to invest it with them, based on its relations with other events and states. One consequence is that action ceases to be what Aristotle thought it was: namely, a fundamental category of reality. No event can ever count essentially as an action, because what makes it actional can only be its relational characteristics, and these never form part of an entity's essence.

To the reductionistically minded, this is a welcome result. And opponents of volitional theories have tended to believe all bodily actions can be reduced to the motions of bodies and their parts, via causal relations with prior, nonactional mental states of the agent. The focus of such theories has tended to fall on intention and related mental states of the agent. Intention is crucial to action, for although not everything we do is intentional, there are no cases of action in which nothing at all that is intentional gets done.[8] I may not intend to startle the speaker, but I do intend to raise my arm; Booth may not have intended to injure his leg when he jumped from Lincoln's box, but he did intend to jump. Intentions are in turn closely related to an agent's reasons, which may be understood as

---

[5] I can, of course, raise my arm in a way that is clearly nonbasic, simply by using my other arm to lift it.

[6] Bishop, *Natural Agency,* p. 11; see also Harry G. Frankfurt, "The Problem of Action," *American Philosophical Quarterly* 15 (1978), 157. The claim is not always this explicit. Often, we are told that action is "behavior" that is caused and guided by appropriate mental states.

[7] For more on this view of act individuation see "The Individuation of Action and the Unity of Agency," Chapter 2 in this book.

[8] Davidson, "Agency," pp. 6–7.

combinations of a desire to achieve some end and a belief that it can be achieved if a certain action is performed. When an action is intentional it is done for a reason. I raise my arm intentionally because I do so out of a belief that by so doing I can get to ask a question, and a desire to accomplish that end. Booth jumped from Lincoln's box intentionally in that he saw doing so as a means of effecting his hoped-for escape.

It looks, then, as though a causal theory of action could take its start from the principle that an intentional action A takes place just in case there occurs a bodily change a, where a is of the sort appropriate for A-ing and a is caused by an intention of the agent to A. Alternatively, one might call for a to be caused by a desire on the agent's part to B and a belief that he can do so by A-ing. So when my desire to signal a question and my belief that I can do so by raising my arm cause my arm to go up, its going up counts as an intentional act of raising it on my part. Because that act has the further consequence that the speaker is startled, I also startle the speaker. But I do not do that intentionally, since I neither intended to do so nor saw it as means to any further end.[9] The case is similar for Booth: his jumping from the box to the stage was an intentional action, since it was caused by an appropriate desire and belief. But his injuring his leg was not, since that was neither desired nor intended.

Causal Deviance

If a theory of this type can succeed, overt bodily actions will effectively be reduced to the motions of bodies and their parts, which will stand as actions just in that they are appropriately caused. If the version that proceeds in terms of causation by desire and belief is successful, an even more ambitious result may be in the offing: it might also be possible to reduce the intentions agents have in acting to their reasons. This second reductive enterprise faces problems of its own,[10] but they have little bearing on the present discussion. The problem of causal deviance remains essentially the same no matter which version of the theory we choose. It arises because in both versions, the causal theory of action rejects the idea that any exercise of will or inner agency is necessary to bring an agent's intentions or reasons to realization. No such occurrence is supposed to inter-

[9]   How my acts of raising my arm and startling the speaker might be held to be related would depend on one's views on the individuation of action. For discussion, see Part I of this book.
[10]   See especially Myles Brand, *Intending and Acting* (Cambridge: MIT Press, 1984), chap. 5; and Michael E. Bratman, *Intention, Plans, and Practical Reasoning* (Cambridge: Harvard University Press, 1987), chap. 2.

vene between reason and intention and the external events the theory holds constitute overt bodily actions. And the problem is simply that without the intervention of agency, the kind of sequence the causal theory calls for is not sufficient for action.

A number of examples have been posed to illustrate this, usually directed against the version of the theory that assigns the pivotal causal role to desire and belief. The best known is one given by Roderick Chisholm: a young man desires to inherit his uncle's fortune and believes he will do so if he kills him. The desire and belief so agitate the nephew that he drives excessively fast and accidentally runs over and kills a pedestrian who, as it turns out, is his uncle.[11] Here it is not obvious that the nephew ever intended to kill his uncle, but in any case he did not intentionally do so. A somewhat different example is offered by Donald Davidson: a climber wants to rid himself of the weight and danger of holding another man on a rope, and knows he can do so by loosening his grip on the rope. The want and belief so unnerve him as to cause him to loosen his hold.[12] In this case it is not even clear that loosening his grip on the rope counts as an action on the agent's part, much less one he performs intentionally. The same applies to a case cited by Adam Morton, in which a man yearns to take vengeance for an insult and believes he can do so by shooting the perpetrator. He aims a gun at his victim, but just then his excitement causes his hand to tremble, and the gun goes off by accident.[13] Here aiming the gun is doubtless an action, but not the shooting or the finger movement from which it stemmed.

It would make no difference to these examples if the causal role were assigned to an intention of the subject, rather than a desire and belief. States like these are never, in themselves, exercises of agency. One can have reasons, even rationally compelling ones, to act, yet never act on them. And one can intend to act, even to act immediately, and still fail to act owing to weakness of will,[14] or to some newly noticed circumstance that prompts a change of mind. So the causal theory is right in this much: if reasons or intentions are the key to bodily changes counting as action, this will have to be owing to some relation between the two. But if the relation is to involve causation, it cannot consist merely in that, for causation is present in all of the cases cited. Yet the outcome is not intentional action in Chisholm's example, and not action at all in the others.

[11] Roderick M. Chisholm, "Freedom and Action," in Keith Lehrer, ed., *Freedom and Determinism* (New York: Random House, 1966), pp. 29–30.
[12] Davidson, "Freedom to Act," in Ted Honderich, ed., *Essays on Freedom of Action* (London: Routledge & Kegan Paul, 1973), pp. 153–54.
[13] Adam Morton, "Because He Thought He Had Insulted Him," *Journal of Philosophy* 72 (1975), 13–14.
[14] See Alfred R. Mele, *Irrationality* (New York: Oxford University Press, 1987), chap. 3.

Modifications of the Causal Theory

In biological terms, the reason for this failure is clear: in all of the offending examples the subject's reason has its effect by operating through his autonomic nervous system, rather than his voluntary one. Insofar as reasons operate in this way, we do not get action at all. But to exclude the counterexamples on this basis is not a comfortable strategy for the causal theory. The question is *why* this pathway to behavior is unacceptable—what crucial element of intentional action is missing—even though the preferred sort of cause is at work. And not all answers are acceptable. In particular, if it turns out that unless the voluntary nervous system is involved, a crucial, inner exercise of agency is lacking, the causal theory will have failed. What the theory must do, then, is place restrictions on the causal relationship between reason and behavior that can plausibly be claimed to capture what is definitive of overt bodily action—restrictions that will exclude the offending examples, while preserving the claim that bodily movements are basic.

One step toward accomplishing this is to insist on a reasonable match between the way an outcome is reached and the way the agent envisions producing it. Intentions and reasons need not be simple. Their content may represent an extended and complex sequence of behavior by which the agent plans to achieve some end. When things go in a way that is not planned, what occurs is usually not intentional action, and may not be action at all. Chisholm's murderous nephew is a case in point. He has a nascent plan for inheriting his uncles's fortune, but no plan as yet for killing him. From the nephew's point of view, therefore, the uncle's death occurs quite fortuitously, in a way he did not even envision, much less desire or intend. So it looks as if we can eliminate this kind of counterexample by requiring that in order for an intentional action to take place, the results that need to be brought about for the action to occur must be produced in a way that matches reasonably closely the way in which the agent intends or desires to produce them.[15]

Such a requirement is no doubt necessary for distinguishing actions that are intentional from those that are not, so we should treat it tolerantly. There will, of course, be borderline cases. Suppose I plan to sink a putt by stroking the ball straight into the hole, but owing to my poor coordination stroke it instead on a line that would carry it an inch or so to the right. Fortunately for me, however, I have also slightly misread the green, and the ball rolls into the hole anyway. What occurs here is not fully in accord

---

[15] Bishop, *Natural Agency*, p. 129; D. M. Armstrong, "Acting and Trying," *Philosophical Papers* 2 (1973), 10; Michael H. Robins, "Deviant Causal Chains and Non-Basic Action," *Australasian Journal of Philosophy* 62 (1984), 266.

with my plan, yet few if any would say I do not sink the putt intentionally. But we might well opt for a different verdict if, for example, I hit the ball 45 degrees off line and it bounces off my playing partner's foot, back to the hole, and in. Human frailty being what it is, we have to allow intentionality in cases like the first, but not, perhaps, the second. That is why the requirement can demand only a reasonable match between plan and execution. This is not really a weakness: virtually any principle for determining when action deviates enough from plan to be unintentional would have to be comparably vague.[16]

Even so, the matching requirement affords at best limited progress with examples like Chisholm's, and it does not address at all the heart of the difficulty our counterexamples raise. The reason is that it relates primarily to what Myles Brand calls *consequential waywardness:* that is, to the path from basic to nonbasic action, and whether an agent's basic acts generate nonbasic outcomes in the way foreseen and intended.[17] That is an interesting matter, but it is not the essential problem for the causal theory of action. That problem concerns *antecedental waywardness*, which occurs when the path from reason to allegedly basic bodily behavior is such that no action whatever is performed, not even an unintentional one.[18] Matching failures can occur here too, of course—especially if the envisioned sequence of behavior is complex or if, as in the Chisholm example, a complete plan has yet to be formulated. But the examples of the mountaineer and the nervous gunman are different. They involve relatively simple bodily actions, and there is no absence of planning, if all that means is envisioning the right movement to achieve the relevant end. And as for the movements themselves, if they are basic there can be no plan for performing them other than simply to engage in them. There is no question of means, so if the anticipated motions occur, the matching requirement is met. What goes wrong in these cases, therefore, must be something else. The preferred sort of cause has led to the expected outcome, but instead of a reduction of agency we have its complete absence.

Can the causal theory eliminate these counterexamples? It might seem an attractive stratagem at this point to insist on a direct causal link between the agent's reason or intention and the events held to constitute action. Basic actions cannot involve other acts as causal means, and insisting on a direct link

---

[16] For an extended discussion of this problem, see Carl Ginet, *On Action* (New York: Cambridge University Press, 1990), pp. 78–83.

[17] Brand, *Intending and Acting*, pp. 17–18.

[18] The Chisholm example is somewhat ambiguous as between the two. The nephew's driving counts as action on his part, so we should probably say he kills his uncle but not intentionally. On the other hand, if the nephew's agitation is alone responsible for some particular item of behavior that causes the car to strike his uncle, there may be room for claiming the killing is not actional at all.

would presumably eliminate the autonomous nervous system as a byway to the behavior's occurrence. Perhaps, then, the way to eliminate the problem cases is to require that there be no causal intermediaries between intention or reason and action.[19] The problem with this move, however, is that it forces us to abandon the claim that overt behavior counts as basic action. The relation between mind and body is, of course, mysterious. But whatever physiological states correspond to reasons and intentions, they would have to be states of the central nervous system. And there is no direct causal link between these and the motions of limbs, digits, or entire bodies. Thus, if we are to insist that reasons directly cause actions, we will have to hold as well that bodily actions begin somewhere in the central nervous system, perhaps in the motor cortex.[20] Such a view would have great promise for eliminating deviant nervous pathways to behavior. But it makes completely implausible the claim that overt bodily actions are basic. If the nervous and muscular events that cause my arm to rise are part of what I *do* when I raise it—as they must be if they are part of my action—then it seems clear that raising my arm involves other actions as causal means after all.

Another poor strategy for defeating the counterexamples would be to insist that the pathway from reason to overt behavior be normal or reliable. This too, no doubt, would eliminate the counterexamples, anxiety being neither a normal nor a reliable means to performing most bodily actions. The fact is, however, that normal and reliable means are not necessary for intentional action.[21] Bouncing a putt off one's partner's foot is neither normal nor reliable as a means for sinking it; but if I plan to make the putt that way and succeed, my action is as intentional as any. Similarly, we could suppose the efferent nerves that figure in my raising my arm have been damaged, so that the signal has to be rerouted through an electronic device. That is not normal, but it would not prevent me from intentionally raising my arm.[22] Nor would it matter if I did not know about the connection. I do not know about many of the causal connections I exploit in raising my arm. Finally, it would not matter if the electronic prosthesis were unreliable, so that it only sometimes caused the desired result. If we define bodily actions carefully enough—for example, doing a complete inward two-and-a-half in the pike position—few of us will be very reliable at performing them. But that does not stop them from being intentional when we set out to perform them and carry them off.

---

[19] Brand, *Intending and Acting*, pp. 20–21. See also his "Proximate Causation of Action," in James E. Tomberlin, ed., *Philosophical Perspectives* 3 (Atascadero, Calif.: Ridgeview Publishing, 1989), pp. 423–42.
[20] Brand seems to agree; *Intending and Acting*, p. 20.
[21] Some authors would disagree with this when it comes to reliability. See, for example, Alfred R. Mele and Paul K. Moser, "Intentional Action," *Nous* 28 (1994), 39–68.
[22] Brand, *Intending and Acting*, p. 21.

Sensitivity and Control

There is, however, another strategy that some philosophers have thought would eliminate causal deviance while preserving the claim that overt actions are causally basic. Behavior produced by anxiety or nervousness on the part of the subject is usually crude, clumsy, and abrupt, and displays little responsiveness to variations in the circumstances in which it occurs. Intentional action, by contrast, exhibits *guidance:* it gets modulated in response to changing conditions, in ways appropriate for achieving the desired result. This can be observed even in relatively simple circumstances. Suppose, for example, that I intend to draw a square. The role of my intention in such a case does not end with the initiation of the action. Rather, because the intention embodies a plan by which to accomplish the drawing, its execution lasts as long as my bodily action does, and requires sustained responsiveness to circumstance as the action proceeds. In drawing a square, the movements of my hand need to be guided so as to produce lines of equal length, right angles, and so on. Even actions performed relatively quickly, such as firing a gun at a target, tend to be part of larger sequences of behavior that involve this sort of guidance. The agent must keep a steady hand, adjust for movements of the target, be mindful of the trigger's sensitivity, and the like. Now it is not at all likely that the clumsy effects of nervousness or anxiety will be found compatible with such refinement. Perhaps, then, the way to eliminate the counterexamples is to require that in order for behavior to count as intentional action, it must not only match the agent's intentions but also exhibit sustained guidance and sensitivity to changing circumstance.[23]

Some caveats are necessary here. First, the requirement needs to be formulated so as not to beg the question. If we are trying to give a reductive analysis of action, then we cannot say that behavior will count as action only if the agent sustains and guides it. To sustain and guide the movements of one's body just *is* action. Rather, we are going to have to speak of behavior as being sustained and guided by the agent's intention or plan, or perhaps require simply that the behavior change appropriately in accordance with environmental feedback received by the agent. Even so, there will be problems. For one thing, mere sustenance of behavior is not enough to guarantee that it is actional. Nervousness can sustain behavior, too—as when it makes one tremble at a job interview. So it looks as if we should ex-

---

[23]   This requirement is suggested by Frankfurt in "The Problem of Action," pp. 158–59, and further developed by Irving Thalberg in "Do Our Intentions Cause Our Intentional Actions?" *American Philosophical Quarterly* 21 (1984), 249–60. See also Robert Audi, "Volition and Agency"; Alfred R. Mele, *Springs of Action* (New York: Oxford University Press, 1992), chap. 8; and especially Bishop, *Natural Agency*, chap. 5.

pect guidance as well. But that has difficulties also. A serious problem is that even when a sustained sequence of behavior does not exhibit guidance, we are given no reason not to consider the *inception* of the sequence actional. After all, the causal theory calls for intentions or reasons to initiate as well as sustain behavior, and the initiation goes off without a hitch in all of our examples. So why not say the agent in each case intentionally *begins* to perform the action at issue, even if things later go awry? Second, some actions are abrupt and simple enough that there is no time for the guidance requirement to take hold. The simple movement of a finger might be an example, or the blinking of an eye. In other cases, variations of circumstance are of little importance. When a paratrooper is poised to jump from a plane, there is only one circumstance that matters. When the sergeant shouts "Go!" he goes. There is not much room for nuance here—even though the soldier might jump in a way that is nonactional if he is startled by the shout.

In still further cases, there will be circumstantial variations that *could* have made a difference to behavior, but in fact should not because the agent's intention is too simple. If my plan for driving home on a snowy day is simply to press through any obstacle or hazard I encounter, then far from being responsive to variations in circumstance, my behavior should not be. Others might slow down for icy patches or steer around drifts, but unless I change my plan I should just plow on. And if I inadvertently lift my foot from the gas pedal at an icy spot, or flinch and veer away from a drift, then that will be unintentional behavior on my part, even if others read it as a sign of guidance. What true guidance requires is not whatever behavior is best for achieving an intended outcome, but rather behavior that manifests an effort by the agent to enact his actual intentions or desires, *whether or not they include responsiveness to circumstantial variations.* But that seems to put us back where we started, for as the examples we have already seen demonstrate, there are many cases where behavior that is not actional will be found to match an agent's intentions, especially when the latter are simple and unsophisticated.

Worse yet, even sophisticated intentions, in which readiness to respond to nuances of circumstance is apparent, can be brought to fruition in such a way that the behavior that occurs is not intentional, if indeed it is action at all. Most recent discussions of this problem involve cases where external agents intervene so as to make an person's behavior conform to his intention. Before discussing these, however, it is useful to see that it is at least in principle possible for autonomic causes to have the same effect. Chisholm's example of the murderous nephew can easily be modified to demonstrate this. In the original example, the nephew has no intention of murdering his uncle by running over him. But there is no reason why he could not have, nor why he could not have intended to do the deed at the very intersection in question. He might also have intended to speed up and steer right into the old codger if he tried to get away. Yet when the time to act arrived, he might have done all of this in a series of nervous spasms, the first of which struck when he recognized that there, sure enough, was the unsuspecting victim, crossing the street on his regular evening stroll.

Nonactional behavior can also exhibit responsiveness to circumstance. The hand of Morton's gunman, for example, might be caused by nervousness to waver—but in just the way the gunman sees is needed to keep the weapon aimed at his victim. Such cases would, of course, be infrequent. But they are perfectly possible, and there is really not much the guidance theory can do about them. To be sure, the behavior of the nephew and the gunman is apt still to be clumsy, and it might not have been responsive to still further subtleties of circumstance. But to require complete expertise or responsiveness is to court trouble with cases like the misread putt, where all does not go according to plan but success is still achieved intentionally. Or consider a novice piano accompanist, whose task is to adjust his playing to the nuances of a singer's performance. The accompanist may wish, even intend, to be responsive. If he is familiar with his soloist's habits, he may even know when it will be necessary to vary the tempo and dynamics of his playing, where a slight pause for breath will be needed, and so on. But suppose that, being new to his art, he is simply not that good, and more or less just pounds through the piece. If so, there will be a clear failure of guidance, and to the extent guidance fails there will be much that is unintentional about the performance. But all that the pianist does will be action, and most of it will be intended.

So just as it is possible for nonactional behavior to exhibit guidance by feedback, so also is it possible for behavior that is actional to fail to exhibit guidance, or to exhibit it only in a clumsy and limited way. This presents an unfortunate prospect for any theory that would make guidance and control necessary for there to be action at all. As the case of the novice pianist illustrates, failed control usually results only in some of what the agent does being unintentional. Yet the resulting performance may be just as wooden and unresponsive as other items of behavior that cannot be considered action at all. It does not appear, therefore, that the sensitive guidance strategy can make out the difference between cases where behavior that matches a subject's intentions counts as intentional action and cases where it does not.

External Interveners

Perhaps the most persuasive counterexamples to the sensitivity strategy involve alien agents who intervene between intention and behavior. Suppose there is a contraption attached to my head that enables a neurophysiologist to read my intentions by monitoring my brain activity, and also enables him to cause overt behavior on my part by sending efferent nerve signals to my muscles. As a result, he is able to preempt whatever is the normal neurological sequence whereby intention issues in behavior and produce bodily movements on my part that match my intentions, but without any exercise of agency on my part. For example, he may know that I intend to make my mortgage payment today but suspect I will fall prey to my usual tendency to procrastinate. As an act of friendly assistance, therefore, he produces the appropriate behavior on my part by punching a few buttons on his console. There is no reason why my behavior should not exhibit complete control and guidance when caused in this way, since presumably the neurophysiologist could read my intentions in complete detail and guide my behavior with complete accuracy and sensitivity to changing circumstances. Yet we would not consider this action on my part. An agent is supposed to perform his own actions.[24]

Is there a satisfactory way to exclude cases like this? One could, of course, simply rule them out arbitrarily. One could require that for action to occur an agent's intention must initiate and sensitively sustain behavior that matches it, and one could insist that the alleged causal sequence not run through the actions of anyone else but the agent. But this is not satisfactory. Besides being completely ad hoc, it ignores the fact that in certain cases alien intervention does not destroy agency. To see this, recall the earlier case in which my efferent nerves are damaged, so that the signals from my brain have to run through external machinery to be safely delivered to my muscles. If, in a case like that, the efforts of the neurophysiologist were necessary to see that the machinery functioned properly, his activity would be part of the event sequence issuing in my behavior, but that would not prevent my intentionally writing the check.[25] On the contrary, it would enable it. If the causal theory is to succeed, therefore, it cannot simply exclude all cases of alien intervention. Rather, it has to discern what it is about the case where the neurophysiologist reads my intentions and puts them into action that destroys my agency, and find a way to eliminate that.

What is pernicious about such cases, obviously, is the way in which my behavior is controlled. In our example, it is the neurophysiologist who

[24]   For similar examples see Christopher Peacocke, *Holistic Explanation: Action, Space, Interpretation* (Oxford: Clarendon Press, 1979), p. 87; and Audi, "Acting for Reasons," *Philosophical Review* 95 (1986), 530–31.
[25]   That not all alien intervention is preemptive is emphasized by Bishop, *Natural Agency*, pp. 158–59.

controls it, not me. Again, however, one must be careful not to beg the question in excluding the example. We cannot say that where action occurs, behavior is caused by the agent's intention or reasons in such a way that he controls it. To control one's behavior in this case just *is* to act, and action is what the causal theory attempts to analyze. Is there an acceptable principle that will exclude preemptive intervention? According to John Bishop, the key to such cases lies in the way feedback is processed. Ordinarily, the modulation of action in response to circumstantial variation involves feedback that goes to the agent's own neural processing system, and issues in the efferent signals necessary to exert control and guidance. But that, says Bishop, is not what happens in cases of preemptive intervention. There the feedback goes to the neurophysiologist's console, from which the necessary efferent signals are sent.[26] Accordingly, we may eliminate the offending examples by insisting that feedback be processed through the agent's own brain. That is, we get a satisfactory causal theory of action by insisting that if the causal process through which behavior is sustained and guided involves feedback, the feedback is routed back to the agent's central mental processes if to anyone's.[27]

Does this modification secure the causal theory against the problem of alien interveners? Not at all, in my view. The reason feedback is important to action guidance is not that it somehow prompts rote enactment of a prior, complete intention. Rather, feedback is important because it enables me to *alter* my intentions regarding the specifics of my behavior, thus filling in the final details of my action plan. Were it not so, then any adjustments to my behavior that result from processing feedback would be *un*intended. Far from being indications that agency was at work, they would actually be manifestations of its absence. But now if the preemptive intervener is able to read my intentions in the mortgage payment example, then surely he can read any changes in them induced by feedback, and so preempt my action further. And even if feedback does not influence behavior by leading me to refine my intentions, surely the process involves some set of brain events the neurophysiologist will be able to read, if only I am properly wired to his console. If so, then he should have no trouble controlling my behavior, even though feedback is being normally processed in my brain.

The only reply I can imagine the causal theorist giving here is that once the preemptive intervener has taken over my conduct, it is too much to expect that feedback will be processed in the normal way. After all, if I am aware that my agency has been preempted in the execution of my inten-

---

[26] Ibid., p. 170.
[27] Ibid., p. 172.

tions, why should I bother to modify them in light of changing circumstances? Doing so will not restore control to me, and if I have no control there is no reason for me to plan alterations in my behavior. Perhaps. But the problem with this reply is that it presumes I would be able to tell the external intervener was at work, without saying how I can tell. If I were unaware of the hookup, or unable to observe his behavior, there is nothing in the causal theory as so far formulated that explains how I could come by this information. And the most obvious explanation—namely, that I am aware of interference because I know I am not engaged in the normal volitional activity by which intentions get executed—is excluded. As formulated, then, the causal theory gives us no reason to think I would have to be aware that my agency is being preempted by an external intervener. Hence we have no reason to doubt that preemptive intervention can occur in cases where the feedback required for sensitive guidance is being processed normally.

Conclusion

The strategy of the causal theory is to hold that overt bodily events count as action by virtue of a causal relation to inner states which are not themselves actional, but which figure importantly in the etiology of voluntary behavior. The problem is, however, that not just any causal relation will do. What is found *between* mental states and overt behavior is decisively important, as the phenomenon of causal deviance illustrates. Faced with this situation, action theory has found essentially two ways to proceed. One is to face the problem directly: to realize that we enter the causal stream leading to overt behavior *as agents* well before the behavior occurs, and to find a locus of agency between intention and action. The other is the strategy of the sensitive guidance theory: to try to refine the alleged cause and its effects so as to exclude offending examples. What the present discussion has shown, I think, is that the second strategy will not work. No matter how much we refine the supposed causal sequence, nothing can rule out in principle the production of overt behavior that is not actional but exhibits all the refinement that would be present if it were. If that is correct, we need a theory of action that finds the locus of agency within the agent.

III

INTENTION, WILL, AND FREEDOM

7

Intrinsic Intentionality

Intention is associated with practical reasoning—that is, with our ability to evaluate and select goals, plan means to achieve them, and carry out those plans at appropriate moments. Thus accounts of intention tend naturally to focus on the relationship between intentional action and the mental antecedents of action involved in practical reasoning. Often, such accounts are causal. They hold that actions are rendered intentional by being caused by prior states of motivation or intention. Some theories go further and seek to reduce intending to other motivational states—usually a combination of desire and belief that, when they cause behavior of an appropriate kind, are held to issue in intentional action. The reductive approach tends, however, to overlook important features that distinguish intending from desire and belief. As a result, it is inadequate even at explaining what it is to have an intention. But even when they eschew reductionism, causal theories of intentionality are problematic. They appear persuasive where action is preceded by full deliberation, since when that is so the intention out of which an action is performed is likely to have been in place before the action commences. But they encounter difficulty with cases where action is intentional but is undertaken so abruptly that there is no time for prior deliberation or intention formation. Sudden displays of temper, actions undertaken in emergencies, and the like seem certainly to be purposive, but appear not to arise out of an intention formed prior to the act. Whether such acts can be intentional, and if so how, thus remains unclear.

In what follows, I want to outline an account of what makes actions intentional that is neither reductive nor causal. Even where the intention out of which an action is performed precedes it, I shall argue, what makes it the case that the action is performed from that intention is not a causal relation but rather the *intrinsic intentionality* of the volitional activity on which the action is based. I shall claim that this same feature accounts for our ability to perform intentional actions without prior acts of intention formation. First I will examine an example of fully deliberate, intentional action and will argue that a nonreductionist theory of intention is needed to do it justice. Next I will present the beginnings of such a theory, and deal with what it is to form and to have an intention. Then I address how intentions get executed. This is taken to occur through the activity of volition, which I argue is intentional in itself regardless of whether it is preceded by a state of intending. Finally I briefly discuss the implications of the account presented, especially as regards the usefulness of causal theories of human action.

The Irreducibility of Intention

Consider the case of Tom, a golfer, who is about to tackle one of the holes on a golf course he seldom plays. The hole is a par four, dogleg left. On the right-hand side, the fairway is lined with trees from tee to green; on the left is a lake, which reaches out to where the fairway bends to form the dogleg. A good drive would place the ball in the fairway just beyond the bend, making it possible to reach the green in the regulation two strokes, as Tom wishes to do. Like many golfers, however, he is not confident in his ability to hit the ball perfectly straight. Instead, he prefers to hit either a controlled slice or a controlled hook, causing the ball to curve in flight from left to right or from right to left as the situation demands. Accordingly, he has two means of executing the shot, each with its advantages and risks. A hook will keep the ball away from the water, but requires hitting it toward the trees. Should the ball fail to curve back to the fairway, Tom will be in the woods and will have to use his second shot to get out, making it impossible to reach the green in less than three. By contrast, a slice will require that the ball begin its flight over the lake. Should it land in the water, Tom will be charged a penalty stroke and in addition will need two more shots to reach the green, making a total of four. Nevertheless, Tom feels more comfortable trying to slice the ball than to hook it. He considers the controlled slice a shot more natural to his game, since it took him less time to master it, and has always felt more confident hitting the ball this way. Notwithstanding the risk of a penalty stroke, therefore, he decides to try to slice the ball into the fairway.

Having settled on his course of action, Tom must now decide how to carry it out. As an experienced golfer, he knows a controlled slice can usually be accomplished through some combination of opening one's stance, weakening one's grip on the club, and executing a backswing in which the club travels somewhat outside its normal arc. Tom decides to use a little of all three maneuvers. With some trepidation he takes a practice swing, addresses the ball, and, to the chagrined plaudits of his playing companions, executes the shot perfectly. The ball sails in a beautiful left-to-right path and lands in the middle of the fairway beyond the dogleg, well within reach of the green.

Tom's hitting a controlled slice is an example of a fully deliberate, intentional action. Unlike other examples of its kind, such as raising an arm or moving a finger, the bodily movements it involves are rather complex. There is much more to driving a golf ball than the few moves described, and successful golfers have to spend a good deal of time coming to understand and master the art. At the same time, the action is not as complex and extended as, say, traveling by car from Massachusetts to Texas. It can be carried out in one continuous performance, and a virtually complete plan can be developed for it in advance. What is it that makes this an intentional action?

Most of the accounts of intention that have dominated discussion in recent years have been causal. Intentional action, it is held, is action that is based on reasons, and what makes it the case that an action is done *for* a reason is that the reason in question causes the action.[1] Absent the causal relation, it is argued, a reason is moot. It may offer putative support for the action, but it cannot explain it, because the agent did not act *out of* the reason. As to how they are constituted, a reason may be viewed as a combination of cognitive and conative states, typically a desire of the agent to achieve some end, and a belief that it will be achieved if a particular means is employed.[2] And if the intentionality of an action is a matter of its being caused by reasons, the question naturally arises whether intention can simply be reduced to the cognitive and conative states that compose them. But although there have been several attempts to effect such a reduction,[3] there are good grounds for thinking reductionist theories of intention must fail. One problem they face begins to emerge if we consider what might be given as a first approximation to a reductive treatment of

---

[1] This view originates with Donald Davidson, "Actions, Reasons, and Causes," *Journal of Philosophy* 60 (1963), 685–700. It has since been endorsed by many authors.

[2] Ibid., p. 686.

[3] See, for example, Robert Audi, "Intending," *Journal of Philosophy* 60 (1963), 387–403; and Alvin I. Goldman, *A Theory of Human Action* (Englewood Cliffs, N.J.: Prentice-Hall, 1970), chap. 3.

Tom's case. Tom desires to drive the ball into the fairway beyond the dogleg, and he believes he will do so if he hits a controlled slice out over the lake. The combination of this desire and belief, we might say, causes his action of hitting a controlled slice into the fairway, thus making it intentional on his part. Accordingly, the desire and belief constitute his intention.

Even if the causal claim here is correct, the reductionist thesis is inadequate. A satisfactory theory of intention has to be able to distinguish cases where we *have* an intention to act in a certain way from cases in which no such intention is present. But to have an intention cannot be simply to have a desire to achieve some end and a belief as to an appropriate means to achieve it. Early in the course of Tom's deliberation, it would have been false to say he intended to hit a controlled slice. Only during the time when he was rehearsing to himself how to hit a slice and then executing the shot was this true. Yet throughout his deliberations he desired to drive the ball into the fairway and believed he would do so if he hit a controlled slice. Moreover, it was true throughout Tom's deliberation, and even during his shot, that he both wanted to drive the ball into the fairway and believed he would do so if he hit a controlled hook toward the trees. Yet he never intended to do that; he only intended to hit a controlled slice. If, therefore, we try to reduce having an intention to simply having the sort of desire and belief that might constitute a reason, we wind up calling for far more intentions than there are.

If, on the other hand, we try to deal with this problem by exploiting the supposed causal relation between reason and action, we will call for altogether too few intentions. Suppose it is claimed that an agent's desire to achieve some end, and his belief that a certain means will do so, constitute an intention only when they cause him to act accordingly. This eliminates our having to say Tom intended to hit a controlled hook, for his belief that he could drive the ball into the fairway by that means played no part in his behavior. Unfortunately, however, to insist that the cognitive and conative states held to constitute an intention must actually cause the agent to act is to require that we execute, or at least try to execute, all of our intentions. And the fact is that there are many instances of intentions that we do not even try to execute. Some are cases of akrasia, in which we develop an intention and retain it until the time for action, only to find ourselves somehow unable to carry it out. Other times we simply change our minds, abandoning one intention and substituting another for it. Suppose that while taking his practice swing Tom had reconsidered, decided to hit a controlled hook after all, and proceeded to do so. If so, there would still have been a period prior to the shot during which he intended to hit a slice. Yet no appropriate behavior would have ensued. We get no account of such cases if we insist that the states held to constitute an intention must lead to action. Moreover, even adding the causal proviso does not explain the fact that as things actually went in Tom's case, he had the desire and belief that found expression in his act of hitting a controlled slice well before he had the intention to do so.

The reason for these difficulties is that to have an intention is to be in a state which, though it need not issue in action, goes beyond simply having a desire to achieve some end and a belief about how to do so. In themselves, desires and belief are not "practical" in any strong sense; intentions are, for to have an intention is to be committed to act. I know exactly how to call up sick and skip classes tomorrow, and I may very much want to do so, yet have no intention whatever of doing it. And even if I were eventually to shirk my responsibilities in this way, my desire and belief need not be accompanied right now by a corresponding intention. For I need not yet have formed the intention to skip class, not yet have settled on the goal of doing so. If not, then I do not have the *purpose* of performing the action in question, and where there is no purpose there is no intention. The need for this further element is especially apparent in cases like that of our golfer, where action is fully deliberate. Here, the element of purpose is introduced by an explicit step of intention formation. Tom makes up his mind, or decides, to hit a controlled slice. Before this step he does not intend to hit a slice; after this step he does, and he develops this intention further when he decides how to carry it out. Should he subsequently change his mind, his purpose, and hence his intention, would be terminated. Yet his desire and belief could persist unchanged through the entire process.

If the element of purpose is to be captured, the reductionist analysis of intention must somehow be strengthened. Most efforts to strengthen it have focused on the conative aspect.[4] For example, it might be claimed that intending to perform an action requires wanting to perform it more than any other.[5] Now if we take the term *wanting* as simply signifying desire— and we shall see there may be other options—then this approach would have it that the key to Tom's case is that he desires more strongly to slice the

---

[4]   One could try to strengthen the cognitive aspect by claiming that intention requires believing one will do the thing intended, or at least not believing one will not do it. See, for example, Audi, "Intending," p. 388. In fact, even nonreductionist accounts often have it that at least rational intentions are subject to such strictures. See Gilbert Harman, "Practical Reasoning," *Review of Metaphysics* 29 (1976), 432–33; and Michael E. Bratman, *Intention, Plans, and Practical Reasoning* (Cambridge: Harvard University Press, 1987), chap. 3. I have argued elsewhere that all such claims are incorrect. See "Rationality and the Range of Intention," *Midwest Studies in Philosophy* 10 (1986), 191–211; also "Settled Objectives and Rational Constraints," Chapter 10 in this book.

[5]   Audi, "Intending," p. 395.

ball than to hook it. A rather different type of treatment equates intention with a judgment that an act would be best overall, or perhaps simply an unqualified judgment that the act would be best.[6] On this view, Tom's intending to hit a slice consists in his judging this to be the best way of getting the ball into the fairway. But at least to the extent that these efforts rely on what it has become fashionable to call "folk psychological" notions—that is, in this case, concepts employed in everyday thinking and discourse about action—they rely on notions that work against one another in such a way as to undermine both claims. Intentions do often accord with strongest desires, and they frequently accord with judgments of what is best. The problem is, however, that strongest desire and best judgment may be out of accord with each other, and then the intention can go either way. It is just not the case that, were Tom to tell his playing partners he thinks a controlled slice would be best, they could conclude he intends to hit a slice: he might intend to do what he most wants, namely hit one of those long hooks the pros hit on television. On the other hand, if he said hitting a hook was what he most wanted to do, he might not intend that either: he might intend to do what he thinks is best, namely hit the slice. As ordinarily understood, then, neither wanting to perform an action more than any other nor judging it to be best is a necessary condition of intending to perform it.

If neither of these concepts alone will suffice, perhaps aspects of them can be combined in a way that will. In one place, Robert Audi defends the claim that intending to do something entails "wanting on balance" to do it.[7] Wanting on balance is certainly conative, since it is a kind of want, but it also has the deliberative overtones associated with a judgment that a certain action would be best. Perhaps, then, what is crucial to Tom's intending to hit a controlled slice is that this is the action he wants on balance to perform. Unfortunately, however, this claim can be secured only if "wanting on balance" is understood in a way that leaves it unclear that any reduction of intention to other cognitive and conative states is accomplished. It cannot be understood as equivalent to strongest desire, for we have seen that intentions sometimes run counter to our strongest desires. Nor could a want on balance be just a desire experienced at the end of a process of deliberation, for this too could be overridden by a decision to do what is judged best overall. Moreover, in taking this position Audi disclaims the view that wanting entails desiring in any passional sense. But then it is unclear just what the expression *wanting on balance* is supposed to signify, or whether any reduction is achieved by its use.

---

[6] See, for example, Donald Davidson, "Intending," in Yirmiahu Yovel, ed., *Philosophy of History and Action* (Dordrecht: D. Reidel, 1978), pp. 41–60.

[7] Audi, "Intending, Intentional Action, and Desire," in Joel Marks, ed., *The Ways of Desire* (Chicago: Precedent Publishing, 1986), pp. 17–38.

Part of the problem here is that the term *want* has a broad use in which it signifies virtually any conative state, including intending. At times, one communicates an intention simply by saying one wants to do the thing intended. In this sense of the term, however, intending is simply a species of wanting. Trying to reduce it to the latter would be like trying to reduce dogs to mammals. The most likely outcome is that *wanting on balance*—an expression at best rarely encountered in the folk psychological realm—will be given what amounts to a technical use in which it simply goes proxy for the more usual *intention*. Some of what Audi says about wanting on balance suggests that is what occurs in his treatment. For example, he holds that if *x* and *y* are jointly unrealizable, one cannot want both on balance, and that to want on balance to do something is to be "motivationally committed" to doing it, in that one will do it if nothing interferes.[8] Claims like this are associated with intention but not with other conative concepts in folk psychology. It is, then, less than clear that talk of wanting on balance leads to any reduction of intention to other states. And even if it does, the fact that this notion of wanting cannot be taken as equivalent to desire suggests the reduction would not be very radical.

Intending and Deciding

The few remarks above cannot be claimed to do full justice to Audi's treatment of intention. They do, however, point up the difficulty of framing a reductionist account that yields a satisfactory distinction between cases where we have intentions and cases where we do not. Efforts to do so either fail or seriously risk reintroducing the concept of intention covertly. I think it is best, therefore, to seek a theory of intention that does not try to reduce it to other states of the agent. Such a theory has to allow for at least two types of mental entity in cases where action is preceded by full deliberation. First, it must allow for mental states of intending distinct from, and hence not reducible to, states of desire and belief. In paradigm cases, states of intending issue from a process of deliberation, and their content eventually finds realization in the actions to whose performance it serves as a guide. Second, the theory has to allow for the phenomenon of *deciding*, or making up one's mind, to pursue a certain end or goal. Unlike intending, which is a state, deciding is an event. It is the mental act by which, in cases of fully deliberate action, reasons and intention are linked. Decisions are acts of intention formation, and so terminate in states of intending. Decisions are reversible, in that an intention formed by one deci-

---

[8] Ibid., pp. 23, 25.

sion can be expunged by a later one, and they can also be made in the service of intentions already formed. That is what happens when, having formed an intention, we choose the means by which to carry it out.

Both intentions and decisions are usually expressed in future tense, first-person statements, such as:

I shall hit a controlled slice into the fairway.

They can, however, be explicated in terms of a model for mental states and events according to which they consist in a certain attitude or modality of thought—that is, a way of thinking something—that is directed on a certain content.[9] The content is a mental representation, usually of some possible item of experience; that is, of an object, event, or state that might actually exist or come to exist. In the case of intentions, as we shall see, this content can be quite complex. It can, however, be summarized in a proposition. Once he has chosen between the two types of golf shot he is contemplating, Tom may be said to have an intention the content of which is summarized in the proposition, "I hit a controlled slice into the fairway." This same proposition might, of course, have been the content of some other mental state, such as a desire or belief. Whether one tries to reduce intention to other states is therefore not a matter of how one understands their content but of how one treats the modality of intending. The modality or attitude is the way in which Tom thinks or conceives of hitting the shot once he decides to do so. The trick of not reducing it is just to let it stand as is. We should, that is, think of Tom's mental state simply as one of intending or purposing to hit the shot. Thus Tom's state of intending may be expressed by:

Intend (I hit a controlled slice into the fairway).[10]

It is worth remarking that although this treatment is nonreductive, it does find room for both a cognitive and a conative element in intention. The cognitive element consists simply in the agent's grasping what it is that he intends. When we are aware of our intentions, their content is before our minds. It is comprehended by us and can serve either as a basis for further planning or as a guide to action. But while cognitive in nature, this aware-

---

[9] For an explication of this model for representing states and events, see John R. Searle, *Intentionality* (New York: Cambridge University Press, 1983), chap. 1.

[10] Hector-Neri Castañeda argues that the content of an intention should be represented not by a proposition but by an infinitival construction he calls a "practition." *Thinking and Doing* (Dordrecht: D. Reidel, 1975), chap. 6. I am not sure this is correct, but such an adjustment could be made to my own account without damage to any of the major theses of this chapter.

ness does not require that any special cognitive modality such as believing be annexed to the content. Rather, such awareness is common to all conscious thought, cognitive or conative. Any attempt to assimilate it to a psychological attitude of narrower range would lead to an infinite regress. Belief, for example, also involves grasping what is believed. As for the conative aspect of intention, it is found in the modality of the state, which is intending itself. This conative attitude is directed precisely on the content whose presentness to the agent constitutes the cognitive aspect of intention. Thus states of intention are not constructed out of other, more primitive states. Rather, the cognitive element is enveloped in the conative one to make a single mental state that does not have others as building blocks.

Tom's intention to hit a controlled slice is formed at a specific point in his deliberation, by means of a conscious act on his part. That act is one of deciding to hit the shot. It may be represented as:

Decide (I hit a controlled slice into the fairway).

As might be expected, the content of this decision is the same as that of the intention to which it gives rise. Indeed, as far as expression in everyday English goes, both Tom's decision and his resultant intention can be formulated the same way. This is because the modality of deciding is of a piece with that of intending, though not exactly the same. Deciding does not produce or cause in the agent a state of intending. Rather, to decide is to *form* an intention—that is, to *progress* to a state of intending, which is simply the terminal state of one's act of deciding. Still, to decide is not to intend: the former is an event, and the latter a state. To intend is simply to have a purpose; it is neither to undergo nor to bring about a change, and there is no "process" of intending. Moreover, since intentions can endure for extended periods of time, there can be long stretches during which we are not consciously aware of intentions we nevertheless have. By contrast, we are aware of our decisions, and though they may be preceded by lengthy deliberation the act of deciding itself is brief. Most important, to decide is to change; it is to pass from not having some intention to having it. The opposite change occurs when we decide to abandon an intention, and both sorts occur when we substitute one intention for another.

Like intending, deciding is a modality of thought that does not reduce to others. It is not the same as desiring, wanting, or even wanting on balance, for like intention these are all states, and deciding is an act—that is, an exercise of agency.[11] Nor is deciding the same as judging what is best

---

[11] For more on this subject, see "The Formation of Intention," Chapter 8 in this book.

overall. Judgments, even of preferability, are cognitive events, whereas deciding belongs to the conative side of the mind, and we have seen that decisions need not accord with judgments as to what is best. Indeed, if *all* an agent ever did were to experience wants and make judgments about what is best, he would form no intentions at all. Rather, decision is a unique modality of thought in which a possible course of action is made the content of an intention. It is, in cases where action is preceded by full deliberation, the preeminent means by which intentions are formed, and it deserves to be accorded its own place in the list of psychological attitudes.

By permitting intentions and decisions to stand as independent mental entities, we can begin to make reasonable sense of the case of Tom the golfer. What happens is that midway through his deliberation, Tom engages in an act of deciding to hit a controlled slice. Once that act is complete, Tom is in a state of intending to hit a controlled slice, whereas previously he was not. And he never intends to hit a controlled hook because, regardless of his desires and beliefs, this is an intention he never forms. But Tom's deliberation does not end with his decision to hit the slice. He goes on to consider how to hit the shot, and makes a further decision as to the means he will employ. Only then is he in a position to carry out his intention to hit a controlled slice, for only then does he have a fully developed plan for doing so. Thus the effect of Tom's second decision is to develop the content of the intention formed by his first one to the point where it constitutes a viable plan for action.

In this regard, it is somewhat misleading to summarize the content of an intention in a single proposition. Many intentions have as their content a representation of an elaborate sequence of behavior that, even if it is conceived as a unit, can be broken down into various segments and subsegments according to the demands of the occasion.[12] This is perhaps most obvious in the case of elaborate, extended actions such as taking a trip. One cannot just take a trip: one has to take it to a particular place, by a particular means of transportation, and according to at least some kind of schedule. An intention to take a trip will come to nothing unless at least the major features of the action sequence that will fulfill the intention are decided in advance. The details of the plan can often be filled in while it is actually being executed; trips require enough time to permit deliberation while they are in progress, and the traveler may encounter unexpected obstacles along the way. But regardless of when they occur, all of the decisions by which we plan such activities can be viewed as filling out the content of the basic intention out of which we act.

[12] Myles Brand, *Intending and Acting* (Cambridge: MIT Press, 1984), chap. 8.

Hitting a golf shot is somewhat different. This act takes very little time, and golfers who make decisions about their shots while in the process of swinging quickly learn the error of their ways. But the very fact that this error is possible indicates that the content of an intention to hit a golf shot can be subjected to rather detailed analysis. A typical lesson in how to hit a golf ball breaks the procedure down under several major headings. Some are preparatory: gripping the club, addressing the ball. Others concern the swing itself: the backswing, the downswing, the follow-through. There are various do's and don'ts under each heading, and differences in what is done in each phase lead to different results for the shot itself. The aim of the analysis is to break the swing down into a sequence of more or less simple moves for the player to master individually. Even relatively inexperienced players are usually familiar with the rudiments of such analyses. The content of the intention they have in making the shot is accordingly complex, and it can be varied, as in Tom's case, depending on the type of shot to be hit. Decisions made in the planning stage of deliberation introduce the necessary variations into the content of the intention.

We should not conclude from this that it is just wrong to summarize the content of Tom's intention in the proposition, "I hit a controlled slice into the fairway." This is exactly what he intends to do, and as far as Tom's practical purposes are concerned, to hit this type of shot just *is* to go through a sequence of movements of the appropriate kind. Moreover, the swing must be executed not in a series of discrete, staccatolike performances but as a continuous act. If there is anything misleading about summarizing the content of Tom's intention in this way, it is that doing so may encourage us to think of Tom as representing his intended action to himself in the same way we would as observers—that is, largely visually, or in terms of some more or less complicated verbal description of the act of hitting a controlled slice. In fact neither is the case: one cannot watch oneself hit a golf shot, nor can the skill be learned simply by reading books on the subject. Rather, a golf swing, like any action performed by moving one's body, has to be comprehended by the agent in terms of how it *feels* to engage in the muscular exertion the act demands. Vocabulary for describing how it feels to execute various types of bodily movements is all but nonexistent. We are forced to address the subject indirectly, in terms of the consequences of the exertion. But then it is no more incorrect for us to represent the content of Tom's intention as we have done than it would be for a professional to try to teach Tom to drive the ball properly by saying such things as, "Take the club back slowly," "Try to keep your left arm straight," and so on.

As so far formulated, then, our account of fully deliberate action calls for it to be preceded by nonreducible states of intending, by acts of decision that give rise to them, and by further acts of decision as needed to articulate the content of the overall intention into a full-fledged plan of action. Nothing less seems able to do justice to our main example. If, however, this is to be our account of fully deliberate action, we may encounter problems with other cases. For although we have so far considered only what it is to form and to have intentions, we seem to be headed for a view according to which what makes Tom's golf shot intentional is that it is related in some important way to an intention that existed *prior to* the action itself, having been developed in advance by Tom to cover this particular occasion. Yet there are many cases in which action appears to be intentional, but where there is no prior deliberation or decision on the agent's part, nor indeed any prior intention whatever.

Perhaps the most troublesome cases of this kind are actions which occur in emergency situations that permit no time for deliberation. Suppose that, on seeing a small child fall into a swimming pool, Mary instantly dives to the rescue. She might later respond to praise by saying she acted "automatically," "without thinking," or the like. Yet Mary does perform an intentional action. She would not deny that she meant to save the child and dived into the water for just this purpose. There is, however, no deliberation or planning in this case, nor does it seem that Mary forms the intention of saving the child prior to doing so. Such examples present a dilemma for theories of intention. If we deny that Mary's act was intentional, we have to explain away the contradiction in saying that an action can be both meant and done for a purpose yet not intentional. If, on the other hand, we accept this as an intentional act, we have to develop our account of intention in a way that allows for actions to be intentional even in cases where they are not undertaken out of any prior intention.

The Execution of Intention

To be able to come to grips with this sort of case, we must first consider how it is that intentions get executed when action is fully deliberate. There is more to this process than some have supposed. We should not think that having once allowed for independent states of intending, we can simply say that when a prior intention *causes* the kinds of bodily and other changes required for action of the sort its content represents, those *changes* count as intentional action, done by the agent *with* the intention that causes them. Besides promising little or no help with actions undertaken without prior deliberation, theories that seek to understand intentional action in terms of this alleged causal relation invariably founder on the problem of causal deviance. Suppose, for example, that I am bored by a seminar speaker and form the intention to disrupt his talk by dropping the cup of coffee I have in my hand onto the tile floor of the seminar room. If my intention causes me to become so agitated that the cup slips from my hand and crashes to the floor, it will produce the results I had planned. But I will not have intentionally disrupted the seminar; in fact, I will not have performed any action at all. My intention will be replicated in my behavior and will have caused it, but I will not have carried out the intention.

The lesson implicit in causal deviance examples is that just when we are most certain motivational states cause behavior, the subjects of such states become their victims, rather than the agents of their fulfillment. Defenders of causal theories have tried to avoid this result, but in the end I think the only solution to the problem these cases pose lies in a volitional theory of overt action.[13] Properly framed, such theories bring agency, and with it intention, into the actual sequence of events that is constitutive of action. The effect is that whether the sequence counts as action, even as intentional action, ceases to depend on any relation to prior states of the agent. Instead, intentionality becomes intrinsic to the sequence, because it is intrinsic to volition. If this approach is correct, then appeal to causation by prior states of intending is neither necessary nor helpful for explaining what it is to act out of a given intention. Moreover, this kind of theory makes it much easier to account for cases like the rescue example, where intentional action occurs without a prior act of intention formation.

When bodily action is preceded by full-blown deliberation and decision, we execute our intentions by engaging in the mental activity of volition, which is normally the basic activity through which overt actions are performed.[14] In Tom's case, having formed the intention to hit a controlled slice and developed the content of that intention into a plan for doing so, it remains for him carry out his plan. This he does by willing the sequence of exertional changes that will cause the movements necessary to make his golf club traverse a certain arc, thereby causing the ball to travel in a path characteristic of a controlled slice. In our example, Tom's volitional activity does cause the series of consequences he intends, and it is because this is so that he intentionally hits a controlled slice. That is, his volitional activity is what accounts both for the fact that he brings about the results he intends, instead of being passive in their occurrence, and for the fact that he brings them about intentionally.

Volition has a number of features that make it ideally suited for this functional role. It is, first of all, an activity—that is, an exercise of agency.

---

[13] See "Agency and the Problem of Causal Deviance," Chapter 6 in this book.
[14] For a defense of these claims, see "Volition and Basic Action," and "Trying, Paralysis, and Volition," Chapters 4 and 5 in this book.

Our engaging in volition therefore counts invariably as action, as do the deeds we perform by means of it. Second, that volition is an activity implies that it is not a momentary mental "click" that *precedes* the bodily changes associated with action.[15] Rather, volition is ongoing: it continues as long as there are exertional changes to be brought about as a means to an action's performance. A proper understanding of it has as little use for the plural noun "volitions" as a correct understanding of physiology has for "livings," "breathings," and "walkings." The bodily changes an action requires are not, as it were, "lined up" in advance, awaiting only the push of a mental button so they can follow in train. Nor is the bringing about of such changes an experience in which we first set the train in motion and then, like Newton's God, intervene periodically to adjust its course. Rather, just as the series of steps needed for Tom to bring off his golf shot has to be performed as a continuous unit, so also must he be continuously engaged in the activity of producing them. Were he to cease this activity in the middle of his swing, the swing would cease as well.

The ongoing character of volition is what makes it possible for us to guide our behavior in response to changing circumstances—a feature often deemed crucial to intentional action. Thus Tom is able to monitor the development of his swing as it occurs, begin his downswing at the appropriate time, and so on. Tom's swing is over pretty quickly, but there are a lot of actions—taking a walk, for example—that require us to make adjustments as we go. We do that by monitoring the action's progress and adjusting the changes that are willed as needed. In no case, however, is it necessary for us to will to act. One acts by virtue of engaging in volition. And when, as in our example, this activity issues in the consequences we expect, we perform actions. Indeed, we perform intentional actions. When Tom's willing issues in the sequence of changes he undertakes to produce by means of it, he hits a controlled slice, and does so intentionally.

What is it, though, that *makes* Tom's action intentional? We might think it is the fact that Tom had the intention to hit the controlled slice *before* he acted, and carried out the plan that intention presented in acting as he did. Some would even wish to say that Tom's prior intention caused his volitional activity, although we have as yet seen no reason to think such a claim is needed. But while the prior availability of a plan is clearly relevant to Tom's action being intentional, that plan need not have been presented in an intention, or in any state that caused Tom to act as he did. For as long as it was performed through the activity of willing the changes he brought about, Tom's act of hitting the controlled slice *had* to be inten-

---

[15]   This is the conception Gilbert Ryle appears to have had in mind in asking how many acts of will are executed in reciting "Little Miss Muffet" backwards. *The Concept of Mind* (London: Hutchinson, 1949), p. 65. The question is tantalizing but totally misconceived.

tional, and would have been so whether or not he had a prior intention. The reason for this is simply that it is not possible for a person to will the changes an action requires without both intending to will them, and intending thereby to produce the changes willed.

One way to become convinced of this is to consider what would have to hold were it not the case. If the initiating element in action were not intentional by its own nature, then the influence of factors associated with causal deviance should, as in the example of the fallen coffee cup, vitiate the claim that intentional action occurs. As it is, however, this is not a problem. Let it be assumed that Tom's prior intention does cause his volitional activity, and let us add the assumption that it does so by first making him nervous, which in turn causes him to act on his intention. He might, for example, have been about to reconsider his plan until agitation drove the thought from his mind. Would this make Tom's action unintentional? Clearly not, for if he did act by engaging in the volitional activity described, it must have been his purpose to do so. Indeed, there are many cases where agitation and distress contribute heavily to the occurrence of actions that, though undertaken with little or no deliberation, are nonetheless intentional. Consider the parent who, distraught by one or another of life's crises, abruptly and without forethought strikes a crying infant. We can protest after doing such things that we did not mean it. But of course we know that the reason this kind of act is offensive and even terrifying is precisely that at the time, we *did* mean it. Sadly, such actions are intentional, even though but for the agent's agitation they would not have occurred and even though they are done with no prior intention. The best explanation of this is that they are founded on a mental activity that is intrinsically intentional.

Tom's golf swing is also founded on such an activity. In fact, it would be self-contradictory to say that Tom unintentionally willed the changes his golf swing required, or did so without intending those changes to occur. There simply are no plausible examples of unintentional volition. We have every reason to think, then, that volitional activity is intrinsically intentional, and hence would be so regardless of any state of the agent that might precede or cause it. Nevertheless, this claim may appear suspiciously convenient and even ad hoc. Something intrinsically intentional is needed to forestall deviant causal chains and to deal with cases where action is undertaken without deliberation, and volition turns out to be just the ticket. The suspicion that this is contrived is, however, groundless. For the fact is that not only volition but also the other mental activities that help guide our behavior display the feature of intrinsic intentionality. Foremost among these is deciding. It is impossible to make a decision without intending to decide, and without intending to decide exactly as we do.

That is why we never hear of anyone accidentally, inadvertently, or unintentionally deciding to do something. And this is exactly what we should expect, for the function of decision in practical thinking is to establish intentions for the future, thereby enabling us to exert some control over our destinies. This function would be utterly defeated if it were possible for us to make decisions we did not intend to make, or to form purposes it was not our purpose to form. The same holds for the decisions by which our intentions are developed into complete plans: it would be no good to adopt a goal intentionally and then inadvertently choose a means to achieve it. Even the process of deliberation itself is likely to involve more than one point at which we selectively direct our attention to some aspect of the problem at hand in order to explore its significance. This phenomenon, too, is intrinsically intentional. To be sure, we do not have complete control over what we think about, even in deliberation. It is possible for content to obtrude itself into our thoughts and divert our attention from elsewhere. But we cannot actively concentrate on content that is already before the mind without intending to do exactly that, and this too is necessary if the process of planning our behavior is to put it under our own direction.

The entire range of thinking that attends fully deliberate action is, then, filled with mental acts that are intentional. Moreover, in the case of decisions the intentionality has to be intrinsic. To say Tom's decision to hit a controlled slice is intentional cannot mean that he made it out of a prior intention so to decide, for if he already intended to decide that way then he had already decided. It should, therefore, occasion no surprise to learn that the activity of volition is intrinsically intentional. The surprise would be if things were the other way around. Causal deviance examples show that if intention is to function in a way that enables us truly to guide our behavior, the execution of intentions has to be intrinsically intentional. And an examination of the other mental activities that enable us to guide our actions shows it to be the rule, not the exception, that they are characterized by intrinsic intentionality.

What makes Tom's act of hitting a controlled slice intentional, then, is that he performs it by willing the sequence of change he understands to be needed to perform such an act. The intrinsic intentionality of volition is alone sufficient to secure the fact that his action is intentional, and nothing less will secure it. But then what is it that enables us to say that Tom acted out of a prior intention? For the significance of saying volition is intrinsically intentional is in part that even if Tom had not intended beforehand to hit a controlled slice, he would have put himself into a state of intending to do so simply by willing the changes a slice required. What is it that enables us to say Tom acted with the intention he already had, rather than out of another intention formed in the act itself?

Part of the answer to this question is to be gotten from the fact that as he prepared to hit the shot, Tom was aware of his intention to hit a controlled slice, and it was this awareness that presented him with the plan on which he acted. Since this is so, it is fair to say Tom acted out of an intention he already had. There is, however, a much more important point to be made here. The fact is that in normal circumstances at least, it is not possible for a person to have two intentions to perform the same action. To be sure, one can intend the same act for more than one reason. Tom could intend to hit a slice not only to put himself in the best position to par the hole, but also to impress his partners with his ability. But this is not to have two intentions. It is to have one in which the same act fits into a larger plan as contributing to more than one goal. Where one might be said to have two intentions to do the same thing, the reason is usually forgetfulness. I might, for example, intend to drive to the university to charge my car's battery and, forgetting this, form another intention to drive to the university to pick up a book.[16] Even here, however, the phrase *the same thing* is misleading, for the two intentions are parts of larger plans that focus on different objectives. They cannot be executed simultaneously unless I overcome my forgetfulness and combine the plans into one, thus ceasing to have two intentions. If I do not do this, then which intention is executed in a given volitional episode would simply be a matter of which objective I conceive as the outcome of the changes willed.

Apart from this type of case, it seems impossible to have two intentions to do the same thing. Indeed, the whole idea of forming two intentions to do the same thing for the same reason has a psychotic ring to it. What shall I do—try form a second intention to complete this chapter, in case the first fails me? That would be an exercise in paranoia—equivalent, in the cognitive realm, to trying to form two beliefs that there is a God so the communists will have to talk me out of it twice. But apart from the nuttiness of the idea, the fact is that the effort just won't work. If I already know I have a certain belief, I can only reaffirm it; I cannot form a second one. And if I know I intend to do a certain thing I can ratify that intention, but I cannot form a second one with the same content.

There is, then, no need to worry that volitional activity undertaken out of an intention already held might give rise to a new intention that duplicates the first.[17] Rather, Tom's volitional activity may be viewed as rati-

---

16   The importance of this type of case was pointed out to me by Myles Brand.

17   I suspect it is partly this worry that underlies certain features of accounts that treat volition as a kind of occurrent intention. Wilfrid Sellars, for example, claims a prior intention "develops into" a volitional one at the time of action. "Thought and Action," in Keith Lehrer, ed., *Freedom and Determinism* (New York: Random House, 1966), p. 133; Brand appears to follow Sellars in this, presenting what he calls "immediate intending" as the last stage of intending a future action. *Intending and Acting*, pp. 128, 153; and Searle's account

fying the intention he already held, for he could not have engaged in it without, by virtue of the activity itself, intending to hit a controlled slice, and his willing the changes he did means he did not opt for any different intention at the last moment. But the intention to hit a controlled slice that is guaranteed by Tom's volitional activity is not any different from the intention he already had. It is and can only be the same one. This may be upsetting if we are inclined to view mental states as either identical with or having a one–one correspondence to relatively localized brain states. For it would appear that a localized brain state—say, a certain physiological state of a few neurons—should be repeatable, and hence that it ought to be possible to have two intentions or beliefs of the same kind. But whatever its implications for the mind/body problem, the fact is that mental states do not individuate that way. Tom's volitional activity would indeed have given rise to an intention on his part to hit a controlled slice had he not already intended to do so. As it was, however, it simply reaffirmed an intention he already had.

Causation and the Will

Perhaps the most interesting feature of the above account is that it allows us to explain what it is for an action to be done *out of* an intention—even a prior intention—with no mention whatever of nomic causation. Actions are not made intentional by a causal relation to *any* prior state of the agent. Rather, even fully deliberate actions are made intentional by being founded on the activity of willing, which cannot be engaged in unintentionally, and given which the agent must intend to bring about the changes willed. This is not to deny the importance of our being able to form intentions prior to acting. Were we unable to do so, it would be all but impossible to coordinate our behavior so as to achieve long-range goals. Moreover, when a prior intention is formed, it is typically an awareness of this intention that presents the agent with the plan he executes in acting. We do not, however, have to have prior intentions in order to understand what it is to act in a certain way, thus prior intentions are not necessary to intentional action.

This last consideration makes possible a reasonable account of cases where action is intentional but occurs without deliberation or prior intention. Cases like Mary's emergency rescue or a parent's striking a crying in-

---

of intention includes a self-referential feature according to which the act intended is always intended to be performed "by way of carrying out this intention." *Intentionality*, pp. 85–86. If the view I defend is correct, these claims are unnecessary.

fant are bound to be puzzling if we think intentional action must spring from a prior intention, or that intentionality consists in a causal relation with such a state. In fact, however, this is not the case. What is necessary for an action to be intentional is not that it arise out of a prior intention, but rather that the sequence of events constitutive of the action instantiate a *representation* of action that guides the volitional activity of the agent who brings them about. And this, in turn, requires only that the agent be presented with such a representation at the moment of action. This can occur without the assistance of a prior intention. Mary can be aware of what it would be to save the drowning child even if she does not yet intend to do so, provided only that she recognizes that a rescue is needed. Similarly, a distraught parent can know what it would be to strike a crying child without intending to do so. From that point on, willing is all that is needed to provide intentionality. We need not, then, be fearful that an account of intention which allows for nonreducible states of intending will be unable to account for cases where no such state exists prior to action.

Finally, it is worth considering briefly the implications of the theory presented here for causal accounts of human action. The claim that actions are causally determined by prior states of the agent is common. It is, however, without empirical substantiation: We have, as yet, no deterministic "laws" of human action. This puts causal claims in danger of being gratuitous in philosophical theories of action, for in the absence of deterministic laws such claims do little actual work in the theory. No doubt it is partly this danger that has prompted some reductionistic approaches to intention. Phenomena such as decision smack of libertarianism anyway: people unspoiled by philosophy are often inclined to believe that if determinism is true, we never "really" get to decide anything. And since the claim that action is caused by prior motivating states has led to the discovery of no laws, it is only natural to try to make it do some work in the theory of action by attempting to show that once a causal account is adopted, separate states of intending, acts of deciding, and the like will be superfluous. As we have seen, this move appears not to work. But even models of intentional action that admit independent states of intending may contrive to be causal in their account of how intention finds expression in action, for fear that unless such a claim is made we will be unable to explain how it is that an agent acts *out of* one intention rather than another.

It ought to have been expected that this invocation of causality would turn out to be unnecessary, for even though we do not know whether human action is caused, we almost always know when it is intentional. And that is exactly how things do turn out. The story of Tom is one of an agent who, cognizant of the options available to him, intentionally adopts one of them as his purpose and then, cognizant of this purpose, proceeds to execute it in a way that is itself intrinsically intentional, and given which he had to be acting with the intention of doing what he did. No further light is shed on what makes his act intentional by adding the unsubstantiated claim that Tom's state of intending caused his volitional activity. Indeed, if the argument presented here is correct, causation by such a state is neither necessary nor sufficient for behavior to be intentional.

Is there, then, no room for a causal account of intentional action? Perhaps there is, for there are important aspects of the example of Tom that I have not sought to address here. Nothing said here explains why Tom chose the type of shot he did, or why he did not change his mind before acting. Tom did, of course, have reasons for hitting a controlled slice. But nothing in our account says he had to act for these reasons, and there were also reasons for hitting a hook. Now it is often urged that we can have no satisfactory account of intention formation that is not causal. Perhaps, then, some motivational state of Tom's caused him to make the decision he did. Perhaps, too, the persistence of this state caused Tom to carry through with his intention to hit a slice instead of reconsidering and changing his mind. In short, perhaps a causal account *is* in order when it comes to explaining why we *form* the intentions we do, and why we carry them through to execution rather than faltering. Perhaps, but there are reasons for being skeptical, and I think this discussion has added to them. One is the fact that the phenomenon of deciding seems incapable of being accidental or inadvertent. Philosophers who insist on a deterministic theory of intention formation often do so on the basis that unless such a theory holds, it could only be by sheer accident that we come to have and execute the intentions we do. But if what has been said here about deciding is correct, then at least from the agent's practical perspective the alleged accidentalness is not even a possibility, much less a problem an indeterministic account would have to work its way around.

There is, of course, much more to be said on this issue, and the present discussion certainly does not justify the conclusion that causal theories of action are incorrect. I think, however, that this much can be claimed: Even if a causal theory were needed to tell us why we form the intentions we do and why we retain them to the moment of execution, causal theories could not tell us what it is for an action to be intentional. The phenomenon of intentionality is much too deeply embedded in action for a relational concept like that of causation to be able to account for it.[18]

---

[18]   I am grateful to Robert Audi, Myles Brand, and Jonathan Kvanvig for helpful discussions of these issues.

8

The Formation of Intention

Perhaps the central concept in action theory is that of intention. Its importance lies in the fact that it is through our intentions, especially intentions for the future, that the voluntary control we exert over our behavior assumes meaningful proportions. By forming intentions we develop plans for guiding our behavior; by carrying intentions out we exercise that guidance, and so incur responsibility for what we do. Not surprisingly, therefore, efforts to understand human action often focus on the formation and execution of intention. And central to those efforts is the issue of determinism: whether the etiology of intentional action is a matter of nomic causation by motivational and belief states, or of some other, indeterministic process. I have argued elsewhere that the execution of intention can be understood without invoking nomic causation.[1] Here, I want to make the same case for intention formation. The central issue to be discussed is how reasons enter into decisions—that is, what it is for an agent to decide *for* a reason. My purpose is to defend a noncausal account of this process.

I shall discuss first some relations between reasons, intention, and decision, and then turn to the distinction between causal explanations of decisions in terms of an agent's mental states, and teleological explanations in terms of the contents of those states. I shall argue that when we explain decisions by invoking reasons, it is the latter sort of explanation that is in-

---

[1] See "Intrinsic Intentionality," Chapter 7 in this book.

tended. Even if reason explanations are not per se causal, however, they could still presuppose a causal account of intention formation, since whether the agent decided *for* the reasons in question could still be a matter of nomic causation. The success of a libertarian account of human action therefore requires a noncausal account of what it is to decide for a reason, and I try to develop such an account. Finally, I consider how well this account addresses the objection that an uncaused decision must count as a violation of principles of sufficient reason, and hence as a kind of accident.

Having Reasons, Intending, and Deciding

The relationship between action and intention is an intimate one, because intention enters into action at its very start. It may be argued that whenever we act something gets done that is intentional, since all action is grounded in mental activity that is itself intrinsically intentional and hence guided by some purpose.[2] But if the relation between action and intention is close, that between intention and reasons is even closer. Actions are intentional just in case they are performed *with* an intention,[3] and the concepts of acting with an intention and acting for a reason are virtually interchangeable. Very roughly, we may be said to have a reason to perform an action *A* whenever we envision it as a means to some end—that is, in the normal case, when we think that by performing *A* we can accomplish some action *B* that we desire, feel obligated, or are otherwise positively disposed to perform.[4] When people act intentionally, we expect their behavior to be guided by such dispositions: that is, it should be undertaken in pursuit of some end the agent values. By contrast, no one is expected to be able to give a reason for, say, inadvertently spilling his coffee or accidentally losing a message. Acts that are not intended are not done for reasons.

The most important sign of the close relationship between acting for a reason and acting intentionally is, however, that the same ends we might cite as reasons for which an action was performed can also be given as intentions the agent had in acting. Suppose, for example, that you ask me what my reason was for taking my son to Swensen's. I might reply that I

---

[2] Ibid. See also Carl Ginet, *On Action* (New York: Cambridge University Press, 1990), p. 74.
[3] For a defense of this claim, which a number of authors deny, see my "Rationality and the Range of Intention," *Midwest Studies in Philosophy* 10 (1985), 191–211; and "Settled Objectives and Rational Constraints," Chapter 10 in this book.
[4] In the limiting case, *A* and *B* are the same action, and the belief element becomes unnecessary.

wanted to buy him an ice cream cone, or perhaps that I was obligated to buy him one since I had promised. Suppose, on the other hand, that you ask me the intention with which I took my son to Swensen's. If my reason was either of the above, I would almost certainly reply that I took him there to buy him an ice cream cone. Indeed, it is hard to see how either a desire to buy my son an ice cream cone or a sense that I was obligated to do so *could* have been my reason for taking my son to Swensen's unless that objective was my intention in taking him there. The reasons out of which we act match the intentions with which we act.

The close parallel between intentions and reasons is doubtless part of what has prompted some authors to suggest that states of intending simply consist in those mental states of agents, such as desire and belief, to which we allude in citing their reasons for acting.[5] There are, however, significant differences between intending to perform an action and merely having a reason to perform it. When I intend to take my son to Swensen's for ice cream, I am committed to doing so: I need to set aside the time, make sure I have adequate means to get there, avoid forming conflicting intentions, and so on. None of this is implicit in my simply having reasons for such a trip. I may desire to buy my son an ice cream cone, feel obligated to do so, and even have a speculative belief that I will eventually settle on a trip to Swensen's as a means to achieve these goals. But if I have not yet made up my mind on the issue, I am under no rational obligation to plan for the trip. Taking my son to Swensen's is not an objective of mine, for I have not yet formed that intention.

While our intentions reflect our reasons, then, they do not reduce to them. To understand the true relationship between the two, we need to see how reasons enter into intention formation. Paradigmatically, this occurs through the mental act of deciding, or making up one's mind, to do something. Deciding, I would argue, is a ubiquitous phenomenon: it occurs whenever we form an intention prior to actually acting on it. But it is most clearly understood by concentrating on cases that involve more than peremptory deliberation—that is, where the agent spends at least a short time considering the reasons for and against the options available, and more or less self-consciously selects the course he will pursue. If we attend to such cases we will observe another interesting

---

[5]   Donald Davidson appears to have been attracted by this reductionist position in his influential "Actions, Reasons, and Causes," *Journal of Philosophy* 60 (1963), 690. The position is modified, however, in his "Intending," in Yirmiahu Yovel, ed., *Philosophy of History and Action* (Dordrecht: D. Reidel, 1978), pp. 41–60. Classic reductionist accounts of intending include Robert Audi, "Intending," *Journal of Philosophy* 70 (1973), 387–402; and Alvin I. Goldman, *A Theory of Human Action* (Englewood Cliffs, N.J.: Prentice-Hall, 1970), chap. 1. Audi offers another account in "Intending, Intentional Action, and Desire," in Joel Marks, ed., *The Ways of Desire* (Chicago: Precedent Publishing, 1986), pp. 17–38.

parallel: our reasons enter into our decisions in much the way they enter into our actions. This is because deciding is itself purposive behavior and hence demands explanation by reasons. And it turns out that the reasons that explain an agent's act of deciding to *A* are none other than those which, if the intention thereby formed is executed, will ultimately explain his *A*-ing.

We need to be careful here to distinguish between one's reasons for deciding at all and one's reasons for deciding as one does. My reasons for deciding at all what I will do this afternoon need have nothing to do with taking my son to Swensen's. No doubt they will have mostly to do with my need to organize my day sensibly, plan my activities, and communicate those plans to others. But these considerations can only explain why I take pains to make *some* decision. What is crucial for questions of freedom is not that,[6] but rather why I select the particular course of action I do: why I decide to take my son to Swensen's, rather than play golf, say, or work on a lecture. And my reasons for deciding as I do are just my reasons for ultimately doing what I decide on. So if what explains my taking my son to Swensen's this afternoon is my desire to buy him an ice cream cone, then that same desire will explain my forming the intention to take him there. If, on the other hand, the explanation is some felt obligation on my part, that explanation too will apply as much to my decision as to the action that ultimately ensues. In short, just as we act for reasons so we also decide for reasons, and the same reasons that explain our actions explain the content of our corresponding decisions.[7] So whatever it is for me to act for a reason, a similar relationship can be expected to obtain when I decide for a reason. Furthermore, we can expect that whatever freedom we have in acting we will also have in deciding to act—so that if we are free at all, we are free in forming as well as in executing our intentions.

What is it, then, to decide to *A* for a reason? It is frequently held that when an agent is said to act for a reason, the *for* must be understood in

[6] I do not mean to imply by this that the relationship between one's reasons for deciding at all and one's deciding is deterministic. On the contrary: I take this relationship to be like the one I sought to describe between intending and willing in "Intrinsic Intentionality," Chapter 7 in this book. But even if it were deterministic, that would not rule out the content of the decision being up to us in the way libertarians suppose, so that we could still claim significant freedom.

[7] An exception may be required for cases like Kavka's toxin puzzle, where there are special incentives for simply intending to perform an action. See Gregory Kavka, "The Toxin Puzzle," *Analysis* 43 (1983), 33–36. I will ignore such cases here. For discussions of them see Michael E. Bratman, *Intention, Plans, and Practical Reason* (Cambridge: Harvard University Press, 1987), pp. 101–6; and Alfred R. Mele, "Intentions, Reasons, and Beliefs: Morals of the Toxin Puzzle," *Philosophical Studies* 68 (1992), 171–94.

terms of nomic causation.[8] If that were true, we should expect the same to hold for deciding. Deciding to *A* is, after all, a step toward *A*-ing and the fact that deciding is itself a purposive phenomenon gives it perhaps the most important of the trappings of action. On this view, then, my reasons for deciding to take my son to Swensen's cause my act of deciding. And it is fair in this context to understand causation as a deterministic phenomenon. That is what is usually intended, and were it not so—that is, if the causation were only probabilistic—then the causal account of my decision would be open to an objection usually reserved for libertarian accounts: that what it cites as a cause offers only an incomplete explanation, since it is compatible with my having decided to play golf instead. But are reasons really causes? Opponents of determinism would claim not. On their view, to give a person's reasons for acting is to cite not a cause but a justification: it is to provide a synopsis of the considerations that, in the agent's *thinking,* made the act worthwhile, and embodied his purposes in undertaking it.[9] Explanation by reasons is teleological, not causal, and it permits the act in question to be free, in the libertarian sense.

Two Models for Explanation by Reasons

The depth of the disagreement here is partially masked by an important ambiguity in language about the mental. Terms such as *belief* and *desire* may refer either to mental states, or to the content of those states. Mental states count as particulars: my believing that today is Thursday is not the same thing as your believing that today is Thursday, nor is my desiring to go to Europe the same as your desiring to go there. Though mental, these states are concrete entities, at least in the sense that they form part of the totality of our experience, that they involve psychological attitudes which come to be and pass away, and that they might not have existed at all. The situation is different with the *content* of mental states. When you and I both believe that today is Thursday, we believe the same thing, and that is

[8] This claim stems from Davidson, "Actions, Reasons, and Causes," p. 693, and has since been made by many authors. Sometimes a more cautious position is taken. For example, Audi holds in one place that to have acted for a reason, one must have acted "because" of it, where this signifies only that the reason helps explain why the agent acted—a view that leaves open the type of explanation at issue. See "Acting for Reasons," *Philosophical Review* 95 (1986), 515–16.
[9] Classic defenses of this sort of position include A. I. Melden, *Free Action* (London: Routledge & Kegan Paul, 1961); Charles Taylor, *The Explanation of Behavior* (London: Routledge & Kegan Paul, 1964); and G. H. von Wright, *Explanation and Understanding* (Ithaca: Cornell University Press, 1971). More recent noncausal accounts of reason explanations can be found in Ginet, *On Action;* and George M. Wilson, *The Intentionality of Human Action* (Stanford: Stanford University Press, 1989).

an indication that what we believe is not a particular but something conceptual, an *ens rationis*. The contents of states of believing are usually called "propositions." These, it is widely held, cannot come to be and pass away, and represent an entirely different sort of entity from the belief-states of which they form the content. The content of states of desiring is somewhat more controversial, but these states are optative in nature, and it is important that their contents be so portrayed. The content of my state of desiring to go to Europe may be represented as, "Would that I go to Europe."[10] Finally, we should allow for the possibility of there being optative states that have specifically to do with obligation. An important philosophical tradition, of which Kant is the leading representative, holds that motives of duty are to be distinguished from those of inclination or desire, and are capable in themselves of grounding decision. If that is correct, we should think of my sense of obligation to buy my son an ice cream cone as embodying a unique sort of optation. We might represent it as: "I must buy my son an ice cream cone."

Once the ambiguity of language about the mental is recognized, the dimensions of the dispute over reason explanations becomes clear. Nomic causation is a relation that can hold only among particulars. When it is said, therefore, that my decision to take my son to Swensen's was caused by my "reasons," it is in fact my reason-*states* that are invoked as explanatory, via an implicit appeal to covering laws. If my reason consisted of a desire to buy my son an ice cream cone and a belief that I could do so if I took him to Swensen's, the explanation might be outlined like this:

(1) (A scientific law or laws)
(2) I desired to buy my son an ice cream cone.
(3) I believed I could buy my son an ice cream cone if I took him to Swensen's.
(4) Therefore, I decided to take my son to Swensen's.

This is intended to approximate a deductively valid argument. It is not one as it stands, for we do not presently have the laws to fill in premise (1). Ideally, however, they would be universal in form and would connect my desire- and belief-states, which are reported in (2) and (3), with the event of my deciding, reported in (4). Depending on how the laws turn out to be formulated, the exact language of (2) and (3) might have to change. In par-

---

[10]   Thus portrayed, the content of my state of desiring comes imbued with the psychological attitude that characterizes such states. In more formal treatments, the content of a psychological state can be separated from modality of thought that operates on it. Thus we might portray my desire as: desire (I go to Europe). I employ this more formal sort of treatment in "Intrinsic Intentionality," Chapter 7 in this book.

ticular, they might have to include information about the strength of my desire.

This is a far cry from the position of opponents of the causal view. For them, "reasons" are not optative- and belief-states, but rather their contents. On this type of account, the point of invoking my reason for the Swensen's decision is not to cite a nomic cause but to make clear the practical reason*ing* that led to my act of intention formation: to report how I evaluated the action at issue, and to point up the considerations that won approval in my deliberation. For the Swensen's case my reasoning might be summarized as follows:

(1′) Would that I buy my son an ice cream cone.
(2′) I can buy my son and ice cream cone if I take him to Swensen's.
(3′) So I shall take my son to Swensen's.

This second sort of sequence is a type of Aristotelian practical syllogism.[11] Unlike the first argument, it offers not even a pretense of logical validity. Deductive logic does not permit inference even to the desiderative "Would that I take my son to Swensen's" from these premises,[12] much less the conclusion of this syllogism, which is the content of my act of deciding to take my son to Swensen's. As we shall see, this content is in fact the intention I form through my act of decision. And there are no logical principles by which desires and beliefs entail intentions.[13]

What this comes to is that the practical syllogism does not present my decision as inevitable, logically or otherwise. Rather, it offers a purported *justification* for my decision, by citing the considerations I entertained in reaching it, and presenting the decision as *called for* in virtue of them. That is, the practical syllogism encapsulates a teleological explanation in which the value of a goal is presented as rationalizing and justifying a decision aimed at achieving it. Unlike causal explanations, therefore, this argument deals not in mental states but in their content. Its "reasons" are the optation and proposition in light of which I made my decision; its conclusion, rather than reporting my act of deciding, reports what I decided. This is

---

[11]   Or at least this is so on one reading of Aristotle. For an interesting discussion of how the Aristotelian practical syllogism should be understood, see Robert Audi, *Practical Reasoning* (New York: Routledge, 1989), chap. 1.
[12]   We could try to fix that by having the second premise treat taking my son to Swensen's as necessary to buying him an ice cream cone. But the resulting inference would be representative of far fewer cases of practical reasoning, since we usually have more than one option for achieving our goals.
[13]   It should not be concluded, however, that logic has nothing to do with the way optations and beliefs are related to decisions and intentions. See especially Anthony Kenny, *Will, Freedom and Power* (Oxford: Basil Blackwell, 1975), chap. 5.

important, because as Thomas Reid long ago observed, reasons in this sense are not the sorts of things that even *can* be causes; they are not events or states but conceptual entities, which can cause nothing.[14] But they can justify, and to the extent that my premises justify the content of my decision, they also justify my act of deciding.

We have, then, two very different conceptions of reasons, and with them different conceptions of how a reason should be taken to explain a decision. And of course the same two types of explanation can be offered for the action that ultimately ensues. Can they coexist? Perhaps. Both conceptions of reasons are legitimate and it may be that the process of my deciding to take my son to Swensen's was one wherein my reason-states caused me to decide as I did, while their content justified the intention I formed by so doing.[15] But if we are concerned about human freedom we should question this. From a libertarian perspective, it may be wondered what the point would be in offering a teleological justification for a decision that, given my states of motivation and belief, I was going to make in any case. Only the most subjective notion of justification—one that virtually equates it with the motivational force of my state of desire—would then seem to have bearing on my decision. And that seems to trivialize the sort of evaluation a teleological account of my decisions invites. It is worth investigating, therefore, which of our two models of explanation we invoke when we offer reasons for our decisions. If it turns out to be the teleological one, we will have reason for questioning whether the causal account has a legitimate place in the theory of intention formation.

Decisions, Reasons, and Causes

I think it does turn out that way. Admittedly, the initial data are ambiguous. Asked to give my reason for deciding to take my son to Swensen's, I might cite either a reason-state or its content. If I focus on the optative side of the picture, I could say, "I wanted to get him an ice cream cone," reporting my desire-state. Alternatively, I might simply say, "To get him an ice cream cone," giving its content. The same holds if I dwell on the cognitive aspects of my deliberation. I might reply either, "I believed I could get him an ice cream cone there," or just, "They sell ice cream cones." So our ways of reporting reasons appear neutral as between the two models for a reason explanation. But if we look further, it begins to emerge that in both giving and evaluating reasons, the content of the

---

[14]   Thomas Reid, *Essays on the Active Powers of the Human Mind* (Cambridge: MIT Press, 1969), p. 283.
[15]   Goldman, *A Theory of Human Action*, pp. 102–3.

agent's optative- and belief-states is the primary focus of attention. One way to see this is to consider how, once given, a reason explanation can come to be rejected. We need to consider two quite different ways in which this can occur. First, it might be claimed that the explanation is false, that the reasons given are not in fact those out of which the agent acted. Second, it can be claimed that the reasons, though accurately described, are inadequate to ground the decision based on them.

If either mode of rejection favors the causal model it ought to be the first. On the causal view, to deny that an agent decided out of the reasons he gives amounts to saying the reason-states in question are not the nomic cause of his decision. But even when we reject reason explanations as false, there is no clear indication that causation is what we have in mind. One way of undermining claims of nomic causation is to show that universality fails to obtain, that in other cases the alleged cause has not had the effect at issue. Given the notorious difficulty of generalizing about human behavior, however, this kind of argument is all but useless. No one would respond to my claim that I decided to take my son to Swensen's because I wanted to buy him an ice cream cone with: "That can't be right, because Smith wanted to buy his son an ice cream cone too and never decided to take him anywhere." In fact, one would not even reject my explanation on the ground that I myself have not consistently acted in this way in the past. We do, of course, expect the behavior of rational agents to have a certain amount of predictability. But not so much as to preclude the unexpected, and what regularity there is does not require causal laws to explain it. All we need do is remind ourselves that rationality demands a degree of uniformity in the motives we act on, lest we fail to achieve any long-range goals in life.

Another procedure we do not usually follow in refuting reason explanations is to try to assess the motivating force of the agent's optative states at the moment of deciding. We have, first of all, practically no reliable independent means of telling whether, when I decided to take him to Swensen's, my strongest desire was to buy my son an ice cream cone. But even if we did, the fact of the matter is simply that we are not very much concerned with that kind of issue. We would be suspicious if there were indications I had no desire whatever to buy my son an ice cream cone, for a desire I do not have cannot be one on which my decision was based. But if we are prepared to grant that the optative state existed, that is usually all there is to the matter; we pay little or no attention to considerations of strength in attempting to determine whether a desire, once present, did constitute the agent's reason for acting.

How then *do* we go about showing that the reasons for a decision are other than what is claimed? The key issue turns out to be what the agent's conduct displays about his *intentions*. Suppose, for example, that after explaining my decision to take my son to Swensen's, I take him there, go in, order myself an ice cream cone, and fail to order him one. You could then rightly suspect that I had not decided to take him to Swensen's out of a desire to buy him an ice cream cone, but rather because I wanted to buy myself one. The same holds on the cognitive side. Suppose I tell you I have decided to take my son to Swensen's this afternoon. You surmise that my reason involves a belief that I can get him some ice cream there. Later, however, you learn that this afternoon I walked into Swensen's with my son, looked around in complete bewilderment, and then said to the salesperson, "Don't you sell hockey sticks?" Here you could conclude immediately that I had not formed my intention for the reason you thought.

What these cases show, I think, is that our real test for determining whether an agent decided for a supposed reason has to do not with nomic causation but with the replicative relationship between reasons and intentions noted earlier: that is, with whether the content of the reason-states in question is reflected in the agent's intentions.[16] We expect that when a decision is made for a reason, the intention formed will reflect the premises on which it is based, so that what was desired or otherwise opted, and the means to it, thereby come to be intended. It is when this situation fails to obtain that we are able to tell an agent did not decide for the reasons he gives. The obvious implication, to which we shall have to return, is that to decide for a reason has to do with bringing this replicative relationship to pass. The important point for the present, however, is that when we reject reason explanations as false, what we have in mind by "reasons" seems not to be optative- or belief-states, but rather the optations and propositions that are their contents.

The same is true a fortiori regarding the second way reasons can be rejected. Often, we accept it that an agent has decided or acted for the reasons he proffers, but reject those reasons as inadequate in a valuational sense. The issue in these cases is not whether the reasons are genuine, but whether they justify the agent's doings. And here there is no question that by "reasons" we have in mind *entia rationis*. This is most obvious in situations where there are considerations the agent did not think of, but which represent a more sound basis for decision and action than those he employed. There may have been better reasons for me to decide not to take my son to Swensen's. Perhaps he is allergic to ice cream, or perhaps I had other, overriding obligations. But to say there were better reasons for deciding differently is not to say I *had* those reasons, in the sense that they

---

[16] Cf. the suggestion of Ginet, *On Action*, p. 145, which calls for substantially the same test.

were reflected in my thinking. I may not have known that my son is allergic to ice cream, or that I had obligations that outweighed getting him an ice cream cone. Or, I might have known these things but not valued them, not had the optations that would ground a decision in their favor. But then what is meant by a "reason" here cannot be an optative- or belief-state. It can only be an abstract consideration, something that would have formed the content of such a state had I thought about it in the appropriate way.

Even when we focus on considerations that did enter the agent's thinking, moreover, it turns out to be the content of optative- and belief-states we have in mind in evaluating his reasons. This can be obscured, unfortunately, by the ambiguity of reason reports. It would be allowed, I think, that if I had no overriding obligation I would be giving a pretty good reason for deciding to take my son to Swensen's were I to say that I wanted to buy him an ice cream cone. But it might be thought that since what I report here is my desire-state rather than its content, it is actually premise (2) of the causal model for explaining my decision that I am presenting as a "good reason," rather than premise (1') of the practical syllogism. On reflection, however, I think it can be seen that this is false.

What is reported in premise (2) of the causal model is the fact that I desired to buy my son an ice cream cone. This, I submit, is not nearly as good a reason for deciding to take my son to Swensen's as what is recorded in the first line of the practical syllogism—that is, what is expressed by, "Would that I buy my son an ice cream cone." For, in the first place, premise (2) of the causal model presents nothing as being worth achieving; it merely records a fact about my psychology, that I have a certain desire. And simply to do that is not to endorse anything. The first premise of the practical syllogism is quite different: it endorses the project of my buying my son an ice cream cone. It presents that idea as worthy of being pursued, as good. And that an undertaking should be good is a much better reason for pursuing it than that it be desired. Second, because premise (2) of the causal model records not an optation but a fact, it is unfit to be the content of an optative-state. It has to be the content of a belief-state. But then (2) can function as a reason for deciding to buy my son an ice cream cone only in an entirely *different* sequence of practical reasoning than the one we are supposing occurred. What is needed is a second-order optation such as, "Would that I satisfy my desires"—the kind of thing that would be justified if, say, I didn't spend enough time enjoying myself. So even were I to indicate my reason by reporting my desire-state, what counts as a "good reason" in our example is not the state but its content. The state itself is not a good reason for anything, and while the fact that it exists could serve as a good reason, this would be so only if my deliberative process had gone entirely differently from the way it did.[17]

Analogous arguments hold when an agent's citation of a reason fastens on the cognitive side of deliberation. That I believe I can buy my son an ice cream cone if I take him to Swensen's is not as good a reason for deciding to take him there as that I *be* able to buy one. The former could obtain even if Swensen's does not sell ice cream, whereas the latter could not. Nor, indeed, am I even likely to cite my state of believing as a reason for deciding unless I am unsure about the belief, or have subsequently found out it was false. Other things being equal, I will simply cite the belief itself. And again, where the fact that I believe something to be true counts, in the proper sense, as a reason—that is, where it counts as something to be considered during deliberation, the situation is apt to be quite different from the one in our example. It would have to be one where the value of following my beliefs is itself a consideration that enters into the deliberative process, which is pretty unusual.

There are, then, excellent grounds for thinking that in most situations what is spoken of as a reason for performing an action, and hence for deciding to perform it, is not any kind of mental state or combination of them, but rather the contents of mental states. Reason-states, in everyday explanations of decision and action, are not reasons. They are not what is offered as having explanatory force, not what we consider when we evaluate an agent's reasons, not even our guide as to whether an agent really did decide or act *for* the reason he gave. Pretty clearly, then, the causal model is not what we are employing when we offer reasons to explain what we do, or decide to do. The import of the *for* in reason explanations is teleological, not causal.

Deciding for Reasons

As they stand, however, these considerations are unlikely to persuade defenders of the causal model, for they do not shed enough light on what actually *happens* in decision making to give substance to a noncausal account of the process. It is not enough, for a decision to be made for one set of reasons rather than another, that it be made in the presence of those reasons. In the Swensen's example, I may also have wanted to buy myself an

---

17   This kind of argument becomes especially compelling if it is allowed that felt obligation counts as a special sort of optative state. The sense of urgency expressed in "I must buy my son an ice cream cone" gives my obligation conative bite. No such thing is provided by the rather innocuous fact that I happen to believe I am so obligated, or even by the belief itself.

ice cream cone and have believed I could do so if I used my son as an excuse. My claim in the example is that my decision was grounded not in this selfish reason, but in my solicitude for my son. But even if my testimony is reliable on this point, it does not explain how my solicitous motives *came to be* my reasons, instead of the selfish motives that were also present. How did it come to pass that my motive was solicitude rather than selfishness, or rather than both? The defender of the causal thesis has an answer. Whether I decided to take my son to Swensen's out of a desire to buy him an ice cream cone, out of a desire to buy myself one, or out of both is settled by whether the corresponding desire-states, together with my states of belief, caused my decision. The arguments of the foregoing section do hint at an alternative—something to do with the correspondence between the reasons that guide a decision and the intention thereby formed. But they provide no substance: they do not tell us what it *is*, in noncausal terms, to decide for one reason rather than another.

There is reason to think, however, that such an account must be available. By itself, at least, the causal account of deciding for reasons gives us no reason to expect the close correspondence between decision-guiding reasons and intentions; in fact, it is in some ways inimical to it. For suppose that besides having reasons for taking my son to Swensen's, I also have reasons for taking my family to Europe next summer: it would make for an enjoyable vacation, which I want them to have. And suppose that by a wayward causal chain, the mental states of which these reasons form the content cause me to decide to take my son to Swensen's this afternoon and get him an ice cream cone. Does it follow that I reached this decision for the sake of the European visit? As so far formulated, the causal view implies it does, which is clearly mistaken. This can be fixed, of course, by adding the proviso that only when the content of a decision matches that of the reason-states that cause it does the agent decide for the reasons in question. But this has an ad hoc air about it. Why should content matter if causation is the key? Even more telling, however, is the fact that we never even hear of this type of causal deviance. With overt behavior it is commonplace: clumsiness or inattentiveness alone can result in my movements failing to square with my reasons for undertaking them. But there seem to be no plausible examples wherein reason-states yield decisions and intentions that fail to match them in content. If the causal account of decision making were true, however, there ought to be such cases. For on that account the crucial relation in virtue of which a decision occurs for one set of reasons rather than another is an extrinsic one, grounded in a process that could in principle go awry. That there are no such cases indicates that reason explanations are not even undergirded by causal ones:

that what makes it the case that I decide for the reasons I do is something intrinsic to the act of deciding.

To formulate an account on which this is so, we need to understand more of the relation between deciding and intending. Deciding is, of course, a modality of thinking, and when I decide an event of thinking occurs. The functional role of such events is to form intentions, but they do not do so by producing a state of intending as a causal product. Rather, when I decide I *progress* to being in a state of intending, which is the end-state or terminus of my act of deciding. That is why the content of my state of intending—that is, my intention—is virtually identical with the content of my act of deciding.[18] When I decide to take my son to Swensen's, I move from a state in which I do not intend to take him there to a state in which I do, and what is expressed by "I shall take my son to Swensen's" is both something I decide and the resultant intention. In fact, however, the practical syllogism given earlier somewhat oversimplifies this case. When the major premise of my practical reasoning is a desire, to decide is to adopt not just the means but the end as well, and the aspects of it that I find desirable. I come to intend not just to take my son to Swensen's but also to buy him an ice cream cone and to achieve by that the things about the enterprise that seem to me good: that my son enjoy himself, that I get to spend some time with him, and so on. Even desires that appear relatively simple can, then, be teleologically complex, and that complexity is replicated in the intentions grounded in them.

Furthermore, intending, like desiring, is an optative state. Once formed, therefore, my intentions can serve as premises for further decision making. Having decided to take my son to Swensen's, I might reason further that to get there I will have to refuel my car, and so decide to stop for gas on the way. A good deal of practical reasoning turns out to be of this general sort, aimed at filling in details and elaborating means–end relationships in broadly conceived projects already decided on. The effect is to create a plan of action that, fully developed, is often quite complex.[19] Action plans may be viewed either as structured sets of individual intentions or as single intentions that are structurally complex. Either way, they have the feature that is of crucial interest: they are structured according to the reasons out of which they are formulated. This structural parallel is essentially twofold: when a decision to A is made for a reason R, the act type A will be optated in the resulting intention for just those features for which

---

[18]   "Virtually" because deciding, in my view, counts as an exercise of agency, whereas intending does not. Whether that makes for a difference in the way the content is thought I am not sure, but I would like to leave room for the possibility.

[19]   The nature and importance of action plans is explored in Myles Brand, *Intending and Acting* (Cambridge: MIT Press, 1984); and Bratman, *Intention, Plans, and Practical Reason*.

it is optated in R, and it will have the same means–end relations to other act types in the agent's action plan that it does in R.[20]

This twofold correspondence provides, as we have seen, an epistemic criterion that enables us to ascertain the reasons for a decision. If the agent's word is in doubt, behavior is usually our guide, as when my actions at Swensen's indicate my real intention in taking my son there, and hence my reason for deciding to do so, was to fulfill my own desire for an ice cream cone. Most often, however, we need not rely on behavior to settle such questions. By and large people have sufficient knowledge of and sincerity about their reasons and intentions that their testimony can be trusted. The central point, however, is this: once the reasons for a decision are known, it is not necessary to ask what intention the decision issued in; the intention can be inferred from the reasons. And once we know in full the content of a decision, we need not ask the reasons for it; the reasons can be reconstructed from the intention formed.

Indeed, the match between what we might call the teleological structure of our intentions and that of our reasons is impressive enough that it might be thought to offer not only an epistemic but also an ontological criterion for deciding for reasons: that for a decision to be made for reasons R just *is* for the resultant intention to be structured in conformity with R. But that is not accurate. It is true that when we decide out of a set of reasons the intention we form is an intention to act for the sake of the goals those reasons embody; in effect, we decide to (eventually) A-for-R. But there is a difference between this and *deciding* for R—a difference, that is, between the goals presented in my reasons being enshrined in the *content* of my decision and their *guiding* that decision. The structural correspondence between intentions and reasons ensures, of course, that the two will go together. When my desire to buy my son an ice cream cone is my reason for deciding to take my son to Swensen's, that objective becomes part of the intention I form, as well as guiding the decision that forms it. Nevertheless, there is a difference between the two—a difference nicely concealed by ambiguous statements like: "I decided to take my son to Swensen's for the sake of getting him an ice cream cone." For a reason to guide my decision cannot simply be a matter of the objectives it embodies forming part of the decision's content. That would amount to a situation in which if only I *have* a set of reasons whose teleological structure corresponds to that of an intention I form, I will have decided for those reasons. There has to be more to it than that; "for" means more than "in the presence of."

---

[20]   Since decisions often modify the agent's existing plans, a more precise formulation would proceed in terms of the changes the decision introduces in the agent's intentions, but this refinement is not necessary for the present discussion.

A more promising idea has to do with our having intentions about our decisions themselves. It might be thought that we actually make it the case that we form our intentions for the reasons we do simply by intending that it shall be so: that is, by intending of our decision that it be a step toward the satisfaction of the desires or felt obligations at issue. A similar suggestion is sometimes made about the relation between reasons and action: namely, that the reasons governing my action are just those that I intend it to fulfill.[21] Thus, what makes it the case that I take my son to Swensen's out of a desire to buy him an ice cream cone would be simply that I intend my behavior to be a step toward satisfying that desire. If this works, then perhaps the same will work for deciding. Perhaps, that is, my decision to take my son to Swensen's will be made out of my desire to get him an ice cream cone provided just that in deciding I am aware of my desire, and intend of that particular decision that it contribute toward satisfying that desire.[22]

This line of thinking is very much on the right track, but as it stands the proposal is unclear on how the intention of which it speaks—that is, my intention regarding my decision—enters the picture. And here we appear to face a dilemma. On the one hand, it cannot be part of the *content* of my decision to take my son to Swensen's that this very decision shall be made in furtherance of my reasons for taking him there. I am not, in deciding to take my son to Swensen's, *deciding to decide*, for these or any other reasons. For one thing, that would demand too much sophistication of decision makers: little children both act and decide for reasons, but they do not have the process well enough conceptualized to be able to have intentions of this complexity.[23] Second, there is something very artificial about this kind of intention. Even conceptually sophisticated agents never report them, and it is hard to see why they would be needed. How, after all, could my decision to take my son to Swensen's *fail* to be a step toward fulfilling my desire to buy him an ice cream cone if, as we have seen, I am in making the decision adopting a plan whose point is that very objective? A third difficulty has to do with the explicit reference, in intentions like this, to particular acts of deciding. This would seem to require that the act begin before the intention can be formulated, since only then will there be anything to which to refer. But then it seems that at the inception of my act

---

[21] See especially Ginet, *On Action*, chap. 6; also Timothy O'Connor, "Agent Causation," in O'Connor, ed., *Agents, Causes, & Events* (New York: Oxford University Press, 1995), pp. 173–200.

[22] Ginet, *On Action*, p. 143; O'Connor, "Agent Causation," p. 192.

[23] Alfred R. Mele offers a similar objection to a view held by a number of authors that the content of states of intending always includes a self-referential component. See his *Springs of Action* (New York: Oxford University Press, 1992), p. 204.

of deciding, I cannot be deciding for *any* reason, since the condition required for that to be the case is not yet in place. Finally, even if, in deciding to take my son to Swensen's, I were deciding that my decision would be made for certain reasons, it does not follow that I thereby *carry out that intention*. And if I do not carry it out, the intention will be idle. But that puts us back where we started: we still need to know what it *is* to decide for a reason.[24]

It is not, then, part of the content of my decision to take my son to Swensen's that that very decision be made in pursuit of any objective, and it would do no good if it were. But—and this is the second horn of the dilemma—neither can I guarantee that my decision will be made for certain reasons through a further, *extrinsic* decision that this shall be so. Here, too, I would still need to carry out the intention thereby formed, so an extrinsic decision will not advance the project either. Furthermore, to invoke an extrinsic decision raises the danger of an infinite regress. For that decision, too, will have been made *for* one or another reason, which we will have to explain by calling for still another decision, and so forth. In short, we shed no light on what it is to decide for a reason by calling for the agent to decide to decide for that reason. Any such formulation simply reinvokes the concept it is supposed to explicate.

The Intrinsic Intentionality of Deciding

It is possible, however, to formulate an account that avoids this dilemma. The key is to realize that the phenomenon of deciding is *intrinsically intentional*. That is, it is not even possible for a decision to be made inadvertently or without our meaning to make it. Along with volition, decision making is by its very nature an exercise of agency.[25] This cannot be a matter of some relation obtaining, such as that acts of decision be caused by reason-states. On the contrary: if that were so, it *would* be possible for decisions to occur without our meaning to make them, by a deviant causal chain or the like. Nor is it a matter of it entering into the content of my decision that it will be made for certain goals. We have seen that that does no good, and in fact it is not even relevant. The intentionality of acts of decision is not an element of their conceptual content; it is a nonrelational and essential feature of the act of deciding itself. When I decide, I intend to decide, and I intend to decide exactly as I do. That is, I intend to progress to having precisely the objective that is put in place by my decision. In my

[24] Cf. O'Connor, "Agent Causation," pp. 190–92.
[25] For more on this subject see "Intrinsic Intentionality," Chapter 7 in this book.

very act of deciding to take my son to Swensen's, I mean to be forming the intention of taking him there.[26] That it must be so is part of the reason why decision belongs in the functional role of planning future actions. It is ideal for that purpose, because it always leaves me with plans I mean to have.

That the intentionality of deciding is intrinsic to it exempts the agent from demands of excessive sophistication: one need only have phenomenal awareness of the act one is engaged in and mean to be so engaged. Nor must the intention involve reference to this particular act of deciding; I simply intend to decide, just as in walking or speaking I intend to walk or speak. Finally, intrinsic intentionality cannot be put in place by an extrinsic act, so there is no need for any further act of deciding, and no danger of a regress. Nor, of course, is there any danger that the agent will not act to fulfill the intention. If he were not doing exactly that, the intention would not exist. Thus the dilemma posed above collapses completely.

The intrinsic intentionality of decision is closely related to a number of other features of it. First, like all intentional behavior, decisions demand reasons. Just as I cannot intentionally take my son to Swensen's if I have no reason for taking him there,[27] so I cannot intentionally decide to take him to Swensen's if I have no reason so to decide. Otherwise, my decision would be a nonrational act, a forming of a purpose without a purpose. And as we have seen, the kind of reason a decision to *A* requires is simply a reason for *A*-ing. This is because to decide to *A* is in itself to make definitive progress toward *A*-ing: it is to make *A*-ing a part of one's agenda, to undertake a commitment to *A*-ing that can only be abrogated by another act of intention formation. Now the fact that I can decide to *A* only in the presence of a reason for *A*-ing has an interesting consequence—namely, that deciding is a modality of thought that is always exercised on content already before the mind. That is part of the reason why our decisions never surprise us.[28] The implicit plan for *A*-ing that is recast as an intention by my act of deciding is already present in the content of my reason-states, which I perceive as offering reasons both for *A*-ing, and for the commitment to *A*-ing put in place by my act of deciding to *A*. This does not mean I have to have a full conceptual articulation of everything I per-

---

[26]   Some have called for deciding to be intentional, but only in that it settles the issue one way or the other, and only out of a prior intention to accomplish that. See, for example, Robert Kane, *The Significance of Free Will* (New York: Oxford University Press, 1996), pp. 138–39.

[27]   There are, of course, cases where we speak of intentional acts as having been done for no reason, but these are usually cases where there is no reason beyond what is implicit in the description of the act itself, as when I hum a song "for no reason."

[28]   We might, of course, be surprised that we "had it in us" to make a certain decision—that is, at what the decision discloses about our character. But we are not surprised in the sense that the decision befalls or happens to us. See "Sufficient Reason," below.

ceive as valuable in the course of action I am considering. But it does mean I cannot decide on a plan of action I have not even envisioned, and toward which I have no optative disposition at all.[29]

Finally, we need to remember that like desiring, deciding is an essentially optative mode of thought. It is, however, optative in a different way—precisely the way that is needed to account for the difference between intentions and desires. To decide is to form a commitment. When I decide, what is presented in my reasons as worthy of doing becomes my settled objective—something that, barring a change of mind, it will be my purpose to accomplish. That is how I progress from having only reasons to having an intention. It is important to keep sight of the active element in this, which is absent from mere desire. To decide is not just to have, or even to come to have, an intention. It is to *create* or formulate the intention, in the only way it can be rational to do so: that is, in cognizance of the reasons that putatively justify it, and in such a way as to replicate their teleological structure in the intention formed. In effect, to decide is to engage in a type of information processing: it is to transform what is presented to us in our reasons, so that the scenario of action they embody comes to be intended, for just those features the reasons give as justifying it. When I decide, I decide not just to A, but to A-for-R.[30]

But I also *decide* for R, and that is where the issue of causation arises. Is the *for* here one of nomic determination? Not, I think, if the above account is correct; rather, it has the sense of *for the sake of*, which is not causal but teleological. For when I perceive a reason for A-ing also as one for deciding to A, I see it as justifying not just the intention I form but also my act of forming it. Thus, the picture that emerges is one of an agent who knowingly and intentionally undertakes a commitment to achieve the very goals he sees as justifying that commitment itself. Of its own nature, therefore, his decision is a conscious and purposive step toward fulfilling those objectives; it is intrinsic to it that the agent intends therein to be settling on the objectives in question, and hence to progress toward their eventual achievement. That this intention is intrinsic to deciding means its presence is not a causal or otherwise relational matter. To be sure, reasons must be present. Like the intention formed through my decision, my intention to decide would be impossible without an optational framework

---

[29]   That is why intentions cannot be formed for reasons in dreamless sleep. In order to decide I have to have something to decide on, and that has to be presented to me in an optational framework. Otherwise, I am given nothing that *calls* for a decision.

[30]   In this respect the view described here is at least very similar to Kane's; see *The Significance of Free Will*, pp. 136–37. In his language the effect of decision is to transform reasons for choosing into reasons for acting, but I think the latter are equivalent to intentions once the decision is made.

to justify it. So the presence of reason-states is a necessary condition for my meaning to decide as I do. But once they are present, causal sufficiency will not be required for me to have decided for the sake of the reasons they embody. I act for the sake of those reasons simply in virtue of the fact that, in cognizance of them, I *do* decide, and so progress actively, consciously, and in a way that is intrinsically intentional toward achieving the goals they present. So when a decision is explained as having been made for certain reasons, it is not only the case that the explanation is not per se causal; it is not undergirded by a causal explanation either.

Sufficient Reason

This account of deciding allows, of course, for libertarian freedom. It is not an unqualified freedom: if what has been said is correct, one cannot decide except in the presence of optations and beliefs that purport to justify the course of action chosen, and hence the decision in favor of it. Nor can one adopt a set of intentions with one teleological structure and truthfully claim it is justified by reasons that are structured differently.[31] Still, there is nothing in this account that requires an agent to decide for one set of reasons rather than another. In principle, selection of the reasons for which one will decide, and hence of the intention one will form, could be settled by nothing other than one's act of deciding—which is exactly what libertarians have in mind by freedom. There remains, however, an objection a defender of the causal view of intention formation can raise. Let it be granted, he may argue, that reason explanations are not in themselves causal explanations. Let it be granted too that the phenomenology of decision making provides for a noncausal account of deciding for reasons. Still, there is a dimension to questions about why agents decide as they do that remains to be addressed. Suppose that in the Swensen's case, I also wanted to play golf this afternoon, and could not do both. If so, the good I saw in golfing would have offered a putative justification for going to the golf course, just as the good in getting my son an ice cream cone justified taking him to Swensen's. Now it is legitimate to ask why one set of reasons, but not the other, came to be replicated in my intentions. And the kind of teleological explanation we have been talking about cannot answer that question. Say what we will about the good I saw in taking my son to Swensen's, I will also have seen good in going to the golf course. And nothing that has been said explains why I chose the one course of action for its set of rea-

---

[31]   One might, of course, be deceived about one's reasons, or lie about them. Such failures aside, however, the reason one gives for a decision will reflect the intention formed therein.

sons, rather than the other course for the other set. Hence, the argument runs, my act of deciding still lacks an adequate explanation. My optations and beliefs may provide a sound teleological justification for it, but they fail to provide a "sufficient reason" in a quite different sense, the sense associated with nomological explanations. They do not offer a set of principles and conditions given which my decision can be seen to have been inevitable. Only a causal explanation in terms of my optation- and belief-*states* can provide that. If such an explanation proves finally to be unavailable, then however rational my decision may have seemed to me, it will still be a kind of irrational occurrence. It will be a random or accidental event—one no observer could have predicted, even given complete information about all the explanatory factors bearing on it. Furthermore, it is hard to see how I could be responsible for an event that is "free" in this way. No one, after all, is responsible for random accidents.[32]

There is a double thrust to this objection. On the cognitive side, it complains that a world in which there are uncaused events of any kind is hostile to our intellects, in that it presents us with occurrences that finally cannot be understood. If contemporary physics is correct, we may in the end be forced to accept the existence of such events, but we should not do so easily or lightly. However morally edifying an uncaused decision may appear to some, the intellectual price of accepting such events is too high for proponents of this objection. If they are right, then insistence that our decisions are caused by reason-states may be in order, even if we presently have no useful laws of decision making, and even if their discovery would undermine everyday teleological explanations of action. Now, in fact, I think the enmity between uncaused events and cognitive understanding may not be as great as it appears. It has to be admitted, however, that this part of the objection cannot be answered by libertarians in the terms defenders of causation demand. If the only way to reach full understanding of events is by discovering independent determining conditions for them, then the price of exempting deliberate decisions from nomic causation is that full understanding of them cannot be had. This does not mean, of course, that such events do not occur. That is an empirical question that at present seems far from being resolved. But if they do occur, we may have to acquiesce in a less than satisfying account of them.

There is, however, a second component to the objection. In addition to saying the cognitive price of treating decisions as exempt from nomic cau-

---

[32] Arguments of this sort appear to begin with David Hume, *A Treatise of Human Nature*, ed. L. A. Selby-Bigge (Oxford: Oxford University Press, 1888) II, III, II. Important modern defenses of the Humean position include R. E. Hobart, "Free Will as Involving Determination and Inconceivable Without It," *Mind* 43 (1934), 1–27; and A. J. Ayer, "Freedom and Determinism," in Ayer, *Philosophical Essays* (London: Macmillan, 1954), pp. 271–84.

sation is too high, it says the practical gain is too low. That is the point of the suggestion that since an uncaused decision would be an accident, the agent ought not to be held responsible for it. There is irony in this, since philosophers who want decisions exempt from causation see this exemption as necessary for the agent to be responsible. Presumably, they would quickly lose interest in libertarian freedom if its implications were just the opposite. Here, however, the objection seems to me mistaken, and our earlier discussion of deciding goes a long way toward showing why. It is possible to distinguish two meanings of the term *accident*. In a strictly cognitive sense, an event may be deemed an accident just in case it is uncaused. To the extent an event is irreducibly random, it counts as a kind of ontological loose end, something whose occurrence is unforeseeable and unaccountable. And if this is all we mean by an accident, then from the observer's point of view there is fairness in the claim that an uncaused decision would count as such. Usually, however, the term *accident* is practical in its import: an event is an accident when it occurs without our controlling it, and in violation of our planned expectations. And in this sense, a decision is anything but an accident, even if it lacks nomic causes.

It would be otherwise if the only way to exert control over an event were by controlling its causes. If that were the case, an event's being accidental in the cognitive sense would render it accidental in the practical sense as well, since it would lack the determining conditions through which control had to be exercised. On the other hand, if events could be controlled only by controlling their causes, an infinite regress would result, and no one would control anything. What enables us to exert control over the world is that some events are intrinsically exercises of control, and deciding is the best example. No one ever reports being overtaken by a decision, or that they decided something inadvertently or by accident. And we can see at least part of the reason for this in the features of decision discussed earlier. If I cannot make a decision without intending to decide as I do, and if decisions have to be founded on reasons of which I am consciously aware, it is hard to see how I could feel a decision of mine had overtaken or befallen me. Its content would already have been envisioned, and while I might not have known beforehand how I would decide, the intrinsic intentionality of decision entails that in the very act of deciding I mean to decide as I do. Practical accidents, by contrast, are events we do not envision and do not intend to occur.

Whether an event is a practical accident appears, then, to have much more to do with whether it is planned than with whether it is caused. If this is right, then the intrinsic features of deliberate decisions discussed earlier are alone enough to render them incapable of being practical accidents. It may be argued, however, that there is an additional aspect to the phenomenology of decision—namely, that it is itself experienced as an exercise of control. When we decide, our sense is that this does not just happen, that we ourselves settle whether our act of deciding will occur and what its content will be. And it seems certain that this feature, too, is important to a decision not being a practical accident: that unless control over decisions is exercised entirely by the agent, and is fully intrinsic to them, our decisions are ultimately out of our control, and out of reach of meaningful justification by our optations and beliefs. This, of course, is the standard libertarian view of deciding, though exactly what this control consists in is too large a question to be explored here.[33] But its implications for the present discussion are important. For if deciding does include this further element, then far from it being the case that the absence of nomic causation would render a decision a practical accident, it is in fact its presence that would do so.

Conclusion

If the arguments presented above are correct, then the intrinsic nature of the mental act of deciding provides for a noncausal account of what it is to decide for a reason, and for at least a partial answer to what is perhaps the strongest traditional objection to the idea of an undetermined choice. I think that essentially the same account applies to most intention formation.[34] We sometimes reserve such terms as *deliberation* and *decision* for weighty occasions, where the options are difficult and practical reasoning is apt to be lengthy and self-conscious. But practical reasoning also occurs where the options are simple, little is at stake, and we hardly pay attention to what we are doing. Intention formation seems to me little different in these cases than in the more complex ones. Here, too, decision is the standard means of intention formation, and its essential features are the same. All it requires is the presentation, however brief, of a scenario of action that includes the optative elements necessary to justify making up one's mind to do something. If this is right, then a noncausal account of intention formation is available whenever intentions are formed prior to action.[35]

---

[33] For more on this topic, see "Agency, Control, and Causation," Chapter 9 in this book.

[34] The exception is cases where the demand for action is so immediate that intention is formed in the very act itself, through the activity of volition, as discussed in "Intrinsic Intentionality," Chapter 7 in this book.

[35] A very early version of this paper was read at the University of Nebraska in 1987, and a later one at Davidson College in 1996; the comments received on both occasions did much to improve it.

9

Agency, Control, and Causation

At the foundation of human action lies the enigma of agency: the phenomenon whereby, as it seems to us at least, our actions are finally to be accounted for solely in terms of our performing them. Agency is an enigma first because it is hard to say what it is. Exercises of agency are at best difficult to describe, and the concept resists any effort at reductive analysis. Second, it is hard to see how exercises of agency are to be explained, or that their explanation can be made commensurate with our notions of an orderly universe. On the other hand, to relinquish the idea of agency is to jeopardize the entire concept of human action, and with it our sense that we are responsible in a distinctive way for the changes we produce in the world. It is therefore worth investigating how viable the concept of agency is. I want to argue that while it is unlikely the objections it faces can be fully dispelled, the concept of agency is quite viable, and that its problems are in the end no more daunting than those that face its usual competitor, the notion of event causation. Agency, if real, results in explanatory discontinuities in the world; but it does not introduce events that have no explanation, or whose existence is any more mysterious than the existence of things in general.

Agency and Responsibility

The word *responsibility* is not always associated with agency. To say the circuit breaker was responsible for the lights going off is just to say that it was the subject of some event that, by natural processes, resulted in the lights being extinguished. And it is to imply that we can rectify the situation with the lights by doing something to the circuit breaker, such as flipping it back on. Sometimes human behavior can be treated the same way. If a muscle spasm causes my arm to strike the lamp, knocking it over and extinguishing the light, then I am responsible for the lost illumination in the same weak sense that the circuit breaker was. And our recipe for preventing such situations from recurring is likely to be about as simple: just keep me away from lamps. The sense of responsibility associated with agency is far graver. If I deliberately knock over the lamp, my doing so is an *action*—a manifestation of agency, for which I would normally be *morally* responsible. Here, my involvement runs much deeper than merely being the subject of an event with untoward consequences, and to say I am responsible implies that I am an appropriate target for much more Draconian efforts aimed at rectifying the situation. It implies that I can be held to account for what I did, that I am liable for the damage resulting from my behavior, that I may be blamed or punished for my action.

It might be protested that blame and punishment are not different in principle from keeping me away from lamps, that they are simply a matter of bringing to bear influences calculated to produce modifications in my future behavior.[1] But that is not the whole story. For one thing, punishing me is supposed to deter others also. More important, however, is the fact that the very same treatment of an individual will count as punishment or not, depending on whether we think him responsible. We incarcerate mentally deranged killers as well as murderers—in both cases working a hardship on the individual in question, and in both cases for the protection of society. But only in the latter case is the hardship viewed as punishment—that is, as justified precisely because it *is* a hardship, appropriately visited on the offender. And while we may hope thereby to motivate a change in behavior, we do not require that. Often, in fact, the agents we are most anxious to hold responsible for their deeds—mafiosi, mass murderers, and the like—are precisely those whose motives we think are least likely to be affected. Finally, and most important, when they work best, blame and punishment do not affect behavior in just any way. The aim is not simply to terrorize the offender into future compliance. We will settle, if we must, for a thief who out of fear of further punishment steals no more. But that much can be achieved even with kleptomaniacs, whom we do not consider responsible. And the problem in both cases is the same: a terrorized kleptomaniac is still a kleptomaniac, and a

---

[1] For a classic example of this sort of view see Moritz Schlick, "When Is a Man Responsible?" in B. Berofsky, ed., *Free Will and Determinism* (New York: Harper & Row, 1966), pp. 54–63.

terrorized thief is still a thief. What we would rather achieve is a situation in which each agent acts out of a proper appreciation for the nature of his action, and the values it involves. In the case of the thief, that requires the sort of transformation of character we call "reform." Ideally, that is what blame and punishment are aimed at achieving. And the problem for the objection we are considering is that a crucial step in the process of reform is that the agent *take responsibility* for his actions. That brings us full circle, for it is obvious that to take responsibility for one's actions cannot be just to come to believe that suffering will inhibit their recurrence.

The true conditions for moral responsibility are somewhat complex. One, which is probably violated in the case of the kleptomaniac, concerns knowledge: the agent has to know what he is doing, the likely consequences, and the valuational standing of the actions they define.[2] Failing this, he can justly be held responsible only if he is also responsible for his ignorance. The condition with which we are concerned is, however, a deeper one: the subject's behavior has to be a manifestation of *agency*. When the motion of my arm is caused by a muscle spasm, it does not matter what I know about it. I am not responsible, for I have performed no action. But if I move my arm—in fact, if I only try to move it—then I have acted, and I am responsible. The locus of responsibility lies, then, in exercises of agency. And these are not to be found on the surface of behavior. The motion of my arm can count, on some views of act individuation, as part of an action of mine. But it never counts as an action in itself. Rather, it is my *bringing about* the motion that counts as an action, and the fact that I can undertake to do this without any physical result ensuing shows that the phenomenon of agency is an interior one.[3]

The true center of agency lies in exercises of what is often called the will—that is, the mental faculty of voluntary behavior. Exercises of the will include such things as the activity of concentrating one's attention on one or another item of mental content; the act of deciding, through which intentions are usually formed; and the activity of volition, by which intentions for overt action are usually executed. The distinguishing feature of these endeavors is that they possess intrinsically the characteristics we associate with responsible action: they are, and must be, intentional exertions

[2]   It is sometimes claimed that compulsive behavior like kleptomania is owing to a deterministic "irresistible impulse," given which the agent had to behave as he did. My inclination is to think that if libertarian free will is a reality this is wrong—that a faculty of free choice cannot be sometimes determined and sometimes not. Rather, I think, situations in which freedom appears to be lost are actually just cases where, in the agent's deliberation, one option overshadows all others, and so becomes the only valid choice. We seldom call this compulsion when the values involved are reasonable, as for example in most cases of self-preservation; but we do tend to do so when they are irrational.

[3]   See "Trying, Paralysis, and Volition," Chapter 5 in this book.

of the sort of control we have in mind when we think of an act as being "up to us." This is perhaps best seen in the case of deciding, which is the most important manifestation of the will for purposes of the present discussion. As I have argued elsewhere,[4] deciding cannot be unintentional or inadvertent: in making a decision, we mean to decide, and to decide exactly as we do. Neither can a decision be involuntary in the way a muscle spasm or a reflex knee-jerk can be. Even when threats or the forces of circumstance "compel" us to decide a certain way, the compulsion is rational, not nomic. The gunman who convinces me to turn over my wallet operates, ironically, not by the use of force but through the persuasiveness of reasons. And if I later say of my decision, "It was involuntary," I mean only that had it been up to me, the reasons would have stacked up differently. I do not mean that I was driven by blind emotion, or even that I could not have decided otherwise: after all, many have. I mean only that by my lights anyway, that would have been an irrational decision to make.

Deciding is, then, an act that possesses intrinsically the features we associate with responsible control of behavior. Along with the other types of exercise of agency mentioned above, it is by its own nature a purposive exertion of voluntariness—something that is essentially action in the fullest sense. That this character is intrinsic to decisions explains why they are not subject to problems of causal deviance. If agency were just a relational matter—a question, say, of being caused in the right sort of way by the right sort of reason—then we should be able to find decisions that would have been exercises of agency, but for being caused by the wrong reasons or in the wrong way. But that does not happen. There are no decisions that fail to be exercises of agency: none in which we do not intend to engage, none that lack the phenomenal character that leads us to think they are *our* doing, something we control. Unfortunately, however, the fact that agency is intrinsic to exercises of will also makes it difficult to understand. I for one see no chance of analyzing it away, of reducing it to concepts more familiar and supposedly less offensive. But neither do I see reason for regret in that. Concepts we cannot get rid of tend to be important sources of insight, and if they cannot be eliminated, they can still receive useful elucidation.

Being Able to Do Otherwise

The concept of agency has it that the operations of my will are fully my responsibility. My decisions and other activities of will are founded in me,

---

4 "The Formation of Intention," Chapter 8 in this book.

not just because as aspects of mine they could not exist if I did not, but because I am active in their appearance, in a way that makes them manifestations of my rational autonomy. This is an essentially positive idea, but it has a negative implication we need to sort out first. If my action is autonomous it cannot be compelled, either from within or from without; it has to be an instance of spontaneity on my part. And for that to be so I must have had some alternative, if only the alternative of forbearance or inaction. Applied to deciding, this means that at the moment I make a decision, it must be possible for me to decide differently—or at least to commence to do so—or to forbear deciding, so that my inactivity, too, would count as a demonstration of my will, of my capacity to decide what I choose when I choose. I understand this to be an essentially libertarian conception: to have decided freely I must, categorically, have been able to do otherwise.[5]

There are two ways the conception can be attacked. One is by way of an argument set forth by Harry Frankfurt, according to which responsible agency does not in fact require the possibility of doing otherwise. It may seem to, since we usually think of any condition that would guarantee my deciding to do something as actually figuring in the etiology of the decision, so that I would be compelled to make it. According to Frankfurt, however, this need not be so. Suppose, for example, that I decide in more or less the normal way, with no interference or coercion, that I will vacation in Italy next summer. Since my decision is neither uninformed nor compelled, I am surely responsible for it. But suppose too that Jones, who is resolved that I shall decide to vacation in Italy, has implanted a contraption in my brain that would enable him to force me so to decide. In the case at hand, he has no need to use it, since I decide that way anyhow. But, the argument runs, had I been about to decide otherwise, Jones, who is an excellent judge of such things, would simply have pushed a button on a little transmitter he carries, sending a signal that would have compelled me to decide to go to Italy. Here, then, I could not have done otherwise. Still, given what actually occurred, there is every reason to hold me responsible.[6]

The plausibility of this sort of argument depends on what conception of freedom is presupposed. Against compatibilist views it has some purchase, since if determinism is true there will be determining conditions for any decision that occurs, so that an early tip-off that I would decide against going to Italy would easily be possible, and Jones could take ac-

---

[5]   This aspect of agency is, of course, widely recognized. Robert Kane calls it the condition of Alternative Possibilities. *The Significance of Free Will* (New York: Oxford University Press, 1996), p. 33.

[6]   Harry G. Frankfurt, "Alternate Possibilities and Moral Responsibility," *Journal of Philosophy* 66 (1969), 835; a more recent defense of such examples can be found in John Martin Fischer, *The Metaphysics of Freedom* (Cambridge: Blackwell, 1994), chap. 7.

tion. Against libertarian views, however, the supposition is far less plausible. It has to be remembered that doing otherwise does not, in this case, necessarily mean deciding otherwise. I need not make any decision at all. In a context where I am deliberating over my options for next summer, this would count as forbearing to decide (as yet), and for that I am responsible. But it is not clear, in a nondeterministic setting, what the early tip-off of such forbearance would be. After all, up to the point at which I actually decide to go to Italy, I am *already* forbearing to decide. Only by allowing me no deliberation at all could Jones prevent that, and then I would not have the chance to decide on my own. So it begins to look as if Jones can be in the position of being able to control my decision only by actually controlling it.

There is, moreover, a general argument that tip-offs of this type are not possible in a libertarian setting. Let t be the time when I commenced to decide to go to Italy, and consider the alternative scenario in which I would decide to go to France instead. Now Jones cannot wait for this to occur before pushing the dreadful button, for then I would already have done otherwise: I would have undertaken to decide to vacation in France. True, I might not have completed the decision: there might, in John Fischer's words, have been only a flicker of freedom.[7] But that, I suggest, does not matter. Moral autonomy is similar to Kant's good will: a flicker shines like a beacon.[8] So the tip-off to Jones must occur prior to t. It must, moreover, be reliable: it cannot be found only on some occasions when I am about to decide otherwise, since that leaves open the possibility that on this occasion it will not appear, and Jones will be unable to head off my decision. So the tip-off, whatever it is, has to be a *necessary* condition of my deciding otherwise. But now it turns out that in the original example, quite apart from Jones's nefarious schemes, I could not at t have decided otherwise than I did. A necessary condition was missing—namely, the prior occurrence of whatever would have tipped off Jones. So on a libertarian understanding of "could have done otherwise," any situation where a Frankfurt-type counterfactual intervener could have succeeded in controlling a decision is one in which there is an independent proof that the agent lacked moral freedom anyway.[9]

---

[7]   Fischer, Ibid. The assumption that Jones's reaction time is less than what it would take for me to complete my decision is, of course, utterly wrong, but it is not logically impossible.

[8]   Immanuel Kant, *Groundwork of the Metaphysics of Morals*, trans. H. J. Paton (New York: Harper & Row, 1964), p. 62.

[9]   This argument is presented by David Widerker, in "Libertarian Freedom and the Avoidability of Decisions," *Faith and Philosophy* 12 (1995), 113–18. Fischer responds in "Libertarian Freedom and Avoidability: A Reply to Widerkur," *Ibid.*, 119–25. See also Kane, *The Significance of Free Will*, pp. 142–43.

If this argument is correct, then the libertarian is secure against Frankfurt examples. He can persist in maintaining that the ability to do otherwise is a necessary condition of moral responsibility, since the examples which purport to show that this is untrue in fact beg the question against a libertarian understanding of that ability. If decisions are exercises of libertarian agency, there can be no completely reliable way for a would-be intervener to read what one will be prior to its inception.[10]

Perhaps, however, the libertarian understanding of what it means to be able to do otherwise is wrong. A second, more traditional line of attack has it that this ability is not categorical but, as Hume said, hypothetical.[11] To claim an agent could have done otherwise is not to say he might have done so in exactly the same circumstances, but rather that had some crucial determining condition been altered, then he *would* have done so. This, of course, is perfectly consistent with determinism, and if it is all there is to liberty then agency may not be so enigmatic after all. To adopt this view is, of course, to raise the specter of the Frankfurt examples again, but as Frankfurt himself points out, one crucial feature of those examples is that in them, the villain does not *actually* influence the agent's behavior at all.[12] So one can still claim that in such cases, action is "free" in the respect with which compatibilists tend to be most concerned: it is a valid expression of the agent's character. Indeed, one can even claim the agent could have done otherwise, simply by modifying the analysis: had the crucial condition been altered, then barring alien intervention the agent would have done otherwise.

The initial plausibility of this sort of maneuver stems from the fact that conditional analyses can account for what is sometimes called freedom of action, as opposed to freedom of the will. The difference can be seen in an example of Locke's.[13] A man held in a locked room lacks the freedom to leave, in that no exercise of agency available to him will get him out. Should the door be unlocked, however, he will be free to go: if he wills the physical exertion necessary to get him out of the room, then that is where he will wind up. So the conditional analysis succeeds. But the problem

---

[10] It is worth mentioning that even if Jones could read my decision in advance, it is hard to see how anything he could replace it with would count as a decision in the libertarian sense. The problem is the same as that with viewing kleptomania as an irresistible compulsion. To treat decisions as intrinsically autonomous while at the same time subject to determination from without is rather like granting that the phenomenon of beta-decay is intrinsically undetermined, yet still claiming to be able to control it.

[11] David Hume, *An Inquiry Concerning Human Understanding*, ed. Charles W. Hendel (New York: Liberal Arts Press, 1955), p. 104.

[12] "Alternate Possibilities and Moral Responsibility," pp. 836–37.

[13] John Locke, *An Essay Concerning Human Understanding*, ed. J. W. Yolton (New York: E.P. Dutton, 1961), vol. 1, pp. 197–98.

here is not one of freedom of the will. It concerns only the pathway from agency to success—that is, from volition to its projected consequences in the world. That is freedom of action. The question of free will has rather to do with the relation between exercises of agency and their antecedents. If the man does not know he is locked in, and decides on his own to remain, his decision will be just as voluntary as it would be had the door been unlocked. And although Locke himself refused to accept the idea, that makes the decision an exercise of free will. The real challenge for compatibilism is to provide a satisfactory analysis of this kind of freedom.

I do not see how the challenge can be met. For traditional compatibilism, freedom in deciding is a conditional matter: typically, a decision is held to be free provided it would have gone otherwise had the agent's strongest, or definitive, or predominant desire been for some other action. But if this is supposed to capture the everyday, preanalytic notion of free will, it seems clearly to fail. For one thing, the analysis misses the target distinction almost entirely. Compulsives, addicts, people operating under duress—virtually everyone whose freedom to will differently we ordinarily view as compromised—would count by this criterion as free. Surely, if determinism is true, they would have willed differently had their strongest motives been different. Yet these are the people whose responsibility for decisions we would question, precisely *because* we think their strongest motive was too influential. Indeed, aside from Frankfurt-type cases, it is hard to think of any examples of impaired freedom of the *will* that we would not have to pronounce fully free by this type of criterion.[14]

The situation changes little if the compatibilist takes Frankfurt-type examples as showing that responsible agency does not require that the agent have been able to do otherwise. We still need to know why responsible agency is compromised in cases of addiction, compulsion, and the like, but not with normal actions. And the task gets no easier. It will not do, for example, to say a decision is responsible provided it arises out of the agent's motives and character, without alien intervention. This is surely true of addicts and compulsives, as well as normal agents. Nor will it do to add that responsible control over one's decisions is a matter of their issuing from processes that would be responsive to good reasons for behaving differently. The problem is that this is too strong. Agents who behave wrongly usually *are* cognizant of good reasons for doing otherwise,

---

[14] Even the science fiction examples cut both ways. Imagine an alien intervener who, rather than preventing my deciding in accordance with my strongest motive, actually speeds up the process by electronic means. Here too, I am unfree, even if we make it out that had my motives been different, the friendly intervener would have made me decide accordingly. Cf. Robert Audi, "Acting for Reasons," *Philosophical Review* 95 (1986), 531.

but do not respond to them. And if we weaken the requirement to demand only that there be some sort of reason which, had it arisen, would have been persuasive to the agent, we are back with the problem that this, too, is true of addicts and compulsives. Kleptomaniacs don't steal if they know they are being watched, and even the powerfully addicted often find motives to get well.[15]

At least as telling is the way people react to compatibilist analyses of freedom and responsibility. Laypersons, in my experience, are bewildered by them, wondering how we can be held responsible if we "really had no choice." Most students simply fail to grasp compatibilism: they insist on taking it as a theory on which causal factors limit one's options to some extent but allow "free will" to operate among those that remain. And the minority who do understand are all but uniformly hostile to the view. Above all, there is the reaction of philosophers themselves—who, if such analyses could indeed capture the ordinary notion of responsible agency, ought to flock to compatibilism, and the neat solution it provides to a profoundly difficult problem. Yet it has produced nothing but division, garnering every reaction from enthusiastic endorsement to indignant disdain.[16] Accurate conceptual analysis should not have that result. One might, of course, view analyses like these as revisionist in spirit: as efforts to lay out the best account of freedom we can have in a deterministic world. But then the classic objections apply. Why should I take myself to be free in my decisions if they are determined by other events over which I finally have no control? Why should I consider myself responsible for them in any sense more important than I am when a muscle spasm causes me to break the lamp? This kind of conceptual revisionism seems, furthermore, to be rather weak-kneed. If the common-sense notion of responsibility is founded on a false conception of what agency consists in, then surely it should be set aside and a new beginning made. Rather than hold offenders morally responsible, we should treat all so-called wrongdoing as essentially compulsive, drop the idea of blameworthiness, and design what we would conceive as therapeutic programs aimed at correcting behavior we do not like.

Neither as reports on common usage nor as proposals for conceptual revision, then, do compatibilist treatments of free will succeed. Moreover, it

---

[15] For more on reasons responsiveness see Fischer, *The Metaphysics of Freedom,* chap. 8, esp. pp. 164–68, on which the discussion given here is based. Fischer suggests that weak reason responsiveness is sufficient for responsibility, but I think that is mistaken.

[16] For an example of the former see R. E. Hobart, "Free Will as Involving Determination and Inconceivable Without It," in Berofsky, *Free Will and Determinism,* pp. 63–95, esp. pp. 72–77; for the latter, see Kant, *Critique of Practical Reason,* trans. L. W. Beck (Indianapolis: Bobbs-Merrill, 1956), p. 99.

is much too early for the sort of capitulation described above. Inevitable though it may seem to some, the day when a deterministic account of the will becomes an established fact appears distant at best, just as it did two hundred years ago. And in the meantime, there is still the sense we have when we engage in exercises of the will that what happens is up to us, a matter of our intentional control. If the argument of this section is correct, part of what is involved in that is nomic indeterminacy: the idea that the agent might have done otherwise in precisely the same circumstances that occurred. In the case of deciding, this means that the agent might have decided differently, or have forborne deciding, without alteration in his information and motives. But this negative condition cannot be all there is to responsible agency. To see why, we need only suppose that, say, the onset of desire were unexpectedly discovered to be an undetermined phenomenon. Were that to occur, we would not consider ourselves any more responsible for our desires than we do now. The onset of a desire, caused or not, is still an event that befalls or happens to us, something in which we are entirely passive. So if we are any more responsible for our decisions, that has to be owing to their positive nature.

Teleology and Explanatory Adequacy

We can begin to appreciate the positive aspects of deciding by considering the sort of objection usually raised against the claim that decisions are not nomically determined. There is, in fact, a cluster of such objections, built around the common theme that such an event can have no adequate explanation. In one form, the complaint is that an undetermined decision must be a random or accidental event over which the agent had no control, and for which he therefore cannot be responsible. Thus Hume held that if actions do not proceed from some cause in the character of the agent, he cannot on their account become an object of punishment or vengeance.[17] A. J. Ayer argued that if it has no causal explanation, my choosing is an accident, for which I cannot be responsible.[18] And R. E. Hobart claimed that insofar as an act of will is uncaused, it is as if one's legs should spring up and carry him off where he does not prefer to go.[19] These views presuppose, however, that only through nomic causation is it possible for an exercise of will to be nonaccidental, or to exhibit voluntary control. As we have seen, the preanalytic data indicate this is false; indeed,

---

[17] *An Inquiry Concerning Human Understanding*, p. 107.
[18] A. J. Ayer, "Freedom and Necessity," in Ayer, *Philosophical Essays* (London, Macmillan, 1954), p. 275.
[19] "Free Will as Involving Determinism and Inconceivable Without It," p. 70.

it would be a self-contradiction for me ever to assert that I had accidentally decided to do anything. What that indicates is that voluntary control is not just present in acts like deciding but is essential to them, in a way that does not reduce to a causal relation to other events.

Voluntary control consists in general in an agent's ability to direct his behavior to ends he selects. Exercises of the will are, by their own nature, manifestations of this ability. There are, I think, at least two important dimensions to this. One has to do with ontological foundations. An exercise of agency has to be spontaneous and active; it is a creative undertaking on the agent's part, to be accounted for in terms of its intrinsic features, not via the operations of other denizens of the world. Second, exercises of agency must be intentional; they have to be undertaken for the sake of some objective the agent deems worthy of attainment. As with other exercises of the will, the phenomenology of deciding indicates we view these features as essential to it. What counts truly as an act of deciding can only be up to me; it must be an act of mine, rather than something I undergo. And I have to mean it: if I decide, then I must intend to decide, and to decide exactly when and as I do. Thus I am responsible for both the act and its content. It is worth mentioning that neither dimension of voluntary control makes much sense without the other. A creative act on my part not undertaken intentionally would be almost a contradiction, and an act that I mean to perform but whose origin lies elsewhere would be one whose intentionality is at best hollow and redundant. But although the two dimensions are inseparable, they can largely be discussed independently. It is best to begin with the matter of intentionality.[20]

To decide is to progress from having reasons to having an intention. A course of action portrayed in my thoughts as appropriate to advancing one or another objective I value conatively is transformed by my decision into a goal or purpose of mine, something I am committed to achieving. I might, for example, see going to Italy as a necessary step toward a desired visit to Florence, and so decide to vacation in Italy next summer. When I do this, vacationing in Italy becomes my intention, and so does visiting Florence, if it was not an intention already. That is, the desires I conceive vacationing in Italy as a means to satisfying become further intentions, further objectives to be achieved by my going there. Most important, however, is the fact that my act of deciding is in itself a step toward achieving those objectives. It settles, as far as an advance decision can, what I shall be doing next summer, by committing me to the trip, as well as to the preparation and coordination with other activities it will require. So when

---

[20] For fuller development of the points in this and the next two paragraphs, see "The Formation of Intention," Chapter 8 in this book.

I decide to vacation in Italy, I am consciously advancing the project of so doing. That is why it is important that deciding be an intrinsically intentional act. Anything else would contradict its functional role, since an unintended decision would be purposeless in itself, and would leave me with a resultant intention I never meant to have.

Because to decide to *A* is to advance the project of *A*-ing, one's reasons for deciding to *A* are, in the usual case, simply one's reasons for *A*-ing. The desires and obligations I can satisfy by vacationing in Italy are reasons for deciding to go there as well as for going. And to decide for the sake of those reasons is simply to mold them into the resultant intention, thereby advancing intentionally the project they represent. Notice that there is nothing of nomic causation in this story. What makes my desire to visit Florence the reason *why* I decide to vacation in Italy is not that it has some force that compels me to decide: if that were so, we could not know what my reason was, since the question whether decisions are nomically caused is at best moot. Rather, my desire is my reason because when I decide I intentionally *make* visiting Florence, and the associated goods portrayed in that desire, the guiding objective of the trip to which I am committing myself. Quite apart from the issue of causation, therefore, my decision has an explanation. It is a teleological one, in terms of the perceived goods that, in my deliberation, justified my decision, and that came to be intended through it. Add to this the factor to be considered more fully in the next section—that our decisions seem to us to be under our voluntary control—and a libertarian decision appears as anything but an accident that befalls the agent. Indeed, it looks as if we would have more to fear in this respect if decisions were nomically caused. That, it seems, would render our sense that we intentionally direct our decisions illusory, making us their victim rather than their perpetrator.

There is little chance, however, that the determinist will be satisfied with this. For, he may argue, even if deciding has features that render it incapable of being accidental from the practical viewpoint of the agent, a satisfactory *theoretical* explanation of it is impossible from a libertarian perspective. Causal explanations satisfy our need to understand because they invoke laws and conditions in terms of which events can be seen to be inevitable. The sort of explanation promised by a libertarian view of deciding does nothing of the kind. It proceeds in terms of the agent's thoughts—the *abstracta* that occupied his deliberations—and it holds that the values and objectives portrayed in those thoughts may be seen to justify the decision based on them. But the problem is that there will also be reasons on the side the agent did not choose. My desire to visit Florence may justify going to Italy, but if I was also considering a vacation in France then no doubt I also had reasons for going there, and they would have been held to explain my decision had I finally opted for that alternative. But what cannot be accounted for is why I chose to go to Italy for one set of reasons rather than to France for the other. We may be able to postpone the moment of reckoning by citing further reasons. I may have wanted to visit Florence in order to go to San Marco, so that I might see the Fra Angelicos there, to ponder their religious significance, and so on. But sooner or later my train of reasons must come to an end. And when it does, so the argument goes, my decision will be finally unaccounted for: there will be no explanation for my choosing to pursue those purposes rather than the ones I could have achieved by vacationing in France.[21]

There is, I think, a legitimate concern underlying this argument, though in the end it not a decisive one. We need to see first, however, that as it stands the argument is badly inadequate. Consider first the claim that my reasons for vacationing in Italy must come to an end, at which point we will be left with no explanation for my choice. And now suppose for a moment that the train of reasons did not come to an end: the riches of Florence, we might imagine, are so profound that any level of appreciation for them I might have leads on to another. And we can imagine that my mental capacity were such as to comprise all of that, so that I could actually appreciate such bounty. Would that refute the objection? Clearly not, for if the riches of Florence are infinite, then surely those of France are as well. If that were so—and for that matter even if it were not—why should prolonging explanations on the Florentine side quiet the determinist's complaint? I still had the French option, and I still might have chosen it. Furthermore, the discussion at this point takes a rather nasty turn for the determinist. For the truth is that the very sort of explanation he favors offers the best available paradigm of failure to solve this kind of problem. Let my decision be nomically caused, and let it belong to a world that is determined to the hilt. Even so, there will be other possible worlds—for example, a world minimally adjusted for my choosing to vacation in France. And even if we conceive of these worlds as infinite in duration, no amount of explanation from *within* the causal sequence supposed to lead to my choosing to vacation in Italy can explain why this world exists, rather than the one in which I decide to vacation in France, or for that matter no world at all.[22]

There is reason to think, moreover, that the position of the libertarian is a good deal more satisfying than that of the determinist in this regard. There

---

[21]   For a recent example of this kind of argument see Thomas Nagel, *The View from Nowhere* (New York: Oxford University Press, 1986), pp. 116–17.
[22]   This kind of charge is associated, of course, with cosmological arguments for the existence of God. The comparison with difficulties about human free will helps to show, I think, that it is quite legitimate.

are, as far as we know, no natural stopping points for causal chains. They either proceed to infinity or come to an arbitrary halt, at least as far as nomic principles are concerned. So if we want to know why we have one sequence of causes rather than another, we must either prolong the sequence, which only postpones failure, or seek another sort of explanation.[23] With sequences of reasons the situation is different. In reason explanations, the appeal is not to law-bound inevitability but to the justifying force of perceived goods. The point is not to detail the ontogenesis of decisions, but to demonstrate their putative value. Given this objective, a sequence of reasons need be prolonged only until an objective the agent deemed to be of *intrinsic* value— that is, something he took to be valuable for its own sake—is reached. Once that occurs, we have reached a natural stopping point. So if the ultimate goal of my projected vacation in Italy is, say, the aesthetic enjoyment of contemplating the frescoes at San Marco, the teleological explanation of my decision need proceed no further. If someone asks why I decided to visit Italy for the joys of San Marco, rather than France for the delights of Chartres, the answer is that I did so for the sake of the joys of San Marco.

Agency and Origination

All the same, the determinist's complaint is founded on a legitimate concern, which begins to emerge more clearly if we realize that the two types of explanation we are considering function somewhat at cross-purposes. As indicated, the primary focus of the libertarian's teleological explanations is not on the ontological foundation of decisions. Practically speaking, there is no need for that, because in practical affairs we concern ourselves with the details of how events come to pass only when we are trying to bring them under control. With decisions this is neither necessary for agents nor possible for observers, if libertarianism is right. By their nature, libertarian decisions are events only the agent controls, and he controls them "at will." Rather, reason explanations address the dimension of action appropriate for dealing with purposive beings who initiate new sequences of change in the world: they focus on the way decisions are inspired. This has reference to beginnings, of course, but not in a way calculated to providing a key to control. The function of reasons is not to control but to persuade.

The concerns of the determinist, by contrast, are much more like those we have when we are not able to control events directly, but must instead

---

[23]   The favored alternative of theists is, of course, none other than teleological explanation, in terms of the purposes of a creator.

will a sequence of change that will eventuate in a desired result. Such indirect control requires understanding how events come to pass, and that is the sort of understanding the determinist would like to have of the operations of the will itself. Here the focus is fully on ontological origins, and in terms of that focus the objection to libertarian decisions is easily renewed. Whatever the shortcomings of nomic causation for explaining why we have this world rather than some other, determinism at least avoids a corresponding failure in dealing with events *within* the world we have. A deterministic world is a seamless fabric: every transformation of things, all that occurs, may be seen to emerge in a law-governed way from what already exists. We can tell where present events come from, it is said, because they are brought about by past events in accordance with scientific law. Within a deterministic world there are no explanatory gaps, because each event is made inevitable by those that went before. The libertarian's world, by contrast, is filled with such gaps. At innumerable junctures, decisions and other acts of will go one way rather than another, and we have no sufficient explanation why. To be sure, the agent's reasons may make his decision fitting. But they do not make it inevitable, and in that sense we do not and cannot know where the decision comes from. It is a discontinuity in the world, an event that simply crops up, and whose ontological origin, if any, is utterly lost to us. In short, however congenial they may be to our theories of moral responsibility, uncaused decisions are anomalous and rationally unacceptable; they violate our expectation that the world be an intellectually comprehensible place.

One response to this version of the determinist's objection is that the issue here is in the end an empirical one: if acts of will turn out to be nomically undetermined, we will simply have to accept that fact, as we have with other natural phenomena, and try to understand them as best we can. Often, however, the libertarian response goes further. That exercises of agency are not subject to nomic causation does not, it may be argued, mean they have no causes at all. Rather, when I decide to vacation in Italy, it is *I*, the agent, who am the cause of my decision. Instead of being brought about by other events, the decision is brought about by *me*, through an exercise of voluntary power. It is therefore wrong to assert that we do not know where undetermined acts of will come from. True, they are nomically discontinuous with the rest of the world; but they come from their agents, who knowingly and intentionally produce them. This may not solve every problem about understanding the will, but it does provide an alternative to the idea that nomically uncaused decisions present a final and impenetrable mystery of ontogenesis. That, the argument runs, is simply an error, which arises from taking nomic causation to be the only acceptable way in which an event may be brought to pass.[24]

There are, however, some problems with this answer. It has reference, of course, to the other aspect of exercises of agency mentioned earlier: the fact that decisions and other operations of the will seem to us not just to happen, but to be manifestations of voluntary control on our part. It is, of course, this dimension of agency that constitutes its core. What makes my decisions exercises of agency is not just that they are not determined by other events and states, nor even that they are intrinsically intentional. There is also the fact that when I decide, I am actively *doing* something about the intention intrinsic to that act. Like intentionality, this feature of exercises of the will is intrinsic and essential to them, and it has a certain *sui generis* character that renders it incapable of being reduced to anything else. When we decide, we take ourselves to be actively carrying out a commitment to deciding which is itself brought to pass solely through that very act, and extends to all dimensions of it. My decision, its timing, and its content are all "up to me," in that I am actively and intentionally given over to them through the act of deciding itself, and there is no condition independent of that act that makes it so.[25]

It is not obvious, however, that we should take this aspect of deciding as providing any useful sense in which I may be said to be the "cause" of my deciding.[26] It is, perhaps, a natural temptation to say that, as a means of trying to capture the unique aspect of voluntariness I have just tried to describe.[27] It may even be fair to think of me as the "source" of my decisions, inasmuch as their occurrence is a manifestation of a power or capacity of mine—as opposed, say, to a power of something acting on me. But a source in this sense is simply a point of origin. A cause is supposed to be more than that: it should have some sort of explanatory priority with respect to the phenomenon to be explained. But that notion has no purchase with substances as such. Qua acting subject, I don't explain anything; I only act. Explanations have to invoke the descriptive and / or val-

[24]   Defenders of agent causation include Roderick M. Chisholm, "Freedom and Action," in Keith Lehrer, ed., *Freedom and Determinism* (New York: Random House, 1966), pp. 11–44; and "Human Freedom and the Self," in Gary Watson, ed., *Free Will* (New York: Oxford University Press, 1982), pp. 24–35; Timothy O'Connor, "Agent Causation," in O'Connor, ed., *Agents, Causes, and Events* (New York: Oxford University Press, 1995), pp. 173–200; and William L. Rowe, "Two Concepts of Freedom," *Proceedings and Addresses of the American Philosophical Association* 61 (1987), 43–64.
[25]   Compare Kane's condition of Ultimate Responsibility, *The Significance of Free Will*, p. 35.
[26]   Kane would agree, Ibid., pp. 188–90.
[27]   Compare the suggestion of Carl Ginet, *On Action* (New York: Cambridge University Press, 1990), p. 13. Ginet, too, rejects the concept of agent causation, but he also finds that it offers the best available simile for describing what he calls the "actish phenomenal quality."

uational aspects of things. And in the case of deciding, as we have seen, explanation is a matter not of nomic determination but of teleology: of the goals an agent is advancing in the act of deciding. This sort of explanation does not require our speaking of the agent as causing his decision, nor is it strengthened by it. Teleological explanations are about goals, not causes.

Even more problematic is the idea that voluntary agency is a matter of my somehow bringing about my decisions, in the sense of conferring existence on them. Again, one can understand the temptation: the active spontaneity of deciding, together with its intrinsic intentionality, may suggest that when I decide, I do something that amounts to producing that very act—*ex nihilo*, as it were. But it is very hard to find coherent content in this idea, taken literally. For in what would the supposed productive relation consist? If it is centered in some operation on my part independent of the act of deciding, then that operation, whatever it is, will become the true locus of agency—posing all of our problems anew, and threatening an infinite regress. If, on the other hand, the productive relation is thought to reside in some aspect of deciding itself, then the occurrence of my act of deciding would seem to have ontological priority. Only with its appearance could the causative aspect find reality, by which point it has no work to do. The idea of agency as a causal or productive relation seems, then, to be of little value. It may help to convey the intrinsically actional quality of operations of the will, and to emphasize the point that we should not look for a "source" for them in the other events of the world. But it creates the impression that there is some higher-order doing by which agents somehow bring their acts of will into existence, and that is not a workable view.

Causation and Origination

When the determinist's objection to libertarian freedom is framed as one about how the operations of will originate, then, the libertarian has no truly satisfying response. The essence of his position is to postulate ontological discontinuity between acts of will and other events and states. Once that is done, it is no longer possible to explain a decision as we would an event like a solar eclipse or the acceleration of a billiard ball—that is, as a natural outcome of the continuing dynamic processes that constitute our world. And the void cannot be filled by other explanatory devices. Teleological explanations may be suited to free decisions, but they are chiefly concerned with matters of content. They address the rational grounds for decisions, not their ontological underpinnings. And agent causation is simply a misfire—metaphysically misconceived, and lacking any real explanatory value. Decisions are, of course, comprehensible in part via their antecedents. They are influenced by character and circumstance, and they are made by rational agents, who in order to achieve anything in life must display at least some stability of purpose. One can expect, therefore, that statistical generalization about decisions will often be possible, and that knowing an agent's character and projects will often enable us to predict how he will decide. But this kind of order is more an upshot of free decision than a limitation on it. If the operations of the will are undetermined, they really do represent discontinuities in the world, and their provenance is as hidden from us as that of the world itself.

This concession is not, however, as damaging as it first appears, for it turns out that provenance is a problem on the other side as well. We have already seen this to be so with respect to the question why we have the world we do, rather that some other, or none at all. Determinism is not equipped to deal with that kind of issue, because there are no nomic processes for getting us to this world from some other, or from none at all. It might be thought, however, that once it is in place nomic principles can, if the world is deterministic, account for its continued existence, as well as the coming to be of new events and states within it. Indeed, it might be thought, this is precisely what the metaphysical seamlessness of a deterministic world consists in: that its history is a matter of law, in which present events produce or bring about future ones, in accordance with principles which, though not logically true, nevertheless articulate a kind of necessity that orders the progress of all things. How else could it be that in a deterministic world we know where events come from, whereas in an indeterministic one we do not?

The matter is not, however, so simple. The idea that present events are somehow able to produce or generate future ones is no more successful than that of agent causation. For, again, in what is the alleged generative relation supposed to consist? It cannot consist in some further event, something the causing event does, or an operation in which it engages. There are not that many things events may be said to *do* in any case, and it is impossible to imagine any operation that would count as one event bringing another into existence. We could, of course, make one up: we could postulate some kind of intervening event—producing, say, or bringing about, or necessitation—and claim that it binds event-causes to their effects. But we could have done the same with agent causation, and it would not have availed very much. Nor does it avail anything here. As Hume pointed out, all such claims are empirically vacuous: we observe no causal nexus in the world, only the orderly succession of events.[28]

---

[28]   *An Inquiry Concerning Human Understanding*, pp. 74–75.

Moreover, as with agent causation, the kind of generational event imagined here would simply raise anew the problems it is supposed to solve. Only now the problem is twofold. First, if causal production does count as an additional event in the world, we will need to explain how events of this sort arise, again threatening an infinite regress. Second, to account for the appearance of the effect the supposed "causing" would have to be independent of it, in which case some new generational relation would have to be postulated to bind these two as well, so that a second regress looms. We cannot, then, postulate occurrences in the world that consist in one event causing another. But if there are no such occurrences, then the claim that events can produce other events has no more substance than the idea that agents can produce the operations of their will.[29]

It might be thought that recourse to scientific laws can save the day at this point—that what is crucial to the relation of causal productivity is that when it obtains, there will be a law which states that events of the kinds in question are bound by a relation of necessitation, by which the cause-event must give rise to the effect. I think, however, that this move only compounds the problem. Scientific laws are, after all, propositions—that is, they are the means by which we report the way things are in the world. But laws do not *operate* in the world: they are not pieces of legislation, and they can neither put in place nor strengthen any real relation between events. Rather, if there is some viable notion of necessity attaching to scientific laws—which is itself a contested question—it has to be because there is already an answering relation in the world, among the events laws purport to describe. But then we are back where we began: the necessity of laws has to be grounded in an appropriate relation in the world, which we are unable to find. Indeed, the invocation of laws as a foundation for causal efficacy actually leads to a new embarrassment. Whereas the causal relation is usually taken to be diachronic, scientific laws, classically at least, are not. Newton's first law does not tell us that a body not acted on by a net force will be at rest or in uniform motion a moment from now; nor does the second law say a force applied to a rigid body at t will yield an acceleration an instant later. Rather, the world of classical physics is one of simultaneous action and reaction, in which changes of state occur *as* a body is acted on, not afterward. I am not fit to judge whether all of physics is this way, but to the extent that it is so, diachronic productive relations among events are not called for by scientific laws. They are, as Hume said, a product of our imagination, something we have added on.

---

[29]   The case against productive causal relations is presented at greater length by Jonathan L. Kvanvig and me in "The Occasionalist Proselytizer: A Modified Catechism," in J. E. Tomberlin, ed., *Philosophical Perspectives* 5 (Atascadero, Calif.: Ridgeview Publishing, 1991), pp. 587–615.

The idea that there are generative relations by which earlier events give rise to later ones is, then, no more successful than the notion that there is a generative relation by which agents produce their actions. But then how is event causation to be understood? And how do we account for our sense, which is surely legitimate, that we understand the origin of nomically determined events far better than that of a free decision? The answer, I think, lies in treating the changes we observe in the world not as a matter of things coming to be and passing away, but as variations in the way what is *preserved* in the dynamic flux of things is manifested.[30] The explanation of a solar eclipse is not that the event of the moon moving between the sun and the earth generates an eclipse. It is that when the moon moves to this position the flow of energy from the sun to the earth is interrupted, which we observe as a darkening of the sun. The explanation for the acceleration of a billiard ball is not that when the cue ball strikes it, an event of acceleration is produced. It is that when the cue ball contacts the object ball a transfer of momentum occurs, which is manifested in the acceleration of the latter. These are not stories about a mysterious nexus by which the universe somehow bootstraps itself into the future. On the contrary, these explanations, and the laws that underlie them, deal entirely with the interplay of masses and of energy, whose existence throughout the processes in question is presupposed. True, that interplay involves the entities of the world assuming new properties with the passage of time. But nomic explanation does not treat this as a generational process so much as a transformational one. The primary concern of science is not the existence of things, but rather their nature; it explains the present constellation of the world as emerging from what went before, not as created by it.

Taken in this way, nomic explanation is freed of the intractable task of describing processes of ontogenesis. True, we have to give up the pretense that the present was brought into being by the past, but that was never anything but a false pretense anyway. Rather, the way in which nomic explanations tell us where events "come from" is by making them continuous with what went before. The nature of the entities composing a deterministic world is essentially passive: their changes of state are entirely interdependent, so that an entity acts only insofar as it is acted on. The effect of nomic explanations is in part to trace those relations of interdependence, so that events need never surprise us. But that is not all. A good explanation will also describe the phenomena in terms that display the common nature of the entities involved, so that their interactions can be

---

[30] For this kind of approach to understanding causality see Phil Dowe, "Wesley Salmon's Process Theory of Causality and the Conserved Quantity Theory," *Philosophy of Science* 59 (1992), 195–216; and Wesley C. Salmon, "Causality Without Counterfactuals," *Philosophy of Science* 61 (1994), 297–312.

seen as transformations of a shared underlying reality. And of course that is what is lost when phenomena are not determined. Entities capable of spontaneous behavior act without being acted on, so that events cease to be completely interdependent, and outcomes are no longer inevitable. In effect, to the extent an event is undetermined, it has no natural ancestry. That is the sense in which we do not know where a free decision comes from. Notice, however, that this is simply a fuller description of the problem we saw in the last section, the problem of explanatory discontinuity. There is not a further problem of a free decision failing to participate in a nexus that would otherwise explain its existence. There is no such thing, even in a determined world.

Conclusion

Thomas Reid held that our idea of active power was derived not from observation of the world, but from the inner experience of voluntary exertion.[31] If that is right, it is only to be expected that the illusion that we generate the operations of our own will should be translated into the world, and reappear as the illusion that events generate other events. A more plausible view results if we give up the idea that causation is a matter of bringing events into existence. Rather, event causation is a matter of present states of the world giving way to later ones by way of ongoing processes, in which the crucial participants neither come to be nor pass away, but simply display new arrangements and manifestations. Agent causation, if we wish for it to be a viable concept, consists in the fact that through the intrinsically actional operations of the will, we are able to enter that causal stream and thereby influence events at a distance from the will. But it does not consist in our somehow "bringing about" the operations of the will itself.

The world that results is not, of course, the orderly world of the determinist, but it is not one for which the libertarian need apologize. It is, rather, the familiar world of experience, in which agents act freely and are responsible for what they do. There is, of course, a large remaining problem about that world: namely, where it, along with the free decisions and actions it includes, comes from. And here *comes from* has the stronger sense that *is* concerned primarily with the sheer existence of things, and worries over why we have this world rather than some other, or none at all. But that was going to be a problem in any case. Relations of event generation, whether by agents or by other events, were not going to solve it

---

[31]   Thomas Reid, *Essays on the Active Powers of Man* (Cambridge: MIT Press, 1969), p. 36.

either globally or in detail, because they do not exist; to believe in them is to adopt a superstition as the solution to a mystery. As to why we do have a world, that is not a problem that can be addressed here, but there are two things to be said. First, it is only one problem, not two: there is not one problem as to why this world exists and then another as to why the events that make it up do. And finally, it is only incidentally a problem for the philosophy of action.[32]

---

[32]   I have sought to address this problem from an entirely different perspective in "Divine Sovereignty and the Freedom of the Will," *Faith and Philosophy* 12 (1995), 582–98.

IV

PRACTICAL RATIONALITY

10

Settled Objectives and Rational Constraints

We may daydream about doing anything, even the impossible, but when we form intentions they usually embody objectives we expect to achieve. This alone is enough to suggest there are constraints on what we may intend, and a number of authors have posed such requirements. One view has it that in order to intend to *A* a person must, at least on pain of irrationality, believe he will (probably) *A*.[1] Others claim this is too strong, and demand only that he not believe he will not *A*.[2] And there is a related requirement that one not have intentions that are mutually inconsistent, in that if one is fulfilled the other cannot be.[3] Such constraints are of interest partly for their antireductionist implications, since other motivational states, in particular states of desire, are not similarly encumbered. Part of the human condition is to have incompatible desires, and we are not criticizably irrational if we want to do what we believe we cannot. Equally important, however, are the implications for the theory of practical rationality. Very roughly, whether an intention is rational would seem to depend first and foremost on whether the objective it embodies is one

[1] See, for example, Robert Audi, "Intending," *Journal of Philosophy* 79 (1973), 388; Wayne A. Davis, "A Causal Theory of Intending," *American Philosophical Quarterly* 21 (1984), 43–44; and Gilbert Harman, "Practical Reasoning," *Review of Metaphysics* 29 (1976) 432.
[2] Michael Bratman has defended this view in a number of places, but see especially *Intention, Plans, and Practical Reason* (Cambridge: Harvard University Press, 1987), chap. 3 and 8. A similar position is presented in Alfred R. Mele, "Intention, Belief, and Intentional Action," *American Philosophical Quarterly* 26 (1989), 19–30.
[3] Bratman, Ibid.

whose pursuit offers an acceptable chance of our changing things in ways we take to be for the better. Constraints like those cited may be viewed as instructions about when the chance is acceptable: that inconsistent objectives are always unreasonable, and that it is never rational to pursue a goal unless we think the chances favor success—or, on the weaker view, unless we at least do not expect to fail. Any of these latter claims would, if true, constitute an important principle of practical rationality.

Unfortunately, all are false. There are a number of examples in which it is rational for agents to try to achieve goals they believe they will not accomplish, and some of the examples involve mutually incompatible objectives. Moreover, it turns out that when, unexpectedly, such attempts succeed, the sought-after goals are achieved *intentionally*, notwithstanding the fact that the above constraints would forbid their being intended. Now ordinarily at least, we expect a person who *A*'s intentionally to have intended to *A*. Thus, a plausible response to the examples in question is to treat them as exceptions to the norm, and allow that in them we may intend objectives that would ordinarily be ruled out. But some authors balk at this, and instead reject what they call the "Simple View"—that is, the principle that anyone who *A*'s intentionally intends to *A*.[4] My purpose here is to defend this principle. Rejecting the Simple View, I shall claim, forces us to assign to other mental states the functional role of intention: that of providing settled objectives to guide deliberation and action. A likely result is either that entities will be multiplied or that the resultant account will invite reassertion of reductionist theories. In any case, the account must drive a wedge between intention and practical rationality, by forbidding agents to intend goals it is rational to seek. Worse yet, the states it "substitutes" for intention turn out to be subject to the same constraints that prompted the substitution, and hence are indistinguishable from intention in the very respect in which they are alleged to differ. Thus, I shall argue, there is no evidence to justify such supposed distinctions, and the Simple View is to be preferred.[5]

The Functional Role of Intention

The best way to understand intention is by comprehending its functional role in deliberation and action—a role that sets it apart from other states to

[4]   The term is owing to Bratman, who argues against this principle in "Two Faces of Intention," *Philosophical Review* 93 (1984), 375–405, and in *Intention, Plans, and Practical Reason*, chap. 8. See also Mele, "Intention, Belief, and Intentional Action," p. 21. The same principle is rejected by Harman, "Practical Reasoning," p. 433.
[5]   I have defended the Simple View in "Rationality and the Range of Intention," *Midwest Studies in Philosophy* 10 (1986), 191–211, but without exploring the theoretical issues pur-

which it is sometimes alleged intention can be reduced. Unlike someone who merely desires to attain some end, a person with an intention has a *settled objective:* he is committed to a goal, which guides his deliberation and which, in the normal case, he will eventually act to achieve. This attitude of commitment qualifies intention for a functional role to which desires, even predominate desires, are unsuited. For one thing, it does not always occur that one of the alternatives over which an agent deliberates elicits a predominate desire in him. In such cases, forming an intention is the standard way to resolve the issue: it settles the agent on one course or another.[6] This same resoluteness characterizes intention generally. Someone who intends, say, to go to the library this afternoon is committed to that course of action regardless of how the commitment arose. It may be grounded in a prior, predominate desire to go to the library, or it may not; even if it is, that desire need not presently persist. The agent may, so to speak, be "locked into" the project of going to the library, without time to plan for an alternative that has since come to appear preferable. All the same, he is committed, and the commitment manifests itself in a number of ways.

The most emphasized dimension of intentional commitment concerns the initiation and sustaining of action. Suppose I intend to go to the Deluxe Burger Bar for lunch. If that intention survives to the time for action, and if I see that the time has arrived, and if nothing interferes, then I will act in accordance with the intention and set out for the Deluxe. And as long as I retain the intention I will sustain my activity accordingly. I will monitor and adjust my behavior in appropriate ways—make the correct turns, obey traffic signals, and so on—to ensure my timely arrival.[7] Desires, however strong, do not carry this sort of commitment. I may desire to go to the Deluxe for lunch yet not do so. There is nothing irrational in this, since this desire needs to be weighed against others, such as my desire to finish grading an examination. As Michael Bratman puts it, desires are only potential influencers of conduct; intentions, by contrast, are conduct controlling.[8]

But there is a second dimension of intentional commitment, also emphasized by Bratman. Future-directed intentions have an important influ-

sued here. See also Fred Adams, "Intention and Intentional Action: The Simple View," *Mind and Language* 1 (1986), 281–301.

6 Such Buridan-type cases appear more frequent than might be supposed. See Bratman, *Intention, Plans, and Practical Reason,* p. 11; and Edna Ullmann-Margalit and Sydney Morgenbesser, "Picking and Choosing," *Social Research* 44 (1977), 761.

7 The role of intention in guiding behavior has been emphasized by Myles Brand, *Intending and Acting* (Cambridge: MIT Press, 1984), chap. 7. See also Irving Thalberg, "Do Our Intentions Cause Our Intentional Actions?" *American Philosophical Quarterly* 21 (1984), 257–59; and Mele, "Intention, Belief, and Intentional Action," p. 22.

8 *Intention, Plans, and Practical Reason,* p. 16.

ence on rational processes—that is, on the thinking in which agents are apt to engage after the intention is formed.[9] First, they introduce a characteristic stability or settledness into practical thinking: once in place, they are not readily subject to reconsideration. If I intend to go to the library this afternoon, I will not normally continue to deliberate about whether to go. But if I have only a desire to go, even a predominate one, this need not be so. I may still deliberate about whether to go to the library or, say, take the afternoon off and garden. This is not to say that intentions are somehow harder to get rid of than predominate desires. On the contrary: strong desires tend to be all but impossible to dislodge, whereas intentions have the reputation, at least, of being changeable "at will." Once I have an intention to *A*, however, I am normally of a settled disposition about *A*-ing: I am unlikely to consider the matter further, especially in the absence of new information. With desires this is not so. I may have a desire to take the afternoon off—a desire, in fact, that I will eventually act to fulfill—yet not consider the matter settled at all. Indeed, I may not even have thought about the issue and may still have a lot of deliberation to go through before I form the intention. If so, I can hardly be said to have a settled objective.

Second, future-directed intentions often set problems for further deliberation, thereby prompting the formation of additional intentions. If I intend to go to the library, I must settle on a means of getting there, on specific details of route, departure time, and so on, and on any preparatory steps I shall take before going. To solve such problems is to elaborate a *plan* of action, which is likely to involve a number of steps. And the steps of a plan are not developed haphazardly or in isolation from each other. For besides posing problems for further deliberation, future-directed intentions limit the admissible alternatives for solving those problems. The most important of these limitations, for purposes of this discussion, have to do with consistency. Plans should first of all be *internally consistent*, other things being equal. We would not normally expect a plan to include intentions that contradict, in that if one is fulfilled the other cannot be. In addition, however, there is a demand that plans be *consistent relative to the agent's beliefs*. To paraphrase Bratman, other things equal, it should be possible for an entire plan to be successfully executed without any of the agent's beliefs being false.[10]

I shall call these the requirements of *internal consistency* and *epistemic consistency*, respectively. The latter is, of course, a version of the weaker epistemic constraint cited earlier, and it is the more sweeping of the two

[9]   The points that follow are based largely on Bratman's discussion. Ibid., pp. 16–18.
[10]   See *Intention, Plans, and Practical Reason*, p. 31, where both of these requirements are articulated.

requirements. Indeed, any case of internal inconsistency in which the agent recognizes the conflict will also be a case of epistemic inconsistency, since to be aware that a pair of intentions are inconsistent is just to believe that they cannot both be successfully executed. And if we view the requirements as arising out of considerations of rationality, we can see a clear-cut justification for both of them. The rationality of intentions, it was suggested above, depends on whether the goals they embody are such that, by pursuing them, we gain an acceptable chance of changing the world in ways we believe are for the better.[11] But surely we will not normally be able to bring about desirable change by pursuing objectives that conflict either with each other or with our beliefs about what we will in fact achieve. I would be criticizably irrational, other things being equal, if I intended both to attend your seminar at two o'clock tomorrow and to play golf at that time. Similarly, though I might intend courses of action whose anticipated difficulty prevents my believing I *will* succeed, I would not normally be expected to have intentions I positively believe I will *not* carry out. I might, for example, intend to go to your seminar tomorrow, yet fear that I am coming down with the flu, and hence have no belief as to whether I will actually go or not. But if I am convinced I will *not* go, how could it be rational of me to intend to do so? The requirements of internal and epistemic consistency do, then, normally constrain intentions. Finally, we should remind ourselves that these constraints also militate against reductionism. There is nothing irrational about my desiring both to go to your seminar at two o'clock tomorrow and to play golf at that time, even though I would be irrational to intend both. Nor is it irrational of me to desire to go to your seminar when I am convinced I will not. Rational agents regularly desire to do lots of things they believe they will not do.

Consistency and the Simple View

If this account of the functional role of intention is correct—and there is a great deal that can be added to it—we have the basis for a strong antireductionist position. Intention appears to play an indispensable role both in practical thinking and in the genesis of action, and hence to deserve independent status in theories of rational agency. The position is jeopardized, however, by an apparent conflict between the consistency demands

---

[11]   I prefer this formulation to Bratman's, which bases the rationality of intentions on whether they maximize expected satisfaction of the agent's desires. But I agree with him that differences over what is fundamental to practical rationality are unlikely to affect the present discussion, since similar standards of reasonableness are likely to emerge on any plausible theory. *Intention, Plans, and Practical Reason*, pp. 52–53.

on intentions and the so-called Simple View: the principle that in order for me to perform an action *A* intentionally, I must at the time intend to *A*. On first hearing, at least, it seems hard to imagine a less offensive principle. Surely if I intentionally mow my lawn, call you up, or slice a golf shot, the natural supposition is that at the time I was in a state of intending to do those things. But the Simple View is threatened: there are a number of cases in which strict adherence to consistency requirements would preclude agents from intending actions that, as it turns out, they perform intentionally. When this occurs, it has been alleged, the Simple View fails.

A pair of examples of Bratman's will illustrate the point. The first is of a common phenomenon: an unexpectedly successful attempt. These occur because there are times when it is rational for us to *pursue* enterprises we expect will fail. Suppose that owing to a storm last night there is a large log blocking my driveway, and that I plan to make an effort this morning to move it. The log is large enough, however, that I believe it will prove too heavy for me, so that in fact I will not move it. Here it is not just the case that I have no belief that I will move the log; rather, I positively believe I will not. Still, I have nothing to lose by trying, as planned, to do so. And if to my surprise I succeed, we would say I had moved the log intentionally. By the requirement of epistemic consistency, however, it seems I cannot rationally intend to move it, for that would be to hold an intention inconsistent with my beliefs. And Bratman offers a further consideration to reinforce this prohibition. If indeed I believe I will fail to move the log, he says, then I should be able to plan on the basis of this belief, and intend to have the tree company move it this afternoon. But if my plan to try first to move the log myself involves intending to move it myself, then my total plan for the day would include both moving the log myself and having the tree company move it. And, as Bratman points out, "it seems folly to plan to cause the log to be moved twice."[12] Finally, we may cite a point recently emphasized by Alfred Mele—namely, that I would be unlikely to avow an intention to move the log. Noting its size you might say to me, "Surely you do not intend to move that yourself!" I would probably not answer, "Yes." I might say something like, "No, but I intend to try."[13]

A second sort of case is less common, but still perfectly possible. Consider an ambidextrous video game player who simultaneously plays a pair of video games, one with each hand. Each game involves directing a "missile" toward a target. The targets are difficult to hit, and there is a re-

[12]   Ibid., p. 39.
[13]   See especially "She Intends to Try," *Philosophical Studies* 55 (1989), 101–6. Also "Intention, Beliefs, and Intentional Action," p. 28.

ward for hitting either one. The games are, however, linked in such a way that if either target is hit, both games end, and if both targets are about to be hit simultaneously, both games simply shut down. Despite this last possibility, the player sees it as worthwhile to have a go at both games at once; she is highly skilled, and the risk of shutting down both appears to her to be outweighed by the greater chance simultaneous play provides of hitting one target, and thereby gaining the reward. Now suppose the player hits target 1. She will have done so intentionally, since her success would be owing to her skill and effort. And the Simple View would then say that she had intended to hit target 1. The example is, however, symmetrical with respect both to the games themselves and to the agent's attitudes toward them. Hence she would also, if the Simple View is correct, have had to intend to hit target 2. This violates both consistency requirements, since these two intentions are consistent neither with each other nor with the player's knowledge that she cannot hit both targets. Hence, Bratman claims, to have both intentions would involve the player in a criticizable form of irrationality. Yet, given the facts of the case, it seems clear that the player need *not* be guilty of irrationality. Her strategy of giving both games a try appears perfectly reasonable. Now if she is not irrational, Bratman argues, then she does not have both intentions. And given the symmetry of the case, this would have to mean she does not have either of them. But then the Simple View has to be false. It has to be possible for the player to play both games, hit target 1 intentionally, yet never have intended to hit either target.[14]

It is important to realize that such cases need not be taken as refuting the Simple View. The alternative is to claim them as exceptions to the constraints of internal and epistemic consistency. Indeed, in Bratman's formulation both requirements carry clearly stated *ceteris paribus* clauses, and he claims that both are defeasible, in that "there may be special circumstances in which it is rational of an agent to violate them."[15] Now my having a go at removing the log from my driveway certainly seems rational, as does the game player's behavior of firing at the targets of both games. And although more needs to be said on the matter, it may be possible to explain the hesitancy of agents in such cases to avow the relevant intentions on pragmatic grounds. Perhaps, then, the game player and I

---

[14] *Intention, Plans, and Practical Reason*, pp. 114–15. Once having abandoned the Simple View, Bratman goes on to apply the distinction between intentional and intended action to cases of oblique intention, where otherwise unacceptable consequences are brought about as unavoidable accompaniments of the agent's main objective (chap. 10). Space does not permit treatment of such cases, which in any case have received other accounts. But they do not form part of Bratman's main argument against the Simple View.

[15] Ibid., p.32.

should be taken as intending to achieve what our behavior is aimed at achieving, and what we will in fact have done intentionally if our endeavors are successful. This, however, is not the strategy chosen by opponents of the Simple View. Instead, they hold that it is *irrational* for me and the game player to intend to achieve objectives that we *are* rational in pursuing. The effect is to introduce considerable strain into the theory of intentional action.

Intention Surrogates

If we are to have blanket enforcement of consistency rules, we need a plausible account of what happens when the agents in our examples succeed in their efforts. That is, we need an explanation of how it is possible for an agent to A intentionally without intending to A. Now surely a person who intentionally A's must have intended to do *something*: otherwise, the theory would have to call for intentional behavior to occur in cases where intentions are in no way operative. Opponents of the Simple View agree, but insist that the intention in virtue of which one A's intentionally need not be an intention to A. For Bratman, one must distinguish what is intended from the *motivational potential* of an intention. The latter is broader in scope, and it is the primary determinant of what acts are intentional. Provided its occurrence is not owing to such factors as deviant causal chains, blind luck, or the like, an action A may be intentional simply by falling within the motivational potential of an intention one is executing. But the intention may be an intention to B, where B is different from A.[16] Similarly, Mele holds that A-ing intentionally requires having some pertinent intention, but not necessarily an intention to A.[17] And the appropriate intention for cases such as those we are considering, it is claimed, is the intention to *try* to A. That is, it is suggested that someone who manages to A in the course of carrying out an intention to try to A will, assuming other conditions standard for an intentional action are satisfied, have A'd intentionally.

On such a view, the correct explanation of how the game player comes to hit target 1 intentionally would be roughly as follows. She wants to hit target 1, and for that reason intends to try to hit it. She executes this intention by firing missiles at the target, and thereby hits it. This result is not due to blind chance or a deviant causal chain. The player hits the target in the way she was trying to, and her success is owing to her skill as a player. Accordingly, she hits the target intentionally. But she never intended to hit it; that would

[16]   Ibid., pp. 119–20.
[17]   "Intention, Belief, and Intentional Action," p. 21.

have yielded a violation of the requirements of rational consistency, since she had to have the same attitudes toward hitting both targets. The treatment of the log moving case is similar. I want to move the log, and for that reason intend to try to do so. I carry out my intention by tugging on the log, and to my surprise succeed in moving it. Again, the outcome is not fortuitous or owing to causal deviance. Hence I moved the log intentionally. Yet I could not rationally have intended to move it given my belief that I would not, for to do so would have been a violation of epistemic consistency.

There is considerable plausibility to these explanations, as far as they go. Our willingness to say both of my act of moving the log and of the game player's act of hitting target 1 that they are intentional certainly has something to do with the fact that each of us was trying to do exactly what we did. Other things being equal, that is enough to secure intentionality, despite my belief that I will fail, and despite the inconsistency of the "wants" that ground the game player's intentions to try to hit each target. But this account of our examples is not yet sufficient to overthrow the Simple View. It depends on the crucial assumption that it is possible for a person to intend to try to *A* without intending to *A*. That assumption is difficult to defend, for the fact is that *trying* is not a name for a kind of action. No matter what skills I have or what experience I can draw from, a bare intention to try to move the log is not an intention I can act on; the same applies to the game player's intention to try to hit target 1. This is because there is no particular type of change we can bring about in the world that counts as a "try." Rather, *trying* is a term that signifies the general business of acting in pursuit of some objective, a term that tends especially to be used when the objective is difficult to achieve. Thus my intention to try to move the log must be carried out by doing something else, aimed at achieving the objective of moving it. In this case, that turns out to be my act of tugging on the log. And the game player's intention to try to hit target 1 is executed by firing missiles at it.[18]

But now it begins to appear that the agents in our examples may yet have the intentions opponents of the Simple View would forbid. For clearly, it can only be the agents' attitudes toward the actions constituting their attempts that make them count as such. Suppose, for example, that by tugging on the log I also succeed in straining my back. What makes my tugging count as an attempt to move the log rather than an attempt to strain my back? And why is it that the game player's firing missiles counts as an attempt to hit the target rather than, say, to burn out the firing mechanism? The answer in each case is clear. It is because I tug on the log *as a*

---

[18]   For a thorough analysis of trying, see "Trying, Paralysis, and Volition," Chapter 5 in this book.

means to the end of moving it that my act counts as an attempt to move the log, and similarly for the game player's act of firing missiles at target 1. It is the place of the actions in our respective *plans* that determines what they are attempts to achieve. Furthermore, there is nothing in our consistency constraints that forbids me from *intending* to tug on the log, since I did believe I would do that; nor does anything prevent the game player from intending to fire at each target, since these intentions are perfectly consistent. But this situation does not differ at all from what we would expect if, confident of success, each of us had adopted the intention of *doing* what, in the examples, we are said only to intend to try to do, and had then chosen the actions constituting our attempts as means to fulfilling our intentions, and proceeded to carry out our respective plans. As far as planning and execution are concerned, our examples differ not at all from standard cases of intentionally *A*-ing. All that is missing, supposedly, is the intention to *A*. But if the agents in our examples do not intend their objectives, what exactly is their attitude toward them?

The problem here is that regardless of whether the game player and I intend to achieve our ends, we are still committed to them as settled objectives, which guide our deliberation and action. Hence theories that reject the Simple View must find some other mental state to play the functional role of intention in our examples. One option here is to claim there are mental states that count as a class of quasi-intentions: that is, mental states of having a goal or purpose that are able to guide deliberation and action, but which fall short of being full-fledged intentions in that they do not carry consistency constraints. Thus Mele speaks at one point of what he calls *intention**, characterizing it as, "whatever is left of *S*'s intention to *A* when we substitute for her belief that she probably will A a belief that she probably will not A."[19] For Mele, either an intention to *A* or an intention* to *A* may guide deliberation and action, and both involve having a plan the *goal* of which is to *A*. An intention* on my part to move the log from my driveway would involve a plan in which moving the log is represented as a goal, and some suitable act such as tugging on it is represented as the means.[20] On this account, then, to have a settled objective is to have a goal. But it should not be thought that to have a goal must in turn be to have an intention in the full sense. That, Mele argues, is false: "When Lydia purchases a lottery ticket with the goal of winning a million dollars and the knowledge that her chances of winning are less than one in a million, surely she does not *intend* to win."[21]

---

[19] "Intention, Belief, and Intentional Action," p. 20. On this characterization, of course, intention* need be nothing other than plain old intention, but Mele's presentation makes clear that he thinks otherwise.

[20] Compare Mele's example of shooting a free throw. Ibid., p. 21.

[21] Ibid., p. 22.

Bratman, too, is attracted by a theory of purposive states that fall short of being full-fledged intentions. There are, he says, two senses in which one may act "with the intention of *A*-ing," and only the stronger sense entails that one intends to *A*. The weaker entails only that I act *in order to A*, which will occur provided I act with the purpose or goal or aim of *A*-ing. This, however, does not require that I intend, strictly speaking, to *A*.[22] Again, the suggestion is that there are mental states of having a goal or purpose that may guide planning and action, but which unlike intention are exempt from the demands of rational consistency. Unlike Mele, however, Bratman does not leave it at this. He seems not to want to treat merely having a goal or purpose as a mental state with full ontological standing. Instead, he speaks as though the functional role that usually belongs to intention is carried out in our examples by a state of desire—what he calls a *guiding desire* to *A*:

> When I endeavor to *A*, I act in order to *A*, my aim or purpose in acting includes *A*. Even if I do not, strictly speaking, intend to *A*, I do desire to *A*, either as a means or for itself, or both. Further, I do not *merely* desire to *A*. My desire is guiding my attempt to *A*: it is a *guiding desire*. Now, in this case my guiding desire guides present conduct. But a desire may also be a guiding desire by virtue of guiding planning for the future.[23]

For Bratman, it is guiding desires that embody our goals and purposes when rational consistency forbids us to intend them. Like intentions, guiding desires frame settled objectives, which direct the planning of anticipated behavior and prompt its occurrence when the time for action comes. Our game player, then, may be taken to have a pair of guiding desires to hit target 1 and to hit target 2, which lead her in deciding to play the games simultaneously. Unlike the case with intending, however, there is no rational pressure for one's desires to be consistent, either internally or epistemically. Accordingly, the game player can allow her planning and her conduct to be guided by these desires without any failure of rationality. Similarly, I can rationally allow my desire to have the log out of my driveway guide my planning and conduct, thereby setting for me the goal or purpose of moving the log without my ever having the intention, properly so called, of doing so.

The Simple View and Practical Rationality

On the Simple View, my act of moving the log from my driveway and the game player's act of hitting target 1 are straightforward intentional

---

[22] *Intention, Plans, and Practical Reason*, p. 129.
[23] Ibid., p. 137.

acts, in which an intended end is achieved by intended means. Our initial beliefs that our attempts would fail may have the pragmatic consequence of inhibiting avowals of our full intentions, but they call for no alteration in the standard structure of intentional behavior. On the alternative approach, the intentionality of the game player's and my acts is held owing to our intentions to try, and our planning and behavior is viewed as mediated by purposive states that are not intentions, and which on one account turn out to be embodied in the agent's desires. Rejecting the Simple View can lead, then, to considerable complication in the theory of intentional action. I think, however, that the postulation of other purposive states to fill the functional role of intentions is neither demanded by our examples nor justified by preanalytic data.

That they are unnecessary is especially evident if, with Bratman, we view the requirements of internal and epistemic consistency as constraining only the *rationality* of intentions. Such a view does not hold it impossible for me and the game player to intend our objectives: it says only that we would be irrational to do so. But if the foundations of practical rationality are anything like what has been suggested above, this is a mistaken claim. In the case of the game player, firing at both targets maximizes expected gain: it increases the chance of hitting one target, thereby winning the reward. As long as they are viewed only as principles of practical rationality, a more obvious exception to the requirements of internal or epistemic consistency could hardly be found. The log moving example is similar. What makes tugging on the log sensible for me is the fact that I *may* thereby move it, thus clearing the driveway sooner and saving the expense of calling in the tree company. The cost of a failed attempt is, by contrast, remarkably low: some lost energy is all. Now it is perfectly consistent for me to believe both that I will not move the log, and that there is a slight chance I *will* move it. Why not, then, adopt the *intention* of moving the log myself, since I can pursue this objective at minimal cost and with a chance of considerable gain? Indeed, if this case does not fall under the *ceteris paribus* clause of the epistemic consistency requirement, one wonders what would.

It turns out, then, that far from it being irrational for the game player and me to intend our settled objectives, we would in fact be irrational to intend anything less. Nor should we accept the argument that if I believe I will fail I cannot intend to move the log, since my belief should then support an intention to have the tree company move it, putting me in the foolish position of planning to cause the log to be moved twice. This argument is far too strong, for it applies equally to my intention to *try* to move the log, and to my supposedly weaker "goal" or "purpose" of moving it. If I believe I will not move it, then clearly I believe that my attempt will fail and my purpose be frustrated. By a similar argument, therefore, I ought to intend right now to call in the tree company. But whether we call moving the log my "purpose" or my "intention," this again puts me in the unacceptable position of having two plans for moving the log. So what is wrong here is not my intending to move the log, but the demand that I be committed unconditionally to a plan that presumes failure. There is no reason for me to decide to call in the tree company before my attempt is made. The most I need have is the conditional intention to call the tree company if I fail.[24]

Principles of practical rationality offer no basis, then, for the claim that the intentionality of the game player's and my behavior is owing to the operation of purposive states other than intention. Furthermore, such states would be theoretically redundant, for it turns out that in the end they too must be restricted by conditions of internal and epistemic consistency. Otherwise, anyone faced with an accusation of irrationality for having inconsistent intentions could circumvent the charge simply by forming "goals" or "purposes" instead. That would be far too permissive. Indeed, the entire idea that there are states of having a settled objective which are exempt from consistency constraints is wrong. Suppose you ask me my plans for tomorrow. I reply that I am looking forward to the afternoon, since at two o'clock I am going to play golf and attend your seminar. Since your seminar is not scheduled for the golf course, you find this a bizarre plan. Gently, you point out to me that I cannot do both. "It's alright," I reply, "I'm not being irrational. Granted, I would be irrational if I were to intend to do both, but I don't have an *intention* either to go to your seminar *or* to play golf at two o'clock tomorrow. It is only my *purpose* to do both—my aim or goal, as you might say. So you can see everything is okay." I do not think this reply would set your mind at ease. Similarly, suppose I tell you that at the next meeting of the APA in Chicago I plan to jump over the Palmer House. That, you might protest, is a silly plan to have, since I can't succeed at it. And it wouldn't change things if I respond that my *intention* only is to *try* to jump over the hotel, that actually jumping over it is merely a goal or purpose of mine. Here, the chances of success are so remote that unless there is some special reward just for trying, there is no point in my making any move toward the objective.

Unless special circumstances obtain, then, it is irrational to have settled objectives that are mutually inconsistent, or conflict with one's beliefs about what one will achieve. And the irrationality is not diminished by treating the having of such objectives as a purposive state that is suppos-

---

[24] Bratman responds that if my belief that I will fail does not support planning it is not truly a belief. Ibid., p. 40. I would disagree, but in any case this argument too would have to apply to all purposive states, and hence must fail in the end.

edly weaker than intending. It is the commitment that goes with having a settled objective that is irrational in these cases, and it remains irrational regardless of what we call it. Nothing worth achieving can be accomplished by my committing myself both to going to your seminar and to playing golf. Unlike the game player's objectives, these cannot even be *pursued* simultaneously. So unless there were something to be gained simply by *having* both purposes, I can proceed more efficiently and with less frustration by dropping one of them. The other case is similar. If the APA were offering a prize for the most convincing attempt to jump over the Palmer House, I would have a good reason to try to do so. In fact, however, there is no reward just for trying, and the chances of actually succeeding are so vanishingly remote that they do not outweigh the effort and embarrassment of the attempt. The entire project is therefore irrational.

The mistake of seeking an alternative route to intentional action is compounded if, with Bratman, one associates it with a special operation of the agent's desires. Such a step cannot avoid consistency demands, but it does invite a reassertion of the sort of reductionism most current theories of intention are at pains to avoid. Unless "guiding desires" play exactly the functional role usually reserved for intention, they cannot yield intentional behavior. My guiding desire to move the log from my driveway must be able to prompt and sustain action on my part when the right time comes. It must be able to call for the selection of a fitting means, since it cannot otherwise be pursued. In order to fulfill these tasks efficiently, guiding desires cannot be constantly open to reappraisal, or viewed by the agent as embodying less than a settled objective. And of course guiding desires must carry constraints of internal and epistemic consistency. It would not do for me to be guided by a pair of desires to attend your seminar at two o'clock tomorrow and to play golf at the same time. But then, the reductionist might argue, guiding desires constitute at least as good a starting point for the rational planning and direction of behavior as intentions. Why not, then, simply get by with them? In the normal case, we can safely suppose that the agent's strongest desire is what serves to guide his deliberation and behavior. Cases where no single desire predominates are less clear, but surely a first approximation would have it that in them a desire gets to be "guiding" through whatever mechanism nonreductionists would claim is responsible for the formation of an independent state of intending. In short, if desires are able to assume the functional role of intentions on some occasions, why not have a theory according to which they regularly do so?

The way to avoid this conclusion is not to let the argument get started. We have already seen that the functional role of intention is different from that associated with desire. What jeopardizes the nonreductionist position is not anything about the way desires usually operate, but rather the effort to adapt desires to the task of providing settled objectives. But this will seem necessary only if, contrary to the evidence, we insist it would be irrational for the agents in our examples to intend actions that they perform intentionally. That insistence is what leads to the postulation of purposive states other than intention, and the resultant temptation to ground them in special operations of desire. There is no need, however, to start down this path. It is perfectly rational for the agents in our examples fully to intend their objectives. In short, these problems arise only because we abandon the Simple View, when a correct understanding of practical rationality indicates we should hold fast to it.

The Simple View and Avowals of Intention

There is, however, a reply available to the opponent, for the requirements of internal and epistemic consistency can be interpreted another way. Instead of constraining the rationality of intentions, they may be taken as conceptual or ontological in import—that is, as limitations on when the purposive states of agents *count* as intentions.[25] On this type of view, to have the settled objective of *A*-ing is always to have the goal or purpose of *A*-ing, and having a goal is not an "alternative route" to intentional action. It is the fundamental purposive state, with ontological standing independent of desire. It is bound by consistency constraints, but our examples illustrate that in exceptional cases one may have goals that fail to be consistent. Such goals cannot, however, be *intended* by the agent (even though they are achieved intentionally), for while internal and epistemic consistency bind only the rationality of goals or purposes, they are now taken as strictly binding over whether a purpose counts as an intention. It is a conceptual impossibility for me to intend to remove the log from my driveway, or for the game player to intend to hit target 1. And the evidence for this is simply what was said earlier about avowals: the fact that if asked whether I intended to move the log, I would avow only an intention to try.

If this view is adopted, the problems raised in the last section can be minimized. The notion of guiding desire with its reductionist overtones has been dropped. Nor is it supposed that states of having a goal or purpose are exempt from being rationally consistent. The strictures of consistency apply, but with a *ceteris paribus* clause that is now clearly understood to cover our

---

[25]   Though he would not be committed to all that follows, Mele inclines toward a view of this second sort. For him, epistemic consistency is a "confidence condition" on intention, one that must be satisfied before an agent can properly intend at all. "Intention, Belief, and Intentional Action," p. 28.

examples. Finally, this position does not proliferate entities, since it does not treat having a goal or purpose as a second way of having settled objective besides intending. On the contrary, my having the goal of moving the log would count as a state of intending but for my belief that I will fail; and the game player's purpose of hitting target 1 would count as an intention if only she did not have the incompatible purpose of hitting target 2.

In one respect, this account parallels the Simple View exactly: it treats all intentional action as arising out of the same sort of mental state, regardless of consistency constraints. It insists, however, that those constraints be satisfied before an agent may be said to intend, rather than just to have a goal or purpose. The issues here are, of course, partly verbal. One is always free to define one's terms in such a way that the game player and I cannot "intend" our objectives. But the Simple View cannot thereby be undone, for it pertains to the everyday concept of intending, not a stipulated one. And there are good reasons for not construing the everyday concept so narrowly. I for one would resist the suggestion that given my epistemic state it is impossible for me to intend to move the log from my driveway, or to jump over the Palmer House. For one thing, such a view makes whether I intend depend on what beliefs I do *not* have. A heedless person could have either intention simply by failing to address the prospect of failure. But intention is not usually taken to be a negative concept, and it is supposed to attend the actions of the judicious at least as much as the foolish. If it does, then I *can* have these intentions; it is just that only the former would be rational. Indeed, to forbid this is to begin to separate intention from the foundations of rationality, by making it impossible for the game player and me to intend goals we are rational to pursue. But we judge the rationality of agents by considering their intentions, not by inquiring about supposedly weaker goals or purposes.

Finally, we need to note that the argument from avowals, by which this understanding of our consistency constraints sets such store, will not withstand scrutiny. Not that the conversation it envisions could not occur: asked whether I intend to move the log, I *can* reply, "No, but I intend to try."[26] The problem is, however, that I can give exactly the same sort of reply no matter how my settled objective is described. You might say to me, "Surely it is not your purpose (goal, plan) to move that yourself." And I could respond, "No, but it is my purpose (goal, plan) to try." Yet we have seen that to be set on trying to *A* must be to have the purpose or goal of *A*-ing. The "No" in these replies cannot, then, be a denial that I have the objective in question, however it is described. Indeed, if we attempt to spell

[26]   I might, but I need not. It is at least as plausible for me to opt for a weaker response like, "Well, I intend to try in any case," thereby avoiding the appearance of denying that I intend my objective.

out the supposed denial, we get a reply I submit would *not* be given—that is, "No, I do not intend to move the log from my driveway, but I do intend to try to do so." The trouble here is that the second conjunct asserts what the first denies: that I have the settled objective of removing the log from my driveway. Instead of taking the "No" as a *dis*avowal of an intention, therefore, we should take it as a pragmatic weakening of the avowal, aimed at diminishing audience expectations about my success. Such weakening is of value precisely because our consistency constraints do normally bind the rationality of intentions. Since this is so, my avowals of intentions can normally be taken as indicative of what I believe I will accomplish and, since such beliefs are usually correct, as a basis for others to develop their own plans. By avowing only the intention to try to move the log, therefore, I signal my awareness of the difficulty, and implicitly warn others not to base their own deliberations on a belief that I will succeed. But I do not completely disown the intention of moving the log, since it is implicit in the intention to try to do so. Furthermore, the same considerations that make it equally misleading for me to avow outright the intention to move the log would also make it misleading for me baldly to avow the goal or purpose of moving it. And as we see above, the preanalytic data indicate I would not do so.[27]

The evidence from avowals provides no reason, then, for thinking that to have a goal or purpose is to be in a mental state on a different conceptual footing from intending. Settled objectives are always subject to consistency demands, but only as regards their rationality, and only with a *ceteris paribus* clause that exempts agents like the game player and me. A similar point applies to the case of Lydia. If we are willing to accept the hortatory "Surely she does not intend to win," this is in part because we would not expect her to avow such an intention. But we can also imagine digging in our heels: "If she does not intend to win, she shouldn't be buying the ticket." There are, however, dimensions to this example that are absent from the others. The fact is that winning a lottery is not so much something one does as something that happens to one. It requires a fortunate concatenation of circumstances, many of which depend on the actions of agents other than the winner. Viewing Lydia's situation in this light, we may well balk at talk of her intending to win. But if we do then we should also reject saying that her goal is to win, or that her purpose is to win. A better description might be that her goal or purpose is to become the winner, or to put herself in a position to win. But of course that is also her intention. Notice, too, that the very considerations that tell against saying Lydia intends

---

[27] For further discussion of this issue, see my "Intending and Planning: A Reply to Mele," *Philosophical Studies* 55 (1989), pp. 107–10.

to win will also count against saying, if the prize falls to her, that she won intentionally. So even if this case does disclose some weak sense in which winning is Lydia's "goal," it is not a sense that supports intentional action, and hence not a sense that threatens the Simple View.[28]

I would venture to submit, finally, that there is no ordinary sense in which terms like *goal* or *purpose* signify objectives that guide deliberation and behavior, but fall short of being intentions. I can think of no plausible case where, *in the same breath*, one explicitly disavows the intention of *A*-ing while avowing the goal or purpose of doing so. (After forty-seven years of faithful participation in the lottery, Lydia finally has her day in the sun. Dazed with euphoria, she accepts the congratulations of the reporters: "Oh, thank you so much! I knew all along that winning the lottery was practically impossible, so of course I never intended to win it. But naturally that's been my goal all along.") Ears differ, but to mine this scenario has standing only as an excerpt from a journalist's nightmare. If that is right, then any goal that guided Lydia's planning and behavior is one she intended to achieve.

Conclusion

If the foregoing arguments are correct, we should not abandon the Simple View. There is every reason to endorse the requirements of internal and epistemic consistency, but only as constraining the rationality of intentions, and only in a form that allows cases like those of the game player and me to count as exceptions. We need not claim the intentional actions that occur in these cases are anything but fully intended. Instead of excluding such a state of affairs, the requirements of rationality actually demand it, and the very same requirements would have to apply to states of having a settled objective that are alleged to fall short of intending. Such states also turn out to be on an equal footing with intention as regards the conditions under which agents may be expected to avow them. Hence they appear not to fall short of being intentions at all. We have every reason to believe, then, that to have a settled objective is to have an intention, and we need not complicate action theory in the ways rejecting the Simple View would require.[29]

---

[28]   It should be noted that Mele does not present the example as upsetting the Simple View, only as showing there are purposive states weaker than intending.

[29]   I am indebted to Michael Bratman, Alfred Mele, and Robert Audi for helpful discussions of these issues, as well as to the comments of an anonymous referee for *American Philosophical Quarterly*. An earlier version of this paper was presented at the 1989 meeting of the Central Division of the American Philosophical Association, and I also benefited from the discussion on that occasion.

11

Practical Rationality and Weakness of Will

On one account, practical reasoning is simply a branch of theoretical reasoning. It is practical in its motivation and subject matter, but its content, like that of reasoning in general, consists entirely of propositions: items that bear a truth value and are fit objects of belief or judgment. On another view, reasoning that is genuinely practical must include not just the agent's beliefs, but also items that are explicitly optational: the contents of states of motivation and will. The first view seems to have attracted more adherents, perhaps because it promises to treat the logic of practical reasoning in more familiar terms. I want to argue, however, that by itself this approach is insufficient. Unless we allow for practical reasoning from optative premises, intention formation cannot be a rational process, and the true relation between an agent's reasons and his intentions is lost. One result is a diminished understanding of the phenomenon of weakness of will, where intention formation departs from what theoretical reason would counsel. A better view emerges when it is realized that even in cases of akrasia, intention formation is itself an exercise in reasoning. This approach makes clear the crucial role motives play in practical rationality, and enriches our understanding of the plight of the akrates, for whom the demands of theoretical reason make little practical sense.

Two Models for Decision Making

There is no question that we sometimes reason *about* our conative states rather than *through* them. The fact that we have some desire, feel an obligation, or hold some intention can, that is, be part of the subject matter of our thinking, and a proposition attesting to the state in question can form part of the content of our reasoning. This can occur, moreover, in cases of practical importance. Suppose, for example, that I have a desire to hear some music of Beethoven. Realizing this, and knowing there is to be an all-Beethoven concert tonight, I might conclude that I should go to the concert. The content of my reasoning would then be as follows:

> I want to hear some Beethoven.
> I will hear some Beethoven if I go to the all-Beethoven concert.
> Therefore, I should go to the all-Beethoven concert.[1]

Does my drawing this inference count as practical reasoning? If it does, it will not be by virtue of its intrinsic features. Admittedly, the subject matter is practical; but reasoning about what actions are advisable is not all we have in mind by practical reasoning. The point of practical reasoning is not to reach judgments about what I should do, but to settle, as far as reason can, what I am *going* to do. That is, it is to settle my objectives, which are a matter not of belief but of intention. The above syllogism does not do that. Indeed, it could be found in contexts where my concern is not intention formation, but rather something theoretical: an exercise, say, in moral psychology or self-analysis, undertaken for its own sake. If so, my reasoning will be practical in its subject matter, but not in its point.

Contrast this with a situation where, in cognizance of my desire to hear some Beethoven and knowing about tonight's concert, I actually make up my mind to go. Here, I reach an intrinsically practical conclusion: I decide in light of my reasons. This appears to be a ratiocinative procedure, but one that goes further than what is represented above. A syllogistic synopsis of it might be as follows:

> Would that I hear some Beethoven.
> I will hear some Beethoven if I go to the all-Beethoven concert.
> Therefore, I shall go to the all-Beethoven concert.

The practical point of this reasoning is inescapable, because it is embedded essentially in the elements of which the syllogism is composed. The major premise here is not a proposition but a kind of *optation*: it encapsulates the content of a state of desire—what it is that we actually think when the desire is experienced or rehearsed. And the conclusion

---

[1]   This is a close variant of what Robert Audi calls the simplest basic schema for practical reasoning. *Practical Reasoning* (New York: Routledge, 1989), p. 99. As Audi points out, numerous variations are possible.

represents another sort of optation: the content of my act of deciding to go to the concert, which is identical with the intention thereby formed. Though propositional in its representation, my intention is not just a proposition, because in one dimension it is not rendered "false" if, as things develop, I am unable to carry it out. It signifies a state of resolution or commitment on my part, which unless I rescind it is in force whether I will make it to the concert or not.

The idea that there are intrinsically practical syllogisms is, of course, an old one,[2] and it is possible to delineate a variety of them. In one variant, the major premise is itself an intention. That would happen if I have already made up my mind to hear some Beethoven and my decision is concerned only with developing a plan for doing so. Another variation would occur if there are psychological states of sensed or felt obligation that do not reduce to desire or belief. For instance, I might have a close friend who will be playing in the Beethoven concert, and feel not just a desire to go, but a sense that it is incumbent on me to do so—something we might express by, "I must go to the Beethoven concert." If there are such states, we can do justice to an important Kantian theme: whether I act out of obligation or desire will depend on whether this intrinsically deontic content forms the major premise of my reasoning.[3] Finally, though I shall not dwell on such cases here, it is possible to think of practical syllogisms as involved not just in the formation but also in the execution of intention. In that sort of case the major premise would consist in the intention that encapsulates my plan of action, the minor would record my recognition that the appropriate circumstances for executing the plan are in place, and the conclusion would be my activity of volition or willing, wherein the sequence of endeavor basic to executing the plan is carried off. This would be a way of doing justice to the position Aristotle appears sometimes to take, in which the conclusion of practical reasoning is held to be action itself.[4]

In terms of flexibility and explanatory power, then, treating the formation and execution of intention as a matter of intrinsically practical reasoning appears a promising strategy. How, then, might the opposite approach come to be adopted? In part, no doubt, because of sheer familiarity. For the most part, we learn our logic strictly in terms of theoretical reasoning, in which only propositions are employed. It is natural, therefore, that they should be our preferred vehicle for representing the

---

[2] It begins with Aristotle, although there are significant problems of interpretation. For contrasting readings see Anthony Kenny, *Will, Freedom and Power* (Oxford: Basil Blackwell, 1975), pp. 71–73, and Audi, *Practical Reasoning,* chap. 1.
[3] Immanuel Kant, *Groundwork of the Metaphysics of Morals,* trans. H. J. Paton (New York: Harper & Row, 1964), pp. 65–67.
[4] See especially *De Motu Animalium* 701a7–36.

contents of reasoning, and it cannot be denied that for at least some of the reasoning that goes on in practical contexts, this is fully justified. Reasoning about rather than through our desires may seem overly detached, but sometimes I do take an analytic view of my motives in deliberation, and when that occurs syllogisms like the first one above may represent my reasoning with considerable accuracy. The same can be true with other topics of deliberative thinking: cases, for example, where I am concerned not with what I desire, but with what it would be good, or perhaps best, to do, or with what I am obligated to do. Furthermore, the premises of such reasoning closely parallel those of arguments represented by our second syllogism. The minor premise seems not to change, and for any optative expression of desire, intention, or felt obligation appearing as the major premise of an intrinsically practical syllogism we can construct a proposition like that in our first argument, which reports the optative state in question. Why not, then, seek to represent as much practical thinking as we can in terms of familiar, theoretical models?

Such an approach may appear to promise a simpler logic, also. In structure, the first of our model syllogisms appears the more straightforward of the two. It is not, as it stands, deductively valid, but at least it affords a case in which a proposition is inferred from propositions. And there may be further considerations that would move us closer to a valid argument. It may be that going to the all-Beethoven concert is not just *a* means for me to hear some Beethoven, but the only or the best means available. And it may be the case not only that I want to hear some Beethoven but that that is what I want most, or what it would be best for me to do this evening. So even if this argument is not valid, further deliberation on my part may yield one. Contrast this with the situation of our second syllogism, in which the premises are not even all propositions, and the conclusion is a decision or intention, a type of thought the modality of which does not even appear in the premises. The hope that a conclusion of this kind might ever be found to follow from premises like those given seems remote. Indeed, it may not immediately be obvious how the intrinsically practical syllogism is even susceptible of logical treatment.

There are, then, complications in treating decision making in terms of intrinsically practical models, and it is not clear what the advantages would be. Perhaps, therefore, we should avoid the complications and proceed strictly in terms of theoretical principles of reasoning. To be sure, not all examples of theoretical reasoning about means and ends will be practical in their import. But we can distinguish reasoning that is fully practical by its motivation, which surely is not just to figure out what to do in the situation at hand, but to get to an intention to do it. The suggestion we must examine, then, is that practical reasoning may be understood without loss simply as theoretical reasoning about what to do, when this is undertaken with a view toward intention formation.[5]

Reasoning About Reasons

There are a number of problems with this suggestion. One is that it proves very hard to deliver on the promise that if we take this view, the logic of practical reasoning will become more perspicuous. Part of the difficulty here has already been hinted at: there may be more than one means available for accomplishing a given end. If so, the search for deductive validity will be impeded. Our theoretical argument on behalf of my going to the Beethoven concert would be strengthened considerably if we could have the converse of its minor premise—that is, if in order to hear some Beethoven I would have to go to the concert. But that is false; all I need to do is put some Beethoven on the stereo. The only way we can narrow my means to one is to portray my deliberation as aimed at discovering the best or most satisfactory way of satisfying my desire. Unfortunately, however, deliberation is not that often concerned with what is best. If you see me at the concert and ask what brings me there, it will suffice for me to reply that I wanted to hear some Beethoven. I need not add that I thought this would be the most effective way to do so, nor would it be reasonable for you to question whether it was. My decision to go to the concert is justified, practically speaking, provided going will accomplish what I want it to accomplish. It does not have to do so in the best way.

A considerably more serious problem concerns the major premise. According to our first syllogism, it is the fact that I desire to hear some Beethoven which, together with further information, leads to the conclusion that I should go to the concert. And there is certainly something to that: cognizant of my desire, and possessed of the information that there is to be an all-Beethoven concert, I might well say to myself, "What I should do is go to that concert." The problem is, however, that it is hard to see what justifies the "should," which seems not to follow from the mere *fact* that I have a certain desire. It looks as if we need a further premise—something to the effect that whenever I have a desire, or perhaps whenever I desire to hear some Beethoven, I should act to fulfill it.[6] But these claims

---

[5] Audi, *Practical Reasoning*, pp. 102–3; see also Alfred R. Mele, *Springs of Action* (New York: Oxford University Press, 1992), p. 229. Mele does, however, allow for other possibilities, pp. 238–39.
[6] Alternatively, one might claim some special rule of inference governs such cases. Again, however, it is not obvious why we should have such a rule, and in many cases this suggestion brings problems of its own. See Mele, *Springs of Action*, pp. 237–38.

are flatly false. Moreover, to introduce such a premise is to misrepresent the reason out of which I decided to attend the concert. One advantage of the second, intrinsically practical syllogism is that it gets that right: it portrays the content of my state of desire as the ground of my decision. If it is to be replaced by a theoretical argument, the theoretical argument should do the same. Something about the value I attach to hearing Beethoven's music has to be given as the basis on which I decided to go to the concert. Neither of the additional premises just suggested does that; rather, they speak about the desirability of satisfying my desires. To introduce them into the theoretical argument reduces the fact that I desire to hear some Beethoven into a minor premise in my reasoning, rather than the major one. This kind of move is sometimes in order, but only when my true motive for deciding to go to the concert is a second-order one—a feeling, perhaps, that I ought to indulge myself more than I do. That is not what is at work in the case described, even when I do tell myself that I should go to the concert.

It does not appear, then, that we will get a satisfactory representation of practical reasoning as in essence theoretical by insisting on major premises that record facts about my states of desire, or how I should react to them. But other tactics are available. What actually guides my decision to go to the concert is the value I see in going: I will get to hear some Beethoven—an experience that, my desire indicates, I would value intrinsically. Perhaps, then, our first model syllogism would have been better framed as:

It would be good to hear some Beethoven.
I will hear some Beethoven if I go to the all-Beethoven concert.
Therefore, I should go to the all-Beethoven concert.

The major premise here no longer mentions my state of desire. Interestingly, however, it seems to come as close as we can in the indicative mood to capturing that state's content, in which the project of hearing some Beethoven is, as it were, comprehended by me as good. And adopting this premise appears to be a step in the direction of logical validity. Ideally speaking, after all, it is a far better reason for performing an action that it would be good to do so than that I happen to desire it. A still more satisfying result will be gotten if, in this or other cases, we can make it out to be my duty to accomplish some end. For surely if I believe I ought morally to accomplish some end, I am entitled to conclude that I should adopt some means to do so. Perhaps, then, practical reasoning is best understood as reasoning not about how to satisfy my optations, but about how to accomplish what is good or obligatory, where this is undertaken with a view toward intention formation.[7]

But this suggestion also has shortcomings. One is that it ignores the fact the previous approach sought to accommodate: that we do at times conclude we "should" do something based on knowledge of our desires alone, without engaging in more objective assessments of what is good or right. A worse problem, however, is that this treatment threatens to put too much distance between practical reasoning and the content of an agent's motivational states. Not that theoretical reasoning about the desirable and the obligatory never occurs in practical contexts: on the contrary, just as I might conclude that I should go to the concert based on knowledge of what my motives are, I might also reach such a judgment based on premises about what is demanded, or worth achieving. No doubt a fair amount of reasoning in practical contexts is of this essentially theoretical sort. The problem is, by itself it need have nothing to do with my motivational states. There is a connection between desire and cognitive valuing: I cannot desire something I do not take to be valuable in any way. But my beliefs about what is good are derived from many sources, and they often have an order and stability my conative states lack. I might well believe, therefore, that it would be good or even best to hear some Beethoven tonight, yet presently have no desire to do so at all.[8] With obligations the situation is, if anything, worse. Beliefs about what is morally required are notoriously apt to conflict with desire. And even if, as I have suggested, there are conative states of felt obligation that motivate us in the way desire does, their content need not match what, under society's influence, one has come to believe is one's duty.[9]

The upshot of this is that whatever its promise in terms of logical perspicuity, to treat practical reasoning strictly as a matter of intrinsically theoretical reasoning about what to do is likely only to increase the distance between it and what is supposed to be its point, namely intention formation. My beliefs about what is good or right cannot influence my decisions if they carry no conative weight with me. Intention formation requires

---

[7]   Ibid., chap. 12. Mele clearly prefers to treat practical reasoning as founded in the evaluative assessments of the agent, not in premises about his desires. Donald Davidson takes a similar view, but suggests our judgments of value always correspond to our motives. "How Is Weakness of the Will Possible?" in Joel Feinberg, ed., *Moral Concepts* (Oxford: Clarendon Press, 1970), p. 95; see also "Intending," in Yirmiahu Yovel, ed., *Philosophy of History and Action* (Dordrecht: D. Reidel, 1978), 43–44. Audi too holds practical reasoning is sometimes grounded in evaluation. *Practical Reasoning*, p. 88.

[8]   This has been denied by some authors. See, for example, David McNaughton, *Moral Vision: An Introduction to Ethics* (Oxford: Basil Blackwell, 1988), pp. 106–10.

[9]   The question whether a belief that an action is one's duty guarantees motivation to perform it is also debated. For a recent discussion, see Mele, "Internalist Moral Cognitivism and Listlessness," *Ethics* 106 (1996), 727–53.

that I be motivated to achieve the end in question, and mere belief neither is nor guarantees motivation. Thus to portray practical reasoning as in essence an effort to reach cognitive conclusions about the right and the good puts us in danger of misrepresenting the considerations that actually guide decision making. In fact, theories that treat practical reasoning as an essentially theoretical exercise seem faced with a dilemma. If, like the first approach we considered, they favor paradigms on which agents reason from information about their own optative states, the models proffered may track the considerations that prompt decisions fairly closely, but they will fail to explain how conclusions about what one ought to do are justified. If, on the other hand, practical reasoning is represented as reasoning about what is good or right, the logic of the models may be clearer, but the considerations that guide decision making may be misrepresented.

The Leap to Intention

An additional tangle of difficulties has to do with how, if we do not allow for intrinsically practical reasoning, intention formation is supposed to occur. Intending is a conative state, and so has dimensions cognitive states do not have. If I intend to go to the Beethoven concert, I am committed to so doing. I need to plan a way to get there, to adjust my other projects accordingly, and so on. Intention formation therefore is action-oriented in a way mere judgment is not. When I decide to go to the concert, I settle what, barring a change of mind, I am *going to do*. Judging that I *should* go to the concert, by contrast, only puts me in possession of a belief that doing so would be in some way appropriate. The gap here is embarrassing, because my arrival at some belief of this kind marks the limit of the progress I can achieve toward intending by using only intrinsically theoretical reasoning. Yet we were told that what separates "practical" reasoning from other theoretical reasoning about what one should do is precisely that it is undertaken with a view toward intention formation.

One way of trying to narrow this gap is to invest the judgments in which practical reasoning is held to terminate with some mark of finality: something that stamps them as an appropriate outcome to the process of deliberation, and perhaps can serve as a signal to the agent's conative faculties that it is now time for intention formation to occur. Thus we might think that practical reasoning should, at least in paradigm cases, issue ultimately in an "all-out," or "best," or "all things considered" judgment, one that purports to be self-consciously made in light of the totality of my relevant reasons, and which I take to represent a sort of final determination on my part as to what action is called for in my situation. In fact, one might even try to close the gap completely, by holding that intention formation simply reduces to making a judgment that an act would be best given the totality of relevant factors—or perhaps simply an all-out, unconditional judgment that the act would be best, period.[10] To think of practical reasoning this way is, however, a mistake. One reason is that judgments about what action would be best are not confined to cases where we reason about what to do with a view toward intention formation. I might well reach such a judgment in the course of a nonpractical project of self-analysis. So if the judgment alone is sufficient for intention formation—and above all if it constitutes intention formation—we are going to find ourselves with some intentions we never expected to have.

The biggest problem, however, is that most episodes of practical reasoning are never aimed at judgments of this kind, and do not issue in them. If I want to drive from my home to Houston tomorrow I have my choice of at least half a dozen routes, one of which would no doubt provide the optimum combination of scenery, speed, and convenience. But I will not even address that issue; rather, I will choose one of the two or three routes I am accustomed to taking, and go. I will do so because those routes all *suffice* for my purpose, which is all practical rationality demands. It does not require that I dredge up all of my reasons for going, puzzle out the best assessment I can of the relative advantages of each route, and reach a solemn judgment that in light of all my reasons, I-45 (say) stands as my best option. The time I spend on that project would be far better spent working on this chapter. It is almost always so: life is too short and the world too complex for rational deliberation to be generally concerned with maximizing. It need only display what is sometimes called due diligence, which is usually just a matter of finding satisfactory means to satisfactory ends. And a lot of practical reasoning isn't even that good. In countless cases we are lazy, or lunge at the first means that presents itself, or ignore relevant information, or even studiously avoid the issue of what would be best, lest we not get our way. None of these are cases in which something that could be termed a best or all things considered judgment is reached. We simply go until we stop. Indeed, as the case of my traveling to Houston illustrates, we need not even reach an *unconditional* conclusion that the option we finally take is the one that "should" be selected. Yet in all of these cases practical reasoning occurs, and intentions get formed.

---

[10]   For this last suggestion, see Davidson, "Intending," p. 56. The difference between all things considered and all-out judgments is the basis for Davidson's account of akrasia in "How Is Weakness of the Will Possible?"

Suppose, however, that we do have a case in which an agent judges that all things considered, a certain action should be performed, or would be best. Even so, the agent does not yet have an intention; it is simply not possible to conclude, based on an agent's claim that he thinks a certain action would be best, that he intends to perform it.[11] And we need to consider how the remaining gap gets bridged. Now the procedure here has to involve the agent's motives, which differ in kind from judgments; but on the present view it cannot be ratiocinative. Presumably, then, what occurs is a causal process, in which the agent's best judgment triggers or gives rise to a desire for the act in question and/or the ends it serves, and this in turn causes an intention to be formed.[12] But if this is the way intention formation works, then practical reasoning is a questionable strategy for forming intentions. If, as in our first model, it simply tracks my existing motivational states, why bother with it? Surely those states will have their causal consequences whether I reason about them or not.[13] If, on the other hand, the aim is to reach conclusions about what would be good or right, which my motives need not follow, then why think of practical reasoning as a reliable means to intention formation? In the end—and indeed this is true on both of our strictly theoretical models—intention formation has to be turned over to what can only be conceived as a nonrational and potentially hostile process. My conative states, presumably through their relative strength, will now determine my act of intention formation, which may or may not accord with the deliverances of "practical" reason.

Worse still, this model makes it impossible to see how reasons can rationalize or justify forming an intention. When I decide to go to the concert tonight, my reason is not the *proposition* that I desire to hear some Beethoven. As was hinted earlier, this fact can count as a reason for going to the concert only in the context of some other motive—for example, a wish to indulge myself more than I do. Rather, what counts as my reason is the conceptual *content* of my state of desire: my conative sense of the value of hearing some Beethoven.[14] But that serves as a premise of my reasoning only in our intrinsically practical syllogism. It does not appear in either of the theoretical ones, and on the present view it does not account for my decision. Rather, my intention is formed through a causal process founded in my *state* of desire—a process that could in principle occur when I am sound asleep. But then what sense is there to the idea, which

---

[11] For an argument to this effect, see "Intrinsic Intentionality," Chapter 7 in this book.
[12] Audi's account is along these lines, *Practical Reasoning*, pp. 129–30.
[13] Mele, *Springs of Action*, p. 238.
[14] For an argument that it is the content of states of belief and desire, rather than the states themselves, that constitutes an agent's reasons for acting, see "The Formation of Intention," Chapter 8 in this book.

seems required if a reason explanation is to be in order at all, that I decide out of an awareness of my desire to hear some Beethoven, and of the availability of the concert? In the end, there is none. On this view, I do not form intentions for the sake of ends represented in my reasons; indeed, there is no strong sense in which *I*, as a rational agent, form my intentions at all.

Akrasia

Some of the significance of these problems can be seen by considering how, on the views we are discussing, akrasia or weakness of will might be treated. Typically, weakness of will involves acting against one's cognitive assessment of the alternatives available. If we allow that in many cases one will not have a best judgment about things, we might say that when akrasia occurs one acts against one's *better* judgment: against one's view of what would accomplish greater good in the circumstances at hand, perhaps, or against what one takes to constitute one's obligation.[15] I might judge, for example, that rather than going to the Beethoven concert tonight, I ought to stay home and work on this chapter. Yet, for the sake of enjoying the Beethoven, I might go to the concert anyway. If so, I will have behaved akratically.[16] In the normal course, I will also have *decided* akratically: the same motives for which I go to the concert are also motives for deciding to go there, and I need to decide in advance so as to plan how I will get to the concert, how to dress, and so on. Is it possible to formulate a plausible and enlightening account of what goes on here if practical reasoning is viewed as a strictly theoretical operation?

Prospects are at their dimmest for accounts that would identify intention with the agent's best judgment as to what should be done. Even if we substitute "better" for "best," the problems seem insurmountable. One is that if I go to the Beethoven concert tonight I will have done so intentionally, and we expect an agent's intentional behavior to match his intentions. But on the present account my intention, even while going to the concert, is actually to stay at home and work, for that was my better judgment. At a minimum, then, this account is committed to the unlikely posi-

---

[15]   Davidson, "How Is Weakness of the Will Possible?" p. 94; Audi, *Practical Reasoning,* p. 7; Mele, *Springs of Action,* p. 87.

[16]   The proviso that this be for the sake of enjoyment may be necessary for the case to count as one of true weakness of will. If, knowing I ought to do something else, I decide to go to the concert out of a Nietzschean impulse to stamp out the voice of morality in my deliberations, we may doubt the action would be one of moral weakness in the full sense, though it would still be one of incontinence.

tion that it is possible for me to go to the concert intentionally without intending to do so. Indeed, the situation is worse yet. For the truth is that if I decide in advance to go to the concert, plan my evening around it, and then carry out my plan by going, I *do* intend to go.[17] What is it to decide to go to the concert if not to form that intention? If during the concert the voice of conscience reminds me that I should be home working, would it do for me to take comfort in the thought that I really don't intend to be where I am? Clearly not. But then the position to which the reductivist must be committed is that I intend, based on my decision, to go to the concert, and at the same time intend, based on my better judgment, to stay at home and work. And that is an absurd position. There is indeed something irrational about akratic behavior, but it is not generally that the akratic agent has directly incompatible intentions.

Do we get a better result by identifying intention with a simple, unconditional judgment? Donald Davidson has suggested that the agent's all things considered judgment is essentially *prima facie* or conditional, in that it is tied to the reasons that justify it. But an intention, he says, is not that: it is simply an all-out, unconditional judgment that a certain action is to be preferred. This distinction promises to allow for akratic intentions and actions, because it permits the agent to judge all things considered that *A* would be better than *B*, while at the same time judging unconditionally that *B* would be better than *A*, and thereby intending *B*.[18] Space does not permit full consideration of this approach, which has in any case been widely criticized.[19] But the view does not provide a plausible account of akrasia. If out of weakness of will I were to decide to attend the Beethoven concert tonight, I would not consider myself to have judged doing so to be better than working on this chapter, either all things considered or *sans phrase*. Nor is it generally true that akratic agents consider their actions superior to the available alternatives.[20] In addition, it is not clear what the provenance of such a judgment would be. If the totality of considerations I take to be relevant justifies my judging that it would be better to skip the concert, then it justifies my proceeding to make that judgment uncondi-

---

[17]   It is sometimes claimed that when one believes it highly unlikely that one will succeed in *A*-ing, one cannot intend to *A*, yet may do so intentionally. I have argued against this view in "Settled Objectives and Rational Constraints," Chapter 10 in this book. But in any case, the example of my attending the concert is not one where there is reasonable doubt of success.

[18]   "How Is Weakness of the Will Possible?" pp. 109–11.

[19]   See Michael Bratman, "Practical Reasoning and Weakness of Will," *Nous* 13 (1979), 153–71; Alfred R. Mele, *Irrationality* (New York: Oxford University Press, 1987), chap. 3; and William Charlton, *Weakness of Will: A Philosophical Introduction* (Oxford: Basil Blackwell, 1988), chap. 7.

[20]   Bratman, "Practical Reasoning and Weakness of Will," p. 160.

tionally. To do the opposite would be an act not of irrationality, but of sheer lunacy. It would be like judging that based on the totality of evidence, it is probable that smoking causes cancer—only to proceed to the "all-out" judgment that most likely smoking does not cause cancer. Weak-willed agents may not conform to every ideal of practical rationality, but they have not gone round the bend. Their intentions represent a failure of will, not of cognitive sanity.

Davidson's approach is not, however, entirely on the wrong track—a fact that emerges once we abandon the effort to make intending out to be a kind of judgment. Like the picture Davidson gives, both of the theoretical models for practical reasoning described earlier allow for the possibility that the process by which an agent reaches judgments about what should be done is different from that by which intentions are formed. That leaves room for the phenomenon that seems essential to akrasia—namely, a certain failure of correspondence between the agent's judgments of value, and the motives that guide his decisions and actions.[21] There is, to be sure, little room for such failure if we treat practical reasoning as reasoning about one's motives alone. Presumably, if that is how things work, I could reach a definitive judgment about what to do only by judging in accord with the strongest motive of which I am aware. But then only if I somehow overlook or suppress awareness of my strongest motive will my best judgment fail to anticipate what will finally be my intention. Such self-deception no doubt occurs in some cases of akrasia, but it is hardly the rule. If, however, we think of practical reasoning as also including consideration of what is good or obligatory independent of my motivational states, there is plenty of room for akratic failure. My judgment that I should foreswear the concert to work on this chapter may or may not be well grounded. It could arise out of a correct assessment of my obligations: of the need for me to meet my professional commitments, to make good use of my talents, and to cease placing pleasure above duty. Alternatively, it may stem from an intellectual obsession with the idea of work, or from an overly strict moral education, in which I was taught to believe enjoyment is never permissible until all one's obligations have been discharged. But whether my judgment is reasonable or not, it need not match my motives: my sense of obligation may be too weak, my youthful enchantment with philosophy too much diminished, my love for Beethoven too great. If so, and if the causal picture of intention formation described above is correct, it may well be that I will come to have an intention to do what I judge I should not. Indeed, it might even be claimed that this ac-

---

[21] For an interesting discussion of some of the ways judgmental evaluation and motives may differ, see Mele, *Irrationality*, chap. 6.

count of akrasia vindicates the view that practical reasoning is simply a type of theoretical reasoning. It is, one might argue, precisely because my reasoning is no guarantee of my intentions or behavior that weakness of will is possible, and that is what the present theory reflects.

Yet problems remain. One is that speaking not of best but only of better judgment makes the theory unclear as to what signals the transition from practical reasoning to intention formation. If the latter process is simply causal, we should expect there to be some indicator in the judgment that precedes intention formation that practical reasoning is now concluded and intention formation may proceed. But a judgment that one action is preferable to another need not necessarily terminate practical reasoning, since other acts could be still more preferable. And even if this difficulty can be resolved, the major one persists: we still have no account of how, on this theory, my decision to attend the Beethoven concert is *guided by* the conceptual content of my reason-states—by my desire to hear some Beethoven, and by the knowledge that I can do so if I attend tonight's concert. This cannot be a matter of my engaging in parallel theoretical reasoning, since if my decision is akratic I will not do that. Nor is it a matter of the sheer strength of my desire for some Beethoven forcing my decision. Strength of desire may figure in my choice, but it does not do so in the dark. Rather, it has to be my *thoughts,* including my desires, that rationalize and explain my decision, and this bespeaks a ratiocinative process that has yet to be articulated. Finally, we should note that while nonreductive theories that treat practical reasoning as theoretical reasoning about what is good or right do make room for weakness of will, they do not shed any special light on the phenomenon. In particular, they do not tell us why, for the akrates anyway, dwelling on what is good or obligatory is so often a fruitless endeavor—one that, however persuasive on the side of knowledge, seems all but powerless to influence decision. Is this strictly a matter of opposite desires being too strong, or does the explanation run deeper?

Intrinsically Practical Reasoning

I think it runs deeper, but to see why we must first understand the virtues of the intrinsically practical model of decision making described earlier. It should be clear that to treat decision making in terms of that model is not to say deliberation never includes theoretical reasoning over what to do; it often includes it, especially in cases of akrasia. Rather, the claim is that decision making, though distinct from reasoning about what would be good or right, is still a matter of reasoning. Intention formation may not always measure up to the standards an ideally rational agent would observe, but it is always rational in the sense that it is an exercise of one's rational faculties. When we decide, the *content* of our optative- and belief-states—as opposed to the fact that we are in those states—is seen as making the intention we form reasonable, in a way we can expect to be portrayed in an argument. That is a major difference from the foregoing accounts, on which for the akrates and the continent person alike, intention formation in itself is a nonrational phenomenon.

In many cases, of course, the considerations on which an intention is founded will be complex; but they can often be summarized in arguments like the practical syllogism with which we began. How is it, though, that the conclusion of that argument is justified by its premises, given that the argument is not deductively valid? To get an answer to this question, we need to appreciate the functional difference between theoretical and practical reasoning. The purpose of theoretical reasoning is to further the conformity of our minds to the world, by adding to our store of true beliefs. The appropriate procedure for that is to begin with propositions we take to be true and advance to further propositions to which, deductively or inductively, they lend support. The object of practical reasoning is quite the opposite: it is to bring the world into conformity with our minds, to structure it according to our preferences.[22] For that, one needs to begin with an optation: a previously formed intention, desire, or felt obligation. One then combines the optation with a representation of a means to satisfying it, and advances toward the action thereby indicated, by adopting the intention to perform it. One selects the means, for the sake of achieving the end.[23]

Once the function of the practical syllogism is recognized, the justificatory relation between its premises and conclusion becomes clear. It is in fact a kind of inverse of modus ponens: my conclusion—that is, my intention to go to the concert tonight—is justified because if the conditional belief that forms my minor premise is true, then carrying out my intention will have the consequence that I get to hear some Beethoven, thereby satisfying the desire which is my major premise. This is not, of course, a case of deductive validity, which on the usual definition applies only to strictly propositional reasoning. But the study of logic would be incomplete if it left no room for arguments like this, for there is clearly a matter of what we might call "practical validity" here: my intention is *justified* by virtue

---

22   This feature of practical thinking has been noted by a number of authors, beginning with G. E. M. Anscombe, *Intention* (London: Oxford University Press, 1957), pp. 56–57; See also John R. Searle, *Intentionality* (New York: Cambridge University Press, 1983), pp. 7–8.
23   This is the procedure for intention formation. When intentions are executed, as noted earlier, one proceeds from the intention as major premise to its enactment, via the mental activity of volition.

of its place in the project of bringing the world into conformity with my optations, and the argument by which it is reached is the practical analog of a familiar deductive model.[24] Relative to the practical premises on which it is based, my intention is as rational as it can get. Indeed, once the function of the intrinsically practical syllogism is understood, its conclusion may be seen to be justified much more easily than those of either of our strictly theoretical models for "practical" reasoning.

Understanding intention formation in terms of the intrinsically practical syllogism makes clear, then, how decision making is ratiocinative, and how our decisions and the intentions we form by them are justified by our reasons. Thus it enables us to overcome the major difficulty with the strictly theoretical model. And it does a lot more. A significant advantage of this approach is that the account of rational decision making it affords does not require that such reasoning be optimific. Indeed, a major impetus toward viewing practical reasoning as an optimizing procedure seems to be that unless we do so practical rationality cannot be explicated using standards of deductive validity. Once we give up the idea that practical reasoning is just a brand of theoretical reasoning, that whole endeavor can be seen to be unnecessary. Practical reasoning and intention formation can be fully rational provided only that through them we adopt means sufficient to our ends. Nor do we have to insist that practical reason terminate in an all things considered judgment, or one that bears some other mark of finality. No such judgment is necessary for decision making to be an exercise of reason, or for a decision to be rationally justified. Furthermore, even when such judgments occur, they do not mark the termination of practical reasoning. Practical reasoning terminates in intention formation, which is based not on best judgments but on motives.

An additional advantage of this approach is that it does not bring with it any of the baggage of determinism. Whether decisions occur according to deterministic laws is an issue on which both philosophers and laypersons disagree. It is, moreover, finally an empirical issue, and hence one on which philosophical analysis ought to remain neutral when it can. The present topic is one on which neutrality is possible. For while people do disagree over determinism, they have no trouble discerning when they or others form an intention out of awareness that it is justified in light of one or another reason. How we discern this is a long story, but that we are able to do so without settling the issue of determinism suggests that nomic relations are not our guide, and that the justificatory relationship—which is first and foremost a matter of the abstract contents of our mental states—

---

[24]   For a development of this approach to evaluating practical arguments see Kenny, *Will, Freedom and Power*, chap. 5, esp. pp. 80–82.

ought not to be confused with any causal relation that might hold between the states themselves. The question what makes intention formation an endeavor of rationality has to do with the justificatory relationship, not the alleged causal one.

Finally, it is worth noting that understanding decision making in terms of the intrinsically practical syllogism makes it possible to explain a phenomenon noted earlier: that we do sometimes conclude on the basis that we hold a certain desire that we ought to perform an action that would satisfy it. Based on the fact that I desire to enjoy some Beethoven, and that going to the concert tonight will enable me to do so, I might well conclude, we noted, that I ought to go to the concert. But we also noted that this conclusion does not follow from the premises cited. How, then, is it gotten? I would suggest it is based on recognition of what is referred to above as the "practical validity" of the corresponding intrinsically practical syllogism. We are aware, that is to say, that the optational content of our state of desire, together with our belief as to the available means, offers practical justification for an act of deciding whose content is, "I shall attend the concert," and we conclude on that basis that we ought to attend. Thus even some of our theoretical reasoning about what to do is founded on an appreciation of the justifying force of intrinsically practical reasoning.

Better Judgments and Worse Reasons

If the position outlined above is correct, then for the akrates and the continent person alike, intention formation is an endeavor of reason, in which decisions are rationally justified by the optations on which they are grounded. Nor does intrinsically practical reasoning find a place only at the conclusion of deliberation. I would suggest that a good deal of deliberation consists in sorting through the optations and beliefs relevant to the different courses available, building justificatory arguments out of them, and making the many small choices needed to develop full-fledged action plans. Resolution of these matters need not be routed through theoretical judgments about what one should do for the outcome to have rational backing. But of course a decision that is rational relative to one set of premises need not be rational relative to others. Just as in theoretical settings it is sometimes wiser to reject the premises of a valid argument rather than affirm the conclusion, so in practical contexts it can be better to forswear the optations that would justify a course of action rather than decide to pursue it.

Presumably, that is what holds in cases of wrong or misguided behavior. If it is truly a mistake for me to decide to go to the concert tonight, it will be because however justified my decision may be in terms of my desire to hear some Beethoven, there are countervailing considerations that outweigh the benefits of going to the concert, and that my decision ought to have respected. Usually, they will be moral considerations, as when my professional obligations are such that I ought to forego the concert in favor of completing this chapter. It may be argued that when this is so, my decision to attend the concert is finally irrational despite the justification my desires offer, in that it puts me in the position of having an intention (to go to the concert) that is in implicit conflict with other intentions of mine: to bring a philosophical project to timely completion, to gain new insight, advance my career, and so on. In any case, decisions that violate moral obligations will at least usually be finally misguided, however well they reflect the agent's conative dispositions. Yet they are all too frequent, which is no doubt why, especially in cases of moral weakness, deliberation will likely include theoretical reasoning about what, morally speaking, one ought to do. Yet this sort of reasoning often has decidedly little effect on the agent's behavior. Typically, he knows perfectly well what he ought to do; he may even intend for a time to do it. But in the end he changes his mind, and the fact that the action finally chosen is wrong, no matter how convincingly it might have been argued, is disregarded. We need to try to understand how that happens.

Doing so requires recognizing the importance of the fact that the major premise of an intrinsically practical syllogism must always be an optation. The reason this is so is that we can only decide and act out of motives— that is, out of desires, intentions, and felt obligations. Mere facts are not enough, because facts alone provide no practical rationale for doing anything. That I will hear some Beethoven if I go to the concert tonight means nothing to me if I don't want to hear any Beethoven; and my belief that I can reach Houston by taking I-45 will prompt no decision on my part if I am not moved to go to Houston. True, we sometimes call such facts reasons, but they are able to influence behavior only if they connect with some motive in a way that practical reason can recognize. By themselves, they are inert. And the same goes for facts about right and wrong. That I should be obligated to stay home and write tonight may, to my theoretical faculties, be grounds for thinking that were I an ideally rational agent I would choose to do so. But to my practical faculties it is not grounds for anything. Decisions are finally grounded not in beliefs but in optations, and unless my beliefs about my duty are seen by me as having bearing on some optative project of mine, they cannot influence my behavior at all.

If this right, then my judgment that I ought to stay home and finish this chapter tonight can enter into my intrinsically practical reasoning only as a minor premise. But what sort of major premise does it fit with? Ironically, there is one important one with which it does *not* fit: namely, my conative sense of duty about finishing this chapter. The idea of specifically deontic conative states is controversial, but I think there is such a thing as a conative sense of obligation, and that instances of it should be distinguished from states both of belief and of desire. If I have a sense of obligation to finish this chapter I will feel that I *must* finish it, that it is incumbent on me to do so. This is not the same as desiring to finish the chapter, in the sense of finding the project attractive. Rather, to feel obligated to do something is to feel that I must do it regardless of whether I like the idea. Nor is it the same as simply believing that I ought to finish the chapter, that this is in fact my duty. Most likely, if I *feel* obligated I will also have this belief. But the reverse need not hold: a judgment that I ought to finish this chapter can derive from abstract considerations, or from my moral training, without there being anything in the thought of the project itself that awakens in me the sense of moral compulsion that defines felt obligation. If so, then I will have a moral belief about what I ought to do, but no corresponding moral motivation.

But even if the moral motive is present, it is not an appropriate major premise for a practical syllogism whose minor is my belief that finishing this chapter is my duty. For one thing, a conative sense that I am obligated to finish the chapter is in itself sufficient reason for deciding to do so, and for adopting means to facilitate and encourage my finishing. If this moral optation is already operative in my thinking, the corresponding theoretical judgment is not necessary. That is why people with a strong sense of obligation tend to go ahead and act, rather than theorizing about their situation. But even if we ignore this point, the fact is that my conative sense that I am obliged to finish this chapter and my judgment that I am obliged to do so do not *connect* logically in the way required to justify a decision. If my belief that duty requires me to finish the chapter is to form the minor premise of a practical syllogism, the kind of major that is needed is an optation *about doing my duty*. The deontic optation we have been talking about is not about that; it is about finishing this chapter.

The sorts of optations that do fit with my judgment are of two types. First, I might have a motive that concerns duty as such: I might desire to do my duty, apprehending it as good and valuable that obligations be observed. Or, the idea of duty might itself awaken a sense of duty in me, so that I experience a kind of second-order sense of obligation, to carry out my obligations. And it is conceivable that out of one or both of these motives, I might decide to finish the chapter. If so, I will have decided for reasons of duty, but not, strictly speaking, the duty to finish the chapter. The second kind of motive that can connect with my judgment is indirect: it may be that carrying out my obligations is a means for me to accomplish something else I desire. I may view doing my duty as a way of gaining the plaudits of others, of pleasing people in authority, or of escaping their wrath. Indeed there can be any number of rewards I covet, which will come to me if only I carry out my obligations. If this kind of motive is the ground for my decision, the argument on which the resultant intention is based will employ three premises: my desire for the reward in question, my belief that if I perform my duty I will receive it, and my judgment that if I stay home and work, I will have done my duty. In this case, however, I will not have decided for reasons of duty, even though my decision is the one duty requires.

With this in mind, consider again my quandary if I suffer from weakness of will. I may know full well that it is my duty to stay home and work, but I lack sufficient motivation, moral or otherwise, to do so. I believe abstractly that I should stay home and finish this chapter, but the raw sense that I *must* do so occupies little if any place in my thinking, and I am not lucky enough to have sufficient compensating motives of desire: little or nothing in the project is attractive to me, at least by comparison with the prospect of an evening of Beethoven. There is little chance, in a situation like this, that it will make practical sense to me to stay at home. Rather, I am likely to be preoccupied with the advantages of going to the concert, and choose eventually to do so.[25] Is it possible for my *beliefs* about my duty to prevail in this sort of situation? Not likely, if the only motives with which they connect are those described above. For consider how suspect those motives are. A sense of duty about doing one's duty may be present in all of us; but it is not likely to be very robust, and its persuasiveness is diminished when, as in the present case, the task to be undertaken does not itself awaken a strong deontic impulse. The same goes for a desire to do one's duty. Besides, how respectable is it to act from a desire to do my duty when the entire idea of duty is that it is supposed to apply regardless of my desires? As for indirect motives, those are not just suspect but downright demeaning. The very idea that the performance of duty should depend on a sufficient reward being in the offing is offensive. Moreover, the rewards of obeying morality are likely to appear not to hang on any one particular act (it's only one concert, after all), and to be more remote than those of self-indulgence.

What this comes to is that while the *fact* that it is my duty to perform a certain act may, from the theoretical perspective, be the best sort of reason to ask me to do it, it is from my own practical perspective a very weak—and perhaps even insulting—reason for complying. And therein lies the

---

[25]   In this respect, the account I offer is similar to many others. See, for example, Mele, *Irrationality*, pp. 93–95; and Audi, *Practical Reasoning*, pp. 135–38.

poignancy of akrasia. The incontinent person knows what duty demands, most likely desires to be a dutiful person, and even feels able to choose rightly. But his *sense* of duty about the prescribed task itself is, if present at all, so weak that a choice in its favor is a kind of moral stab in the dark. He has little or no desire for the task considered in itself, or the issue of morality might never have arisen. And indirect motives favoring the prescribed decision are apt to appear morally perverse, and in any case subject to easy rebuttal. Now it is not impossible for such a person to choose rightly. Weak-willed agents sometimes do make sound decisions. But they may be infrequent, and the intention formed will be difficult to sustain as the time for action draws near. That is why the cure for weakness of will, if there is one, is not further deliberation involving one's present motives. Rather, what is needed is a consistent, arduous, and perhaps even ruthless program aimed at reforming those motives, and avoiding the situations they do not equip us to handle effectively.

Conclusion

No theory of human action can be complete if it fails to recognize the importance of intrinsically practical reasoning. What makes decision making an exercise of our rational faculties is that it is ratiocinative. An intention does not only embody a commitment to action: it is the conclusion of an argument, of which the motives and beliefs in which it is grounded are the premises. Were it not so, intention formation would in itself be a blind process, however much it might be surrounded by theoretical reasoning, and the decisions of all agents—whether weak-willed or strong—would be not so much irrational as simply nonrational. Furthermore, what makes akratic agents irrational is not that their decisions are in themselves exercises in poor reasoning. On the contrary: akratic agents are perfectly sane, and an akratic decision is likely to have as much practical validity as any other. The problem is rather that in akratic agents theoretical and practical rationality are divorced: available motives do not justify a practical conclusion that accords with the counsels of theoretical reason. Admitting intrinsically practical reasoning into the theory of action makes for a plausible account of this phenomenon, and so helps us to understand more fully the problem of weakness of will, as well as the strengths and limitations of moral considerations in guiding our behavior.[26]

---

[26] An earlier version of this paper was read at the University of South Carolina, and I benefited from the discussion on that occasion. I am also grateful to Robert Audi and Alfred Mele for comments and discussion.

Index